KW-224-838

CATHOLICS IN A PROTESTANT COUNTRY

By the same author

Éigse na hIarmhí *(Gaelic poets from Westmeath)*

The second city: portrait of Dublin 1700–1760

A Georgian celebration: Irish poets of the eighteenth century

Dublin's turbulent priest: Cornelius Nary (1658–1738)

An Irish bishop in penal times: the chequered career of Sylvester Lloyd OFM (1680–1747)

Ireland in the Stuart papers, *editor*

Divided loyalties: the question of the oath for Irish catholics in the eighteenth century

Catholics in a Protestant Country

The Papist Constituency in
Eighteenth-Century Dublin

Patrick Fagan

FOUR COURTS PRESS

Set in 10.5 on 12.5 point Ehrhardt for
FOUR COURTS PRESS LTD
Fumbally Lane, Dublin 8, Ireland
e-mail: info@four-courts-press.ie
and in North America for
FOUR COURTS PRESS
c/o ISBS, 5804 N.E. Hassalo Street, Portland, OR 97213.

© Patrick Fagan 1998

A catalogue record for this title
is available from the British Library.

ISBN 1-85182-417-0

All rights reserved. No part of this publication
may be reproduced, stored in or introduced into
a retrieval system, or transmitted, in any form or by
any means (electronic, mechanical, photocopying,
recording or otherwise), without the prior
written permission of both the copyright
owner and publisher of this book.

Printed in England by
the Martins Printing Group, Bodmin, Cornwall

Contents

Preface

> ... if you have any sagacity, you will make reflections on every incident and reap instruction and, whatever it be, strive to adapt it to the rank you are to fill hereafter: that of a Roman Catholic in a Protestant country, that of one in a low way, obnoxious to the laws.
>
> Charles O'Conor of Belanagare to his son, Denis,
> in Dublin, 17 November 1751

That Irish catholics were confronted with the reality of a protestant state and a protestant ascendancy throughout the eighteenth century cannot be doubted, but were they really in such a 'low way'? The ensuing chapters seek to explore the involvement during that century of catholics in different sectors, professional, commercial and industrial, principally in Dublin. It will be seen that Dublin, the citadel of protestantism at the beginning of the century with a population almost 70 per cent protestant, had by the end of the century been reduced, mainly by the infiltration of catholics from the provinces, to a situation where the population was little more than 30 per cent protestant. Chapter 2 shows to what extent, and with what effect, various anti-catholic measures were challenged by an *ad hoc* catholic body taking advantage of the Irish parliament's dependence on the English privy council and of the situation where, for the first half of the century, Britain's main ally in Europe was the catholic emperor of Austria. Chapter 3 explores the catholic presence in medicine and shows that from the beginning of the century, a significant number of Dublin's physicians, surgeons and apothecaries were catholic. In the case of the legal profession, it will be seen from chapter 4 that, although catholic solicitors were eventually silenced by the act of 1734, it remained possible throughout the century for catholics to qualify as barristers at one of the inns of court in London, although they could engage only in a chamber practice. The extent to which catholics were trooping into the Freemason lodges in Dublin in the 1750s and 1760s (chapter 5) is scarcely indicative of people 'in a low way', nor indeed the extent to which catholics were throughout the century involved in trade and manufacture in the city (chapter 6).

However, there was one aspect of life where catholics made only a slight impact, and that was literature. Of the thirty poets surveyed in my *A Georgian cel-*

ebration: Irish poets of the eighteenth century, only two (Laurence Whyte from Westmeath and Thomas Dermody from Clare) were, possibly, born catholics, but, if so, there can be little doubt that both of these in later life abandoned the catholic for the protestant faith. The paucity of catholic poets was due to the inferior education enjoyed by catholics, to the fact that the majority of catholics, unlike protestants, still spoke the Irish language and to their exclusion till late in the century from a university education at home.

At first sight Irish dramatists of the eighteenth century (although the leading lights, Sheridan and Goldsmith, were clearly protestants) might appear to offer prospects of a considerable catholic participation with in their midst such Irish and catholic-sounding names as Charles Coffey, Charles Molloy, Kane O'Hara, Arthur Murphy, Leonard McNally, Hugh Kelly, John O'Keeffe and Charles Macklin (McLaughlin). But on a closer examination it will be found that O'Hara, Coffey, Molloy and McNally were bred protestants, while nearly all the others mentioned, though born catholic, appear to have defected to the established church later. It is certain that Macklin did so and probably also Kelly and Murphy both of whom practised at the bar in London at a time when catholics were excluded from so doing. O'Keeffe may have been the only one of the above to die a catholic, although some dalliance with the established church must be suspected in his case also, for a son of his was a minister of the church of England. The obvious poor showing of catholics in literature in the eighteenth century has meant that the original intention to devote a chapter to catholic involvement therein could not be sustained

I would like to thank the Grand Lodge of the A.F. & A. Masons of Ireland, and in particular Ms Alex Ward, curator, for access to their records in Freemasons' Hall, Dublin for the purpose of researching material for the chapter on catholic involvement in freemasonry. My thanks are also due to Fr Benignus Millett OFM, editor, *Collectanea Hibernica,* for the use of material from the Vatican Archives edited or calendared in that journal by the late Fr Cathaldus Giblin OFM and to my son, Desmond, for helping with the checking of the proofs.

I am indebted to the staff of the following institutions for their help and cooperation in my research work: National Library of Ireland, Royal Irish Academy, the National Archives, Gilbert Library (a branch of the Dublin Public Libraries), Public Record Office, Northern Ireland and the libraries of Trinity College, Dublin, St Patrick's College, Maynooth, the Dominican Priory, Tallaght, the Representative Church Body, Dublin, the Society of King's Inns, Dublin and the Royal College of Physicians in Ireland.

The population of Dublin in the eighteenth century with particular reference to the proportions of protestants and catholics*

When we come to consider the population of Dublin in the eighteenth century we find ourselves faced with a concept in some respects rather arbitrary and in other respects somewhat fluid. It is arbitrary in the sense that at the start of the century several parishes, taken to be integral parts of the city, had rural hinterlands, whose populations, not being capable of estimation by themselves, have to be included in that of the city. At the end of the century we have the reverse situation where the city had by then not only spread through the hinterlands mentioned, but beyond them into the contiguous villages, and we have Whitelaw assuming quite arbitrarily for the purpose of his 1798 census that the city proper was bounded by the two canals and the two circular roads, as appropriate, and ignoring developments outside these limits. With regard to the fluid aspect of the concept, there is the matter of the hordes of homeless vagrants, who thronged the streets but who find no place in the statistics of population because they were unquantifiable. At the other pole, socially, there was the Winter Season which had the effect of swelling the numbers, particularly in the second half of the century, again to an unquantifiable extent, of the upper classes and their servants in the five months from November to March each year.

The purpose of this chapter is to give an overall view of trends in the population of Dublin in the eighteenth century by reference to the several estimates made at different times by contemporary writers as well as by reference to recent studies. In particular the chapter will attempt to chart, through a veritable mathematical quagmire, the course by which the city changed from being mainly protestant at the beginning of the century to being mainly catholic at the close of the century.

There are four methods by which statistics of population for Dublin city may be arrived at for the period in question. The first method is enumeration. Provided the enumerators can be depended upon to have gone about their task assiduously, this is clearly the best method. Secondly, an estimate of population may be made by multiplying the number of houses in the city at a given time by

*This chapter is a re-working of an article which appeared in *Eighteenth-Century Ireland*, vol. 6 (1991), pp 121–56

an average number of people per house. A third method of calculating population is the number of deaths in a given year taken in conjunction with the death-rate, and a fourth is the number of births in a given year taken in conjunction with the birth-rate.

With regard to the first method, there have been only two enumerations of the population of the city relevant to the present exercise – South's enumeration in 1695,[1] which is a useful starting-point, and Whitelaw's detailed and comprehensive census of 1798,[2] which is the only one of the many estimates of the population of the city made throughout the century which can be depended on to any degree.

With regard to the second method, figures of the number of houses in the city are ready to hand at various dates throughout the century in the hearth tax returns.[3] These returns, for reasons mainly to do with the corruption and carelessness of the tax collectors, have been regarded by some modern commentators as an unreliable guide to the actual number of houses *in the country as a whole*. For example, Connell assumed that the returns were deficient by at least 50 per cent for the period 1712 to 1785.[4] More recently, however, Daultry, Dickson and Ó Gráda concluded that 'the result of the test [spatial autocorrelation] on the eighteenth-century data suggest on the face of it relatively good hearth tax returns for

1 Gilbert, J.T. (ed.), *Calendar of the ancient records of Dublin* (CARD), VI, pp 575–81.   2 Whitelaw, James, *An essay on the population of Dublin, being the result of an actual survey taken in 1798*, Dublin 1805.   3 House figures for Dublin city up to 1760 are available as follows: *1695* (South): 5,999 (5,150 inhabited); *1696* (CARD): 6,124 (5,407 inhabited); *1701–5* (CARD): *1701*: 6,604, *1702*: 6,727, *1703*: 6,908, *1704*: 7,140, *1705*: 7,369; *1706* (Molyneux): 7,505; *1712* (CARD): 9,162; *1718* (CARD): 10,004; *1725* (Dobbs): 11,466; *1726* (Dobbs): 11,525; *1728* (Dobbs): 11,086 (inhabited); *1733* (Monck Mason): 11,718; *1732–3* (Bindon): 12,942; *1744* (Watson): 11,923; *1745* (Rutty): 12,148; and the following from *Watson's Dublin Almanac: 1749*: 12,407; *1752*: 12,575; *1753*: 12,857; *1760*: 13,461. There is a question as to whether the figures for the years 1701–6 include 'waste' (uninhabited) houses, and in this connection we have to consider which is the more logical progression: (a) from 6,124 in 1696 by an average of 96 each year to 6,604 in 1701, and given actual increases of 125 between 1695 and 1696 and 123 between 1701 and 1702, or (b) from 5,407 in 1696 by an average of 239 each year to 6,604 in 1701, given an actual increase of 257 between 1695 and 1696 and 123 between 1701 and 1702. The more logical progression would appear to be (a). It appears then that the figures for 1701–6 do include 'waste' houses. The figures for 1712 and 1718 should also be regarded as including 'waste' houses since they are compared with the figures for 1701 in CARD, VII, p. 577, the 1718 figure stated to be 'as taken by survey in March 1718'. The figures for 1725 and 1726 must also include 'waste' houses since a figure for inhabited houses for 1728 is less than the figure for 1726. The figure for 1732–3 for the reasons later stated relates to inhabited houses, as also evidently Monck Mason's figure for 1733. The figures for 1744 and 1745 are deemed to be for inhabited houses on a comparison with the figure for 1726 which includes 'waste'. As for the figures from 1749 to 1760, the indications are that they are for inhabited houses. If the figure for 1749 were to include 'waste' houses, then on making even a conservative reduction in respect of such houses (say 7.3 per cent as in 1798), the 1749 figure would be found to be considerably less than the 1745 figure.   4 Connell, K.H., *The population of Ireland 1750–1845*, Oxford 1950, p. 13.

the first half of the century, a perceptible decline in their quality after mid-century, and improvement setting in only at the end of the 1780s'.[5]

But however much opinions may differ about the country as a whole, it is apparent that in the specific case of the city of Dublin the hearth tax returns up to, say, 1760 can be accorded a much higher reliability status than for the rest of the country for the following reasons. Firstly, the tax collectors in the capital, being directly under the eyes of the administrators of the tax, were much less likely to indulge in corrupt or careless practices than in more remote areas far removed from authority. Secondly, there are in the case of Dublin a number of independent bench-marks against which estimates of population based on the hearth tax returns can be viewed and tested. We have at the end of the period under review Whitelaw's reliable statistic of 15,199 inhabited houses in 1798.[6] For 1778 a figure of 1,400 houses[7] emerges from a municipal tax on houses and for 1755 a count of the houses in Rocque's very detailed map of the city can be compared with figures from the hearth tax returns around that time.[8] For the early part of the century a figure of total population can be extrapolated from Archbishop King's abstract (early1716) of men capable of bearing arms,[9] and this can be compared with the population arrived at on the basis of the number of houses in the hearth tax returns.

Hearth tax returns up to 1760 present us with a logical, gradual progression of the number of houses in Dublin city which it is suggested should be accepted as reasonably credible. Figures available from the hearth tax returns after 1760 are, however, a different matter. A figure for 1766 of 13,194 houses from those returns appears in *Watson's Dublin Almanac* for 1767 and is repeated for several years thereafter. There is then a jump to 17,151 houses for 1777,[10] and this figure is repeated in the almanac for the ensuing ten years. Figures repeated in this fashion for several years cannot be taken seriously; the figure of 17,151 is in any event demonstrably far too high when compared with Whitelaw's 1798 figure.

5 Daultry, S., Dickson, D. and Ó Gráda, C., 'Eighteenth century Irish population: new perspectives from old sources' in *Journal of economic history*, vol. 41, no. 3 (September 1981), p. 613.   6 Whitelaw, J., op. cit., Appendix p. vii.   7 Dickson, David, 'The demographic implications of Dublin's growth 1650–1850' in Lawton, R. and Lee, R. (eds), *Urban population development in Western Europe from late eighteenth century to early twentieth century*, Liverpool 1989, p. 179. See also CARD, XII, pp 536–7.   8 Rocque's map of Dublin was first published in 1756 but it was based on surveys carried out in 1754 and 1755. The map purports to show 'every dwelling-house, warehouse, stable, yards, backhouses and gardens'. It does not, however, cover the parish of Donnybrook nor the extremities of several parishes. A count of the houses in the map yields a figure of 11,645 houses. If 550 is added in respect of Donnybrook parish – it was 452 in 1733 according to the Monck Mason ms in Gilbert Library, Dublin – the total is 12,195 (say 12,200). The difference between this figure and the hearth tax figure of 12,857 for 1753 could be explained by the extremities of several parishes not being included in Rocque's map. In any event the comparison shows that the hearth tax figure for 1753 is reasonably close to actuality.   9 The Archbishop King abstract is reproduced in George T. Stokes, *Some worthies of the Irish church*, Dublin 1899, pp 246–8. The dating of this abstract is discussed later in this chapter at the appropriate place.   10 *Watson's Dublin Almanac* for 1767.

As to the other factor in the calculation – the average number of persons per house – for most of the century it was generally accepted as ten. This figure appears to have been more in the nature of a hunch than one arrived at by actual sampling, although sampling of some kind was done from time to time. The figure of 11.2 persons per inhabited house emerging from Whitelaw's 1798 census shows the average of ten to have been a conservative estimate. As suggested below, the probability is that the average number per inhabited house increased progressively throughout the century from 9.2 in 1695 to 11.2 in 1798, or, if 'waste' (i.e. vacant) houses are included, from 7.8 in 1695 to 10.4 in 1798.[11] The generality of contemporary writers from the late 1720s onwards accepted ten persons per inhabited house as a conservative average.

Of the two factors in the calculation, the average number of persons per house is by far the more critical and indeed the least certain. For example, if we take the year 1725, when the hearth tax returns show 11,466 houses, a figure of eight persons per house yields a total population of 92,000 while a figure of ten yields a total population of 115,000, a quite significant difference of 23,000. Nevertheless, apart from South's 1695 enumeration, the hearth tax returns multiplied by an average number of persons per house is the best basis we have of estimating the population of the city up to, say, 1760, but, given that both factors in the calculation are to an extent uncertain, the most that can be claimed for population figures arrived at even on this basis is that they are rough estimates.

As to the third method of calculating population mentioned above – the number of deaths in a given year taken in conjunction with the death-rate – it had been computed by a Doctor Halley that one person in every thirty died each year.[12] This would be equivalent to a death-rate of 33 per 1,000. Estimates of the population of Dublin using this method were made by Arthur Dobbs in 1728[13] and by John Rutty in 1753,[14] but both rejected the results as far too low, and had to fall back on the more familiar method of estimating the population by reference to the hearth tax house returns. In recent years Dickson has dismissed this (death-rate) method as of no use in calculating total population, or even the protestant portion of it, for the reason that the figures of deaths available are only of those buried in Church of Ireland graveyards, and, while dissenters and many catholics were buried in such graveyards, poor catholics tended to be buried in non-consecrated free burial grounds and wealthier catholics were often buried in cemeteries outside the city.[15]

As to the fourth method above – the number of births in a given year taken in conjunction with the birth-rate – the problem here again is that the accessible figures of births relate to baptisms of persons belonging to the established church,

11 Whitelaw, J., op. cit., Appendix p. vii. The figure of 11.2 is an adjusted figure after the inclusion of Donnybrook parish and the Ormond Market.   12 Dobbs, Arthur, *Essay on trade and improvement in Ireland*, Dublin 1731, part 2, p. 9.   13 Ibid., p. 9.   14 Rutty, John MD, *Chronological history of the weather and seasons and of the prevailing diseases in Dublin*, London 1770, p. xliv.   15 Dickson, D., op. cit. in note 7, p. 182.

and the birth-rate is a matter of conjecture, although a rate of 35 baptisms per 1,000 persons has acquired some credence. It is conceivable that figures of catholic baptisms/births could be gleaned from parish registers generally available from the mid-century onwards, but the trouble entailed in such an exercise would be out of all proportion to its possible value. Rutty has provided figures of baptisms in respect of the established church for the period 1699–1770 with twelve years missing,[16] but one's faith in these figures is not enhanced by the glaring inconsistencies in the proportion of males and females baptized. However, Dickson has derived decennial averages from Rutty's figures from which he estimates the protestant population for different periods, based on 35 baptisms per 1,000 people.[17]

A point to be remembered is that the calculation of population from statistics of births and, to a lesser extent, of deaths does not take proper account of sizeable net migration into the city, a factor of considerable relevance in the growth of Dublin in the eighteenth century.

Having adverted to these general considerations, it is appropriate, then, to begin our survey in 1695 with a city of a dozen civil (or Church of Ireland) parishes, of which the following included a rural area – St Michan's which comprised the entire north side of the city, SS. Catherine & James's, St Andrew's, St Nicholas's Without and SS. Peter & Kevin's. Donnybrook was entirely a rural area, centred around the villages of Ringsend, Irishtown and Donnybrook, but this parish was nearly always included as part of the city because it had formed part of the city liberties ever since the charter of 1192.[18]

Not all of what could logically be called the city of Dublin came under the jurisdiction of the lord mayor and corporation. On the south-west and south of the city the earl of Meath's liberty of Thomas Court and Donore (originally monastery land which the earl acquired on the dissolution of the monasteries), the archbishop's liberty of St Sepulchre and the dean of St Patrick's liberty constituted quite an extensive area where the lord mayor's writ did not run. The earl's and the archbishop's liberty had each its own crude system of local government, with such officials as a steward and registrar as well as a parish watch. Each had its manor court presided over by a seneschal. They did not countenance any

16 Rutty, J. op. cit., p. 20. The following are some examples from Rutty of inconsistencies in the figures of births of males and females: *1699*: 783 M, 536 F; *1706*: 702 M, 400 F; *1720*: 704 M, 527 F. For the period 1699–1723 (eight years missing) 10,451 males were baptized as compared with 8,368 females. While up to 1724 there were each year (with one exception) more males than females, from 1724 to 1745, although the inconsistencies continued, high differences in favour of males in one year were balanced by equally high differences in favour of females in other years. From 1746 to 1770 the differences between the figures for males and females would, apart from five years, be broadly acceptable. Despite all the inconsistencies, for which no acceptable explanation can be found, the total numbers of males and females baptized in the period 1699 to 1770 (with twelve years missing) are acceptably close at 47,192 males and 46,214 females.   17 Dickson, D., op. cit. in note 7, p. 183.   18 Blacker, Beaver H., *Brief sketches of the parishes of Donnybrook and Booterstown*, Dublin 1860, p. 60.

intrusion by the lord mayor or his officials. Indeed, the lord mayor, corporation and city guilds in their triennial marking out of the city liberties, called riding the franchises, were very careful not to trespass on these other liberties. Dean Swift said of his own little liberty of St Patrick:

> I am Lord Mayor of 120 houses, I am absolute Lord of the greatest Cathedral in the Kingdom; am at peace with the neighbouring Princes, the Lord Mayor of the City, and the A. Bp. of Dublin, only the latter, like the K. of France, sometimes attempts encroachments on my Dominions ...[19]

The dean's liberty was only about 5.5 acres in extent, but by 1798 the number of houses, according to Whitelaw's census of that year, had increased to 162. Although parts of these various liberties would today be included within what is known as 'the inner city' (for example, Kevin Street and Patrick Street), they continued to be designated as Dublin county down to the 1850s.

In the case of most of the surveys of population carried out in the period under review, the three liberties mentioned are regarded as part of the city of Dublin. It will be seen that as the century advanced the rural parts of the parishes were gradually built upon and by the end of the century an overspill of population into areas beyond what was regarded as the city's perimeter had begun. Furthermore, the original parishes were in many cases subdivided as new areas were built upon and the population had sufficiently expanded. Thus, on the north side, where there was only one parish in 1695, there were five parishes in 1798. On the south side the new parishes of Saints Anne, Mark, Luke and James were established in the first two decades of the century. Appendix 1 (at p. 47 below) is a map showing the location of the different parishes.

JOHN SOUTH'S ENUMERATION, 1695

The earliest figures of population and houses relevant to the present exercise are for the year January 1695 to January 1696. These come to us under the hand of John South, commissioner of revenue in Ireland, and they are set out in Appendices 2 and 3, pp 48–9.[20] For practical purposes they can be taken to refer to the year 1695. South had this survey published by the Royal Society, London, and in the course of a letter to the president of that body, he stated: 'The whole [survey]

19 Williams, Harold (ed.), *The correspondence of Jonathan Swift*, London 1965, vol. 4, p. 171, letter dated 8 July 1733 from Swift to Pope.   20 CARD, VI, pp 575–81. William Shaw Mason in *A statistical survey of Ireland*, vol. 3, p. xvii states: 'The next attempt [at estimating the population of Ireland] was made by Capt. South in 1695. It is grounded on a poll tax, returns of which are stated for three counties and the city of Dublin, and an average struck for the rest of the Kingdom.' Thomas Newenham in *A view of Ireland*, London 1809, p. 9 Appendices states that the three counties concerned above were Armagh, Louth and Meath.

is wrought with a great deal of care and exactness and is, I believe, the most particular and certain account of the kind that has appeared in the world'.[21]

South presents us with two sets of figures – (a) the number of houses and hearths in each parish in 1695 derived from the hearth tax returns and (b) figures of population for each parish totaling 40,508, compiled about the same time in connection with a poll tax. There were several poll taxes in Ireland and Britain between 1660 and 1698, this latter one being the last in Britain. The tax could be levied weekly, quarterly or annually; for instance, the poll tax of 1697 involved a weekly tax of one penny on all persons not receiving alms.

The two sets of figures at (a) and (b), therefore, were independent of each other, and should to an extent act as a check on each other. In the first table South sets out, parish by parish, the number of houses, and shows for each parish the number of one-hearth houses, two-hearth houses, three-hearth houses and so on. He divides the houses into three categories, good, poor and waste. Good houses he defines as those 'tenanted by people of some condition', and these accounted for 78 per cent of the total. Poor houses he defines as 'houses tenanted by those who receive alms' (8 per cent of total). The third category, waste, that is unoccupied houses, accounted for 14 per cent of the total. Hearth tax was not payable on either poor houses or waste houses. The figure of 8 per cent for poor houses was about double the proportion for such houses experienced later in the century. The total number of houses was 5,999, of which 849 were unoccupied, giving a total of 5,150 inhabited houses. On the face of it, the average number of persons per house (including 'waste') in the different parishes worked out as follows: St Audoen 10.9, St Michael 11.7, St John 9.1, St Werburgh 7.2, St Andrew 5.8, St Nicholas Within 10.2, St Nicholas Without 3.8, SS. Peter & Kevin 5.5, St Bridget 5.5, Donnybrook 4.5, St Michan 8.1 and SS. Catherine & James 7.7.[22] It will be seen that some of these figures are called in question below.

It should be noted that South's house figures and population figures come from two entirely different sources. With regard to the population figures, there is convincing evidence that they do not refer to the same area as the hearth tax house figures, and that, while the latter relate, as they invariably did, to the city of Dublin and *all* the liberties, the population figures are for the city of Dublin and the *city* liberties only, and exclude the earl of Meath's liberty, the archbishop's liberty and the dean of St Patrick's liberty, these latter being officially and legally part of the county Dublin.

Indeed, if we go back to the census of 1659, a parallel situation will be found.[23]

21 CARD, VI, p. 580. 22 For the number of waste houses in each parish see CARD, VI, p. 577. As to why the number of persons per house, including waste houses, has been calculated instead of the number per inhabited house, this has been done in the interests of comparability, for it appears, as already argued in note 3, that house figures available from 1701 to 1726 include waste houses. The low average number of persons per house in St Andrews parish is due to the exceptionally high number of waste houses (21 per cent) in that parish. If only inhabited houses had been taken into account, the average in that parish would be 7.3. Reasons for low averages in other parishes are dealt with in the text. 23 Pender, Séamus, *A census of Ireland*

That census and the poll tax of 1660 are believed by some historians to have been based on the same collection of statistics. It is pertinent that in the 1659 census St Kevin's parish (which included what was later St Peter's parish and was partly in the archbishop's liberty) St Patrick's Close (elsewhere called the dean's liberty) and the earl of Meath's liberty of Donore are all included in County Dublin. St Catherine's parish is included with the city but it is not at all clear whether it includes the earl of Meath's other liberty of Thomas Court, although the earl is listed among the tituladoes of the parish. In any event there is in this 1659 census the bones of a precedent for including the dean's liberty, the archbishop's liberty and the earl of Meath's liberty under the County Dublin rather than the city.

At the time of the 1695 enumeration there were four parishes which were partly in the city liberties and partly in one or two of the other liberties mentioned – St Nicholas Without, SS. Peter & Kevin, SS. Catherine & James and St Bridget. In the case of St Nicholas's Without the house and population figures as they stand give an average of 3.8 persons per house. A comparison with the other parishes shows that this is far too low and seems to indicate that, while the population figure relates only to the part of the parish in the city liberty, the figure for houses applies in addition to that part of the parish in the earl of Meath's liberty and to a lesser portion in the archbishop's liberty. The part in the earl of Meath's liberty was indeed large enough to be hived off as the separate parish of St Luke from 1713. The average of 5.5 persons per house for SS. Peter & Kevin also appears too low and again apparently for the reason that this parish straddled the city liberty and the archbishop's liberty. The figure of 5.5 persons average per house for St Bridget is low presumably because the dean of St Patrick's liberty is covered by the houses figure but not by the population figure. While the average number of persons per house in the case of SS. Catherine & James might appear reasonable at 7.7, this scarcely reflects the very crowded conditions in the trading areas, such as Thomas Street in the heart of St Catherine's, referred to by Dobbs.[24]

Since, as demonstrated, the *non-city* liberties have been excluded from South's population figures, we have to consider what should be added to those figures so as to include those liberties.[25] A rough estimate can be arrived at by taking the parishes of St Nicholas Without, Peter & Kevin and Bridget and determining

c.1659, Dublin 1939, passim.   24 Dobbs, A., op. cit., p. 9. The suggestion that the house figures for St Bridget's included those in the dean of St Patrick's liberty may not be correct, but it is difficult otherwise to account for the low number of persons per house in St Bridget's, since that parish does not appear to have included any part of the archbishop's or the earl of Meath's liberties.   25 It may be objected that the low average number of persons per house in some parishes could have been due simply to devastation resulting from the late war. However, if we take the case of St Nicholas's Without with an average of only 3.8 persons per house, a reliable barometer of devastation ought to be the percentage of waste houses in that parish, which at 9.8 per cent was one of the lowest in the city and compared with 14 per cent for the city as a whole, with 21 per cent in St Andrew's and with 17 per cent in St Michan's. It will be seen later, in the case of the Archbishop King survey in 1716, that the average number of persons per

what increase in population in those parishes is required to bring the average number of persons per house up to, say, eight. The answer is 6,500 and if we add, say 1,000 for St Catherine & James (which had already nearly eight persons on average per house), we arrive at a figure of 7,500 as the addition to be made to South's total figure. We thus arrive at a figure of 48,000 as the population of the city in 1695. This includes certain institutions mentioned by South (see Appendix 3, p. 49 below) but not the garrison. Information on the latter was excluded probably because it was regarded as too confidential and sensitive for publication in a public document so soon after a major conflict. The exclusion of the garrison is common to all estimates of the population of the city down to 1798 when Whitelaw's census included a figure of 7,000 for that purpose. As the garrison formed part of the population of the city, there is now no valid reason for excluding it and an addition should be made in that respect to the figure of 48,000.

The standing army in Ireland in the early eighteenth century amounted to 12,000 men, made up, according to information available in the 1720s, of 37 troops of cavalry and 212 foot companies, of which three troops of cavalry and thirty foot companies were stationed in Dublin.[26] It appears from this that Dublin's share of the 12,000 was about one-seventh, or 1700 men, which with some addition for non-army personnel, wives &c., and to take account of the unsettled state of the country in 1695, could be increased to, say, 3,000. In this connection it is of interest that in the period 1701–4 a barracks of impressive proportions, capable of accommodating four regiments (about 4,000 men) and in military use as Collins Barracks until recently, was built. The inclusion of the suggested figure of 3,000 brings the estimated population of the city up to 51,000 in 1695. Had the times been normal the population would, on the basis of the number of waste houses, have been higher than this by, say, 7 per cent, but we are not concerned with what might have been. On the basis of the revised estimates for certain parishes set out above and excluding the institutions mentioned by South, the average number of persons per inhabited house in the city as a whole in 1695 was 9.2. But if waste houses are included, the average comes down to 7.8. Since house figures, at least for the first two decades of the eighteenth century, appear to include waste houses,

house in St Nicholas's Without had by then increased to 7.5, and this after the portion of the parish in the earl of Meath's liberty had been hived off as the separate parish of St Luke.   26 In a letter dated Dublin, 19 November 1726 Sylvester Lloyd, later successively bishop of Killaloe and Waterford & Lismore, disclosed detailed information to the Stuart court in Rome as to how the army was deployed throughout the country – see Patrick Fagan (ed.), *Ireland in the Stuart papers*, Dublin 1995, vol. 1, pp 87–90. Later, in 1728, the same information was made publicly available in Herman Moll's set of maps of Ireland, published that year. The latter is available in TCD early printed books library. According to Thomas Newenham the strength of the army in 1756 was 11,646, including invalids, and 8,616 in 1777, this low level being no doubt due to the withdrawal of troops for service in America. The permanent military establishment as settled in January 1692, Newenham gives very precisely as 12,284 (Thomas Newenham, *A view of Ireland*, London 1809, p. 182). Since catholics were debarred from joining the army until the 1790s, the Dublin garrison can be regarded as totally protestant prior to that date.

the average of 7.8 is taken to be the more acceptable for comparability purposes in the short term.

A noticeable feature of the population figures for the various parishes is the substantial excess, when children and servants have been excluded, of females over males in certain parishes, viz. St Nicholas's Without, St Audoen's, SS. Peter & Kevin's, St Andrew's, SS. Catherine & James's and St Michan's. Four of these – St Nicholas's Without, St Audoen's, SS. Catherine & James's and St Michan's – emerge from Archbishop King's abstract (see below) as among the more catholic parishes, but two, SS. Peter & Kevin's and St Andrew's, were protestant strongholds. The excesses might be accounted for by male casualties in the late war, or, in the case of the protestant parishes, by males still serving in the army, or, in the case of catholic parishes, by Jacobites unwilling to show their faces. But, if so, one would expect the pattern to be repeated more uniformly over all the parishes. Whatever the cause of the discrepancy, it does not seem to have much to do with religion, and when all is said and done, the simple explanation may be just plain carelessness in transcribing the figures by someone somewhere some time.

There are some further points arising from South's survey which call for comment. Firstly, in 1695 around 77 per cent of the population of 51,000 were living on the south side of the Liffey. There was still in 1695 only one parish on the north side, St Michan's, which was indeed to be divided into three parishes two years later. Secondly, just over 10 per cent of the houses in the city and all the liberties had only one hearth. More than half the houses in the parish of Donnybrook had only one hearth, indicating that this was largely a country area with small thatched houses. St Nicholas Without also had a high proportion of small houses, just a third being houses with one or two hearths. At the other end of the scale in the parishes of St Michael, St Werburgh and St Nicholas Within, houses with five hearths or more accounted for 68, 64 and 75 per cent respectively of houses in those parishes, indicating that these were areas where substantial houses, inhabited by the wealthier classes, were the norm.

Thirdly, the average number of servants per house in the different parishes is of interest. It does not come as any surprise that those parishes, already mentioned, where substantial houses were the norm, are to be found at the top of the list when the average number of servants per house are calculated for each parish. Thus St Nicholas's Within had 2.1 servants per house, St Michael's 2.0 and St Werburgh's 1.9. On the other hand, St Nicholas's Without, a mainly artisan and working-class area, had an average of 1.1 servant per house and rural Donnybrook only 0.6. In calculating the figure of 1.1 for St Nicholas's Without, regard has been had to the assumption that the number of servants, like the total population of that parish, for the reason already stated, has been considerably understated by South. It is clear from the figures that even in wealthy, middle-class parishes, the average number of servants per house was not large. Indeed, these figures should dispel any preconceived notion that there were hordes of servants at the disposal of the better-off in the Dublin of that time.

Fourthly, it is not entirely clear what South means by the term 'children'.

Thomas Shortt, writing in 1750, defined children as persons under sixteen years of age and adults as persons over sixteen years.[27] According to the 1841 census, the first to include details of age distribution, persons under sixteen years then accounted for 31.3 per cent of the population. The total of 11,515 children in South's enumeration accounted for 28.4 per cent of the population of the city as recorded by him. The difference between these percentages could be explained by alterations in the intervening period in age distribution or to some persons under sixteen years being recorded as servants by South. It seems probable, then, that South applied the same definition of children as Short.

Fifthly, on the basis of the figures presented by South and excluding the amendments suggested, the number of females in the city exceeded that of the males by 2,984, females representing 54 per cent of total population and males 46 per cent. However, when the garrison, which is taken to include some females, has been included, there is little difference between the proportions of males and females, although the latter still have a slight edge over the males.

THE MOLYNEUX PAPERS, 1706

These papers[28] present us with a figure of 7,505 houses in Dublin in 1706 and a population of 60,224, arrived at obviously on the basis of eight persons per house, an average apparently taken from South with whose work Molyneux was familiar. It is stated that the number of houses was taken from the hearth tax returns which 'were presumed to be very near the truth'. Hearth tax figures of the number of houses, available from another source, for the years 1701–5 were respectively 6,604, 6,727, 6,908, 7,140 and 7,369. When related back to South's figure of 5,999 houses, including waste, in 1695, the probability is that the figures above for 1701–5 and the Molyneux figure for 1706 also include waste houses. Molyneux propounded the rather simplistic rule-of-thumb that the number of people per house averaged 4.5 where houses had only one hearth and 8.5 where houses had more than one hearth. Since 88 per cent of houses had more than one hearth, the overall average number of persons per house, on this basis, would be eight.

THE ARCHBISHOP KING SURVEY, FEBRUARY 1716

A document in Marsh's Library, Dublin, endorsed in Archbishop King's hand, purports to give the numbers of catholics and protestants capable of bearing arms in each parish 'in the city of Dublin and the liberties thereof'.[29] The document is reproduced as Appendix 4 to this chapter (see pp 50–1 below). It appears that the

27 Short, Thomas, *New observations on city, town and country bills of mortality*, London 1750, p. 231. 28 Trinity College, Dublin ms 883, papers of William, Samuel and Thomas Molyneux, part 12, folio 330. 29 Stokes, G.T., op. cit., pp 246–8.

words 'city of Dublin and the liberties thereof' have here to be interpreted strictly, that only the city liberties are included and that the earl of Meath's liberty and the archbishop's liberty have both been excluded, but there is some doubt as to the position of the dean of St Patrick's liberty. My reason for this interpretation is that in the case of those parishes which were partly in the city liberties and partly in the archbishop's or the earl of Meath's liberty, the computed population for those parishes does not match the number of houses therein. In the case of St Catherine's (since 1708 divorced from St James's), which was partly in the city liberties and partly in the earl of Meath's liberty, the computed population is 4,330, but when this is related to the estimated number of houses in the parish in February 1716 (1,067), the average number of persons per house is only 4.1. Apparently then, King's figures do not relate to the entire parish and it seems that the portion in the earl of Meath's liberty has been excluded. Similarly in the case of St Peter's parish (partly in the city liberties and partly in the archbishop's liberty), when the computed population of 2,996 is divided by the estimated number of houses in February 1716 (710), the average number of persons per house is only 4.2, indicating that the part of the parish in the archbishop's liberty has been excluded. The averages of 4.1 and 4.2 suggest that something more than half the population of these two parishes has been excluded. Also excluded is what was from 1713 the parish of St Luke with about 530 houses entirely in the earl of Meath's liberty. Part of St Nicholas's Without in the archbishop's liberty has been excluded, but it is not possible to even hazard a guess at how many houses were involved. Ignoring this exclusion, the average number of persons per house in this latter parish is a credible 7.5 persons. We have here then precisely the same kind of difficulty as was encountered in the case of South's population figures for 1695.

King's survey is undated but when Stokes published it in his *Some worthies of the Irish Church* he was of the view that it related to some date between 1708 and 1713, since St James's parish was included and St Luke's was not, and suggested *c*.1710 as the likely date.[30] However, since St Luke's was entirely in the earl of Meath's liberty, it would not have been included even if the figures related to a date subsequent to 1713. Stoke's suggested date is not, therefore, well-founded.

Archbishop King was appointed a lord justice in September 1714 and, as such, was one of two or three men who effectively ruled the country in the lengthy absences of the lord lieutenant. The ascertainment of the number of men in Dublin capable of bearing arms would be a matter much more pertinent to his position of lord justice than to his position of archbishop. Furthermore, following King's appointment as a lord justice, there was a real emergency in 1715–16 arising from the abortive Jacobite invasion of Scotland in December 1715, a situation that might necessitate the formation of a militia. In fact militias were raised in Dublin and some other cities at this time. In the deliberations of Dublin Corpo-

30 Ibid., pp 246–7.

ration for October 1715 the raising of a city militia of three regiments of foot and one of horse is mentioned.[31] In January 1716 the lords justices and privy council ordered all mayors, sheriffs &c. to put the militia into a condition for service, arising out of the recent landing of the Pretender in Scotland.[32] At the same time the lords justices, in view of the great number of disaffected persons who had lately flocked into the city, required the lord mayor to take an account, distinguishing protestants from papists, of the names of all the housekeepers, lodgers and male servants in the city and its liberties. The lord mayor ordered the alderman of each ward to start the investigation on 31 January 1716 and to take with him the deputy alderman and constables to assist him.[33] Although there was nothing in the lord mayor's order restricting the investigation to men capable of bearing arms, it appears very likely that King based his abstract on the lord mayor's investigation. Terming it an abstract at all implied that it was derived from more detailed information. On this basis, then, the King abstract can be dated quite precisely as February 1716.

The inclusion of catholics in the survey can scarcely mean that King was prepared to admit them to the militia, more particularly as the lords justices at the same time ordered that the laws against papists were to be strictly enforced. It may be that King was simply ascertaining the relative strengths of protestants and catholics in the city in the event of open hostilities.

King's survey shows a total of 17,709 persons, presumably all male, capable of bearing arms in the city and city liberties. It is assumed that this was approximately the number of men aged between 17 and 45 years. There would be a somewhat similar number of women in the same age group, making a total of 35,500 for that age group. As to what proportion of the entire population of the city this 35,500 represented, the earliest census for which reliable figures of age distribution are available is that for 1841, when the 17–45 age group accounted for 43 per cent of the population.[34] In the same census the over–45 age group accounted for 14.8 per cent. Bearing in mind the advances made between 1716 and 1841 in the treatment of diseases, particularly smallpox, the percentage over 45 in 1716 would be significantly less than the 14.8 per cent recorded in 1841, and the percentage in the 17–45 age group would consequently be somewhat higher than the 43 per cent recorded for that group in 1841. This appears to

31 CARD, VI, p. 547.   32 National Archives, MIA 52.166 – State Papers Office misc. letters and papers.   33. CARD, VII, p. 576. The lord mayor's investigation does not appear to have survived. I am assuming that actual capability to bear arms was not taken into account by King. The age limits for military service provided for in the Irish Militia Act 1793 were 18 to 45 years, but it seems clear that age limits of 16–45 years were applied in some parts of the country; see Henry MacAnally, *The Irish militia 1793–1816*, Dublin 1949, 29 & 232. E. Wakefield in *An account of Ireland, statistical and political*, London 1812, p. 692 mentions a 'return of men ... between the ages of sixteen and forty-five years, fit to serve in the militia'. In the case of the King abstract I have assumed age limits of 17–45 as a sort of compromise on the differing age limits above. Incidentally, under the US Universal Militia Law of 1792 all males aged 18–45 years were liable for military service.   34 *Census of Ireland 1841*, p. xlviii.

point in the direction of 46 per cent as the proportion of Dublin's population in the 17–45 age group in 1716. The figure of 35,500 already computed for that age group would thus be 46 per cent of the total population of the city and city liberties in 1716, which latter can then be calculated as 77,000. But if, say, 12,000 is added in respect of the two liberties mentioned,[35] the population of Dublin *and all its liberties* was something of the order of 89,000 (plus, say, 3,000 in respect of the garrison and 1,000 for certain institutions) in 1716. On the basis of an estimated 9,580 houses (including waste) in Dublin city and all the liberties, the average number of persons per house would be 9.3 as compared with 7.8 in 1695.

As to the relation which the number of men capable of bearing arms was believed to bear to the total population, it is of interest that Thomas Newenham, writing in 1805, stated that it was generally found to constitute at least one-fifth (that is, possibly something more than 20 per cent) of the population.[36] This is near enough to the 23 per cent (that is, half of 46 per cent) which emerges above as applicable to men in the 17–45 age group.

An important aspect of King's survey is that it enables a calculation to be made of the proportions of protestants and catholics in the city's population. It will be noted from King's abstract that of male servants capable of bearing arms (i.e. between the ages of 17 and 45), 2,251 were protestant and only 882 were catholic. But King here presents only one side – the male side – of the coin, and if he were to present the other, the female, side, an entirely different picture of female servants, where it is suggested catholics would be in the majority, would emerge. Furthermore, it is necessary to take into account the total servant population of the city and here it will be seen from South's enumeration above that male servants accounted for 7 per cent of the population and female servants for 10 per cent. If we apply these percentages to the computed population of the city and city liberties of 77,000 in 1716, an estimated 5,390 male servants and 7,700 female servants are arrived at. Now, it is entirely credible that the vast majority of the better class of servant (butler, cook, *valet de chambre*, coachman etc.) would be male and protestant, but it is equally credible that the vast majority of the more menial servants would be female and catholic.[37] Accordingly, the figure of 13,090 for all servants, male and female, in

35 The figure of 12,000 is calculated as follows. The number of houses concerned is estimated at 1,380, made up of: St Luke's 530 – a reliable figure from CARD, VII, p. 577 – St Catherine's 500 and St Peter's 350, on the basis already suggested that half the houses in St Catherine's and St Peter's were in a non-city liberty. 1,380 houses with nine persons average per house gives a total of 12,420 (say, 12,000) persons.   36 Newenham, Thomas, *A statistical and historical inquiry into the progress and magnitude of the population of Ireland*, London 1805, p. 316.   37 There is a difference between the figure for male servants of military age (3,133) disclosed by the King abstract and the total of male servants (5,390) arrived at on the basis of 7 per cent of the population which cannot be explained by the number of servants under or over military age. The probability is that one of these figures understates, while the other overstates, the position. The number, according to King, of male protestant servants invites comment. It is probable

all age groups, might be expected to break down as something of the order of 6,000 protestant and 7,000 catholic. Adjusting and extrapolating King's figures to meet this new situation, and allowing, say 3,000, all protestant, in respect of the garrison, it will be found that in the city and city liberties about 65 per cent of the population were protestant and about 35 per cent were catholic.[38]

In this connection there are two further, and to an extent counter-balancing, factors which need to be mentioned. Firstly, the proportions arrived at above for protestants and catholics are in respect of the city and city liberties, but the archbishop's and earl of Meath's liberties could be expected to be more protestant and less catholic. As against that, the calculation of the population for the city and city liberties assumes that the catholic proportion for the 17–45 age group was repeated in the under-17 age group. There is evidence that it would be incorrect to make such an assumption. The bills of mortality for Dublin city and suburbs for the seven years 1712–18 show that, of the total number who died in that period, 55 per cent were under sixteen years. The poorer stratum of the population, generally catholics, can be assumed to have accounted for far more than their fair share of these deaths of persons under sixteen years.[39] It must follow from this that catholics made up a higher, though unquantifiable, proportion of the under-16 age group than of the over-16 age group, and that accordingly the catholic proportion for all age groups would be something higher than that estimated above. However, if we assume that this factor more or less counterbalances the other factor mentioned above, then we can regard the proportions of 65 per cent protestant and 35 per cent catholic as applying to Dublin city and all the liberties.

It could be reasonably expected that the average number of persons per catholic house was significantly higher than the average number per protestant house. An examination of the figures in the King survey provides evidence of this and indicates the coefficients concerned. It will be seen that the number of house-keepers (i.e. heads of houses) was 6,371 (4,693 protestant and 1,678 catholic) as com-

that they were mostly dissenters, a high proportion of whom would be working-class, particularly if they were from the north of Ireland. Some also came from Britain, for in the survey attributed to Bindon (see below) there is mention of 'the many servants from Great Britain who have settled among us, who are all Protestants'. In contrast to this by the end of the century Whitelaw was claiming that servants in protestant houses in Dublin 'were mostly of the Church of Rome'; see letter dated 20 June (year not given) from James Whitelaw to Edward Wakefield quoted in the latter's *An account of Ireland statistical and political*, London 1812, vol. 2, p. 793. The evident erosion of the protestant working class as the century advanced can be seen as one of the factors contributing to the decline in the protestant share of the population.   38 According to the King abstract the total numbers of protestant and catholic housekeepers, inmates and lodgers, capable of bearing arms, were respectively 9,797 and 4,779. It is a matter of extrapolating from these figures, in the manner already set out, the total number of protestants and catholics, and keeping in mind that this excludes servants. We thus arrive at 42,600 protestants (to which should be added 3,000 for garrison) and 20,800 catholics. With the addition of 6,000 protestant servants and 7,000 catholic ones totals of 51,600 protestants and 27,800 catholics are arrived at, that is, a population which was 65 per cent protestant and 35 per cent catholic, total population being somewhat higher than previously estimated.   39 CARD, VIII, p. 578.

pared with an estimated total of 8,200 houses in the city and city liberties in 1716. The term 'housekeeper' is here restricted to housekeepers capable of bearing arms, and hence the number of housekeepers does not equate with the number of houses. It is calculated that housekeepers were in the proportion of 47 protestant to 17 catholic, and if we similarly apportion the houses, we get 6,000 protestant houses and 2,200 catholic. By relating these figures to populations of 49,000 protestants and 28,000 catholics, figures averaging 12.7 (say, 12.5) persons per catholic house and 8.2 (say, 8) per protestant house emerge. It should be borne in mind that these figures are in respect of the city and city liberties only, and to take account of the other, more protestant, liberties, these coefficients should be adjusted to 12 and 8.5 respectively. It also appears to be the case that the higher coefficient per catholic family was due, not so much to catholic families being larger, but to the larger number of families crammed into some catholic houses. That these coefficients are, if anything, conservative is evident from Whitelaw's census of 1798 where an average of sixteen persons per house in the poor and, by then predominantly catholic, parishes of St Luke and St Michael, contrasts with an average of 8.7 in the rich and very protestant parish of St George. Admittedly, the above calculations disregard catholic servants in protestant houses.

The fact that in St Mary's parish it was not possible to discover the religious persuasion of 26 servants indicates that some effort was made to ascertain religious persuasion generally. King's abstract enables us to make a rough estimate of the proportions of catholics and protestants in the different parishes, but in arriving at the number of catholics and protestants in each parish, the same considerations arise in relation to the number of protestant and catholic servants as was noted in regard to the population of the city as a whole. However, in attempting to determine the total number of servants, male and female, in each parish we cannot apply the proportions of 7 per cent male and 10 per cent female of total population thrown up by the South survey, since these are averages for all parishes, and some parishes would be above the average and some below. In arriving at an estimate of the number of servants in each parish, it seems best to take the average number of servants per house in each parish, also available from the South survey, and multiply this by the estimated number of houses in each parish in February 1716 (i.e. the mean of the figures available for 1712 and 1718). Bearing in mind these considerations, the catholic percentages in the various parishes would work out at the following percentages: St Audoen's 67, St Catherine's 65, St Michael's 54, St Nicholas's Without 50, St Paul's 47, Donnybrook 46, St James's 44, St Michan's 40, St Mary's 31, St Peter's 31, St John's 30, St Nicholas's Within 28, St Bridget's 24, St Werburgh's 23 and St Andrew's 20. St Luke's was not covered by the King abstract since it was entirely outside the remit of the lord mayor and corporation. St Anne's does not figure in the abstract since it was not operational at the time in question.

It appears from this exercise that there were only two parishes in the city with a catholic majority in 1716 – St Audoen's with 67 per cent and St Michael's with

54 per cent. St Catherine's shows a catholic majority of 65 per cent but this is only in respect of the part of the parish in the city liberties, that is Thomas Street and the part of the parish north thereof. The situation in the remainder of the parish may be divined from the earl of Meath's attitude to catholics as reported by an English visitor, John Dunton, in 1698: 'There are not four Papist masters of families dwelling in all this liberty, so little is that noble lord an encourager of such people'.[40]

But can the King abstract be relied on to give a true picture of the catholic and protestant proportions of the population of the different parishes? In the case of St Bridget's, it will be seen that the percentage of catholics given above is reasonably close to that included in returns from that parish in 1718 referred to later in this chapter. In the case of St Michan's, however, a survey in 1723 showed that only one-third belonged to the established church.[41] After taking account of protestant dissenters, total protestant population could not then have amounted to much more than 40 per cent, with catholics thus accounting for around 60 per cent. That this was the more likely scenario than that shown by the King abstract is borne out by the estimated number of catholic baptisms of 300 in the civil parish of St Michan in 1726, which on the basis of a probable birth-rate of 35 per 1000 would point to a catholic population of about 8,500. The earliest records for catholic parishes in the city are those for St Michan's and St Mary's, which date from end-February 1726; I have taken into account that St Michan's catholic parish was about four-fifths of St Michan's civil parish in terms of population. The total population of St Michan's in 1726 was about 14,000 (i.e. 1,150 houses x 12 persons per house as disclosed by the 1723 survey) and accordingly on this estimate also the catholic proportion emerges as just 60 per cent. While part of the discrepancy could be explained by continuing catholic infiltration of the parish between 1716 and 1726, the conclusion must be that the King abstract, as extrapolated, significantly under-estimated the proportion of catholics in St Michan's parish. A further proof of catholic strength as early as 1697 in the parishes of St Michan's and St Paul's is the presence there at that date, according to a government source which also names the priests concerned, of eight secular and four regular priests.[42] It is also pertinent that all four orders of nuns established in the city between 1712 and 1730 were located initially either in St Michan's or St Paul's (one order subsequently moving to the south side), a further indication that these two parishes were staunchly catholic from early in the century.

In the case of St Mary's, the estimated number of catholic baptisms in 1726 was 140, pointing to a catholic population of about 4,000. When related to total population in the parish in 1726 of about 12,000, a catholic proportion of 33.3 per cent emerges and this is very close to the 34 per cent arrived at from King's

---

40 John Dunton's letters included in Edward MacLysaght, *Irish life in the seventeenth century*, Dublin 1969, p. 385.   41 Henry Monck Mason Ms, Gilbert Library. This matter is treated further at p. 32 following.   42 *Irish Builder*, vol. 34 (1892), passim.

abstract. I can find no independent data against which to check the percentages of catholics in the remaining parishes disclosed by King's abstract. However, the report on popery 1731 (see below) identifies, through the absence of catholic chapels or schools, St Andrew's, St Nicholas's Within, St Werburgh's, St John's and St Bridget's as protestant strongholds, and this is broadly in accord with the results deduced from King's abstract.

EXPANSION OF THE CITY, 1700–20

The early decades of the eighteenth century was a period of unprecedented expansion in the city. A significant part of this expansion can be presumed to be due to migration, mainly catholic, into the city from the provinces. A resolution of Dublin Corporation in 1707 made reference to the fact that 'great numbers of Irish Papists of late repaired to this city and follow several trades therein'.[43] A case in point was the guild of barber-surgeons (predominantly barbers and peruke-makers) which was so swamped by 'foreigners' – that is, barbers and peruke-makers from the provinces – that the number of these 'foreigners' in the early years of the century exceeded the number of free brothers of the guild.[44]

The total number of houses in the city in 1718 was 10,004, or an increase of two-thirds on the 1695 figure of 5,999. The peripheral parishes accounted for over 90 per cent of the increase of 4,000 houses in the twenty-three year period in question. Clearly, there could be little expansion in centre-city parishes which were hemmed in by other parishes and whose lands had already been fully built on in 1695. The increase in the number of houses was most striking on the north side of the city where the old parish of St Michan (divided into the three parishes of St Paul, St Michan and St Mary since 1697) saw the number of houses increase from 1,101 in 1695 to 2,414 in 1718. On the south side parishes with rural hinterlands also had large increases in the number of houses. St Andrew's showed an increase of 469 houses, St Bridget's 212, St Nicholas's Without and St Luke's 473, St Catherine's and St James's 572, St Peter's 332 and Donnybrook 267. The increase in population on the south side led to the creation of the four new parishes of St Mark, St James, St Anne and St Luke in 1707.[45]

---

43 CARD, VI, p. 379.   44 Trinity College, Dublin Ms 144/7. The term 'foreigners' was derived from the Old French *forain* and the Latin *foris* (outside) and here simply meant people from outside the city.   45 While the act for dividing several parishes in Dublin 1707, 6 Anne c. 21, established the new parishes of St Mark, St Anne, St Luke and St James, these parishes did not become operational until several years thereafter on the occurrence of vacancies for rectors in the parishes divided. St Mark's was hived off from St Andrew's and St Luke's from St Nicholas's Without. St Anne's was formed from parts of St Peter's and St Bridget's. The new St James's parish resulted from the abolition of the united parish of St Catherine, St James and St John of Kilmainham, and the substitution therefor of two parishes, St Catherine's and St James's, the latter including what was formerly St John's of Kilmainham.

ARTHUR DOBBS'S ESTIMATE OF POPULATION, 1728

Dobbs in his *Essay on trade and improvement in Ireland*, published in Dublin in 1731, sought to estimate the population in 1728 by reference to the number of deaths in the city in that year, which he calculated as 3,000, related to a death-rate of one in thirty (33.33 per 1,000 of the population).[46] He compared the resulting figure of 90,000 with figures arrived at by multiplying the number of inhabited houses from the hearth tax returns for 1728 (11,086) firstly by 12.5 people per house (computed by a Dr Tisdall) and secondly by ten people per house, which he remarked 'some think is a low enough computation, considering how many live in a house in the trading part of the city (where seventy persons have been known to live in a house, there being a family sometimes in each room, oftentimes on each floor and in the cellars)'.[47]

It is apparent that Dobbs had little faith in estimates of population arrived at from the total number of deaths in a year and that he rejects this method in favour of the number of houses in the hearth tax returns multiplied by an average number of people per house, which he was apparently unwilling to accept as lower than ten and which resulted in a population figure of 110,860 for 1728. To this should be added, say, 3,000 in respect of the garrison and, say, 1,000 for institutions.

Dobbs's remark in the same book that 'catholics and dissenters were equal in number to, if they did not exceed, members of the established church' is interesting, coming as it does from a protestant commentator more likely than most to be objective in his views. In order to translate Dobbs's comment into what should be the proportions of catholics and protestants (i.e. members of the established church plus dissenters), it is necessary to attempt some assessment of the proportion of dissenters in the Dublin population in the 1720s. Although by the beginning of the nineteenth-century protestant dissenters of all kinds accounted for about 4 per cent of the population of the city,[48] there are grounds for believing that the proportion was appreciably higher in the early decades of the eighteenth century. Their problem was similar to that of the established church in that as the century advanced their numbers tended to remain static, while the catholic proportion was swollen by migration from the provinces as well as by a higher fertility rate.[49] While no precise statistics of the total number of dissenters in the city

---

46 Dobbs, A., op. cit., part 2, p. 9. A member of the Irish house of commons, Dobbs was appointed surveyor-general for Ireland *c.*1730. 47 Ibid. 48 Warburton, John, Whitelaw, James & Walsh, Robert, *History of the city of Dublin*, London 1818, vol. 2, p. 848. Following the deaths of Warburton and Whitelaw, the work was finished by Walsh. 49 The higher fertility rate of the poorer classes (generally catholics) is mentioned in several contemporary books and pamphlets, e.g. Dobbs, A. op. cit., part 2, p. 13; *An abstract of the numbers of protestant and popish families*, Dublin 1736, p. 11; *A serious proposal for the entire destruction of popery in Ireland*, Dublin 1732, p. 1; Letters of a 'French visitor' in the *Dublin News-letter* for 8–12 December 1741. The 'French visitor' stated: 'I believe the poor Irish are the most broody people on the face of the Globe.' However, the higher fertility rate has to be balanced against a higher mortal-

in the first half of the century have been uncovered, there are certain straws in the wind to be considered. Figures furnished by the minister of the established church in St Nicholas's Within in 1718 showed that in that parish the established church accounted for 51 per cent of the population, catholics for 25 per cent and presbyterians for 24 per cent.[50] A similar return in 1718 for St Bridget's showed that the established church accounted for 77 per cent of the population, dissenters for 9 per cent and catholics for 14 per cent.[51]

More significantly still, out of a total of 2,272 free brothers (all by definition non-catholics) from twenty-five city guilds who appeared in lists for the 1749 election in Dublin, 389, or 17.1 per cent, were dissenters or quakers.[52] Since this sample is sufficiently large and represents a cross-section of different trades and manufacturers, it follows that the percentage of 17.1 thrown up by the sample ought to be broadly true for the protestant population of the city. If all protestants in 1749 made up around 50 per cent of the city's population – a reasonable premise – it would follow that dissenters in 1749 accounted for about 8.5 per cent of the population. In the 1720s and 1730s, when protestants made up a higher proportion of the city population, the dissenter proportion could be expected to be around 10 per cent. On this reasoning, and accepting Dobbs's view above, the protestant proportion of the population of the city in 1728 would have been around 60 per cent and the catholic around 40 per cent.

Dobbs gave the following figures of the number of houses in the city for the years mentioned: *1712*: 9,176; *1718*: 9,505; *1725*: 11,466; *1726*: 11,525. As regards the figures for 1725 and 1726 for the entire country, Dobbs remarked:[53]

> The difference between the returns in 1725 and 1726, as I apprehend, is occasioned by the Collectors not making a regular return of the houses of the poor, who are certified to live on alms and don't pay the tax; some in their abstracts returning them, some in part and some not at all.

Since some collectors did not make a return of the houses of the very poor and since these would be predominantly catholic, this represented a further factor in the under-estimation of the number of catholics in the city.

For the 1730s several estimates of the population of the city have come down to us. Edward Lloyd in his *Description of the city of Dublin*, printed in 1732,[54] estimated the city population at 150,000, while a French visitor, writing about 1734,[55] estimated it at 120,000, this latter on the basis of 12,000 houses with an

ity rate among catholic children.   **50** Monck Mason, H., op. cit., part 3, p. 328.   **51** Ibid., part 3, p. 343.   **52** Haliday pamphlets, Royal Irish Academy, no. 214 (1749). The list of freemen of Dublin for the 1749 election is annotated in the Academy's copy to show freemen who were dissenters or quakers.   **53** Dobbs, A., op. cit., part 2, p. 7. Dobbs's figure for 1718 (9,505) compares with 10,004 for that year in CARD, VII, p. 577. It is probable that Dobbs's figure in this instance is in respect of inhabited houses.   **54** Lloyd, Edward, *Description of the city of Dublin*, London 1732, p. 2.   **55** *Dublin News-letter*, 8–12 December 1741.

average of ten persons per house. Other more elaborate estimates for the 1730s are dealt with below.

THE REPORT ON POPERY, 1731

This report was compiled from returns made by the minister of each parish, the lord mayor and the seneschals of the liberties on the directions of the Irish house of lords in November 1731.[56] While it does not provide any figures of population, it does provide some pointers as to which parishes had the higher percentages of catholics in 1731. Thus St Catherine's had in the part of the parish in Thomas Street and north thereof three mass-houses, twenty priests and four schools, indicating that this area was principally catholic; the presence of four schools in the part of the parish in the earl of Meath's liberty south of Thomas Street indicated a significant catholic infiltration into this part of the parish also.[57] St Nicholas's Without also emerges as a catholic stronghold with two mass-houses – one of these, in Francis Street, the largest in the city – fifteen priests and sixteen school-masters. That there was a catholic overspill into the adjacent largely protestant St Luke's is clear from the presence there of six catholic schools.[58]

St Michael's, which was estimated to be 54 per cent catholic in 1716, no doubt had by now swung further in favour of the catholics with two mass-houses, ten to twelve priests and five schools.[59] St Audoen's, which had an estimated 67 per cent catholic majority in 1716 must have had in the meantime extended that majority even further with two mass-houses, a quite extraordinary number of priests (forty to fifty) and three schools.[60] In St Michan's civil parish there were three mass-houses, twelve schools but the number of priests could not be ascertained.[61] It was reported that there was one mass-house with one priest, but no school in St Mary's parish. Although St Paul's is listed as having no mass-house, priests or school, in fact the catholic parish of St Paul had a chapel which happened to be in the civil parish of St Michan, the boundaries of the catholic and civil parishes not coinciding. For the same reason four of the twelve schools in the civil parish of St Michan belonged to the catholic parish of St Paul.

A catholic beachhead had emerged in the south-east of the city in the new civil parish of St Mark where there were two schools, one mass-house and seven priests who looked after the parishes of St Anne, St Andrew and St Peter as

56 The report was published in *Archivium Hibernicum*, vol. 4 (1915), pp 131–49. 57 Ibid., p. 138. To describe them as schools is to give a wrong impression in the majority of cases. At the beginning of the nineteenth century William Carleton claimed that nearly half of the Dublin schools were 'hedge-schools taught in private rooms by men, who were unworthy to be compared for a moment with the great body of country hedge school masters of Ireland. They were for the most part, if not illiterate, excessively and barbarously ignorant' (Carleton, William, *Autobiography*, originally published London 1896, republished Belfast 1996, p. 167). 8 *Archivium Hibernicum*, vol. 4 (1915), pp 146–7. 59 Ibid., pp 140–1. 60 Ibid., pp 137–8. 61 Ibid., p. 141.

well.[62] The absence of any priests, mass-houses or schools in the parishes of St Anne, St John, St Nicholas Within, St Werburgh and St Bridget mark these out as parishes with strong protestant majorities. In the case of St Bridget's it was stated that 'priests in Francis Street [St Nicholas's Without parish] and Hawkins Street [St Mark's parish] perform what occasional duties happen among the Popish inhabitants'.[63] Of four schools stated by the seneschal to be in the liberty of St Sepulchre, the archbishop's liberty, one was in St Patrick's Close in the deanery of St Patrick and the other three were probably in the part of St Peter's parish in the archbishop's liberty, although the minister of that parish did not return them. Donnybrook was reported to have one mass-house with one priest at Irishtown.[64]

SURVEY ATTRIBUTED TO DAVID BINDON, 1732–3

The purpose of this survey, which covers the whole country, was to find out the number of protestant and catholic families, and it is quite apparent that the author set out to prove to his own satisfaction that the catholic majority in the country as a whole was not nearly as great as it was generally supposed to be.[65] He states that his abstract was taken from the returns made by the hearth tax collectors to the hearth tax office in Dublin for the years 1732 and 1733, 'those being reckoned Protestant and Popish houses, where the heads of the families are either Protestants or Papists'.[66]

For Dublin city the abstract shows that there were 12,942 families , 8,823 of which were protestant and 4,119 catholic. Although the abstract refers specifically to *families*, the author, in his observations on the abstract, at times uses the terms *families* and *houses* as synonymous. It also appears from the instructions given to the hearth tax collectors at the time of the enumeration that *families* and *houses* were regarded as interchangeable.[67] Furthermore, the English writer, Thomas Short MD, came to the conclusion that *families* were synonymous with *houses* in the case of an enumeration carried out in Dublin in 1745.[68] It seems safe to conclude, then, that the figures for families given above are in fact the figures for houses. The fact that the figure of 12,942 houses which emerges here is some 10 per cent higher than the hearth tax house figure (11,718) for 1733, may be attributable in part to this figure of 12,942 being based on the hearth tax returns for two years 1732 and 1733, and presumably to houses being included if they appeared in the returns for either year, in which case the figure of 12,942 is probably excessive. It may also be the case that, since the figures were required for the

62 Ibid., pp 139–40.   63 Ibid., p. 144.   64 Ibid., pp 148–9.   65 *An abstract of the numbers of protestant and popish families*, Dublin 1736, attributed to David Bindon in the Gilbert Library, Dublin catalogue.   66 Ibid., p. 1.   67 Dickson, D., Ó Gráda, C. and Daultry, S., 'Hearth tax, household size and Irish population change 1672–1871' in *Proceedings of the Royal Irish Academy*, 82 (C) 1982, 141.   68 Short, Thomas MD, *New observations on city, town and country bills of mortality*, London 1750, p. 238.

particular purpose of estimating the proportions of protestants and catholics in the population, the collectors exercised more care than usual in collecting them. There is the further consideration that the figure of 12,924 would include houses of the poor not subject to the tax.

It has already been calculated that, in the case of the Archbishop King survey, catholic houses averaged 12 persons per house and protestant houses 8.5 persons. By applying these factors to the figures for catholic and protestant houses in the 1732–3 survey, the number of catholics emerges as 49,500 and the number of protestants as 75,000, giving a total of 124,500, which was 40 per cent catholic and 60 per cent protestant. But by using the hearth tax figure for 1733, with ten persons average per house, a total population of 117,000 emerges. Again, something, say, 4,000, requires to be added to both figures in respect of the garrison and institutions. It is of interest that in the preparation of this survey, sample surveys of the average number of persons per house were carried out in different parts of the country and that in Dublin the average was found to be 'near ten souls to a house'.[69]

Scheme of the proportions which the Protestants of Ireland may probably bear to the Papists, 1732

The author of this pamphlet presents us with two separate calculations of the population of Dublin. In the first, on the basis of a figure for houses of 13,427 and thirteen persons per house, he arrived at a population of 174,500, which he 'supposed' could be broken down in the proportions of three protestants to one catholic. In a second calculation he arrives at 48,000 as the catholic population, based on the capacity of fifteen chapels with four Masses each on Sundays, implying an average capacity of 800 persons per chapel, and 74,000 as the protestant population, this latter arrived at in a convoluted way from Petty's 1672 estimate.[70] Total population in this latter case would be 122,000 and the proportions would be 40 per cent catholic and 60 per cent protestant. Despite his unorthodox methods, then, his final results were remarkably close to those extrapolated from the survey attributed to David Bindon. He divulges the interesting snippet that protestant servants employed in catholic houses 'can be no inconsiderable number',[71] although this was flatly contradicted by Bindon's abstract above which stated that there were 'few or no Protestant servants in Popish families'.[72] The reason for the employment of protestant servants in wealthier catholic houses was that such servants, unlike their catholic masters, could bear arms and therefore could afford a degree of protection. The practice was prevalent enough for the government to take note of it in a 1739 act for disarming papists, section 14 of which prevented protestant servants in catholic houses from bearing arms.[73]

69 Bindon, D. attrib., op. cit., p. 8.   70 Anon., *Scheme of proportions which the protestants of Ireland may probably bear to papists*, Dublin 1732, pp 10–11.   71 Ibid., p. 14.   72 Bindon, D., attrib., op. cit., pp 9–10.   73 13 George II c. 6.

MONCK MASON MANUSCRIPT, GILBERT LIBRARY

This survey was copied from original sources by Henry Monck Mason in the nineteenth century. It purports to give the number of houses and the population in each parish in 1733. The purpose of the survey was to discover whether the existing churches were sufficient to cater for the needs of the members of the established church. It found that the number of churches was quite insufficient to cater for the needs of what it called 'the conformist population' and went on: 'From this want of churches it is easy to foresee how few are likely to be brought over to the Established Church, and what danger there is that popery and licentiousness should increase among us.'[74] It attributed the frequent Sunday riots to the influence of popery and licentiousness.

An average of twelve persons per house for the city as a whole was arrived at on the basis of an enumeration in St Michan's parish. A note to the survey states:

> The number of souls is twelve times that of the houses, it having been found by counting the houses and inhabitants in St Michan's parish in 1723 that there were exactly twelve souls to a house and as the buildings and inhabitants of that parish seem to correspond for fullness and thinness with the several parts of the other parishes, it is apprehended that this proportion of twelve souls will hold true throughout the city.[75]

The survey sets out the number of occupied houses in each parish and, by allowing twelve persons per house, purports to compute the population of each parish. Populations of parishes arrived at on this basis are, of course, totally unreal because the average number of people per house, as we have seen from other surveys, varied greatly from parish to parish. It was quite incorrect, for example, to apply an average of twelve to Donnybrook, where the average was probably at that time no more than six, and thus doubling the population figure for that parish. On the basis of a total of 11,718 houses and an average of twelve persons per house a population of 140,616 was arrived at.

Quite extraordinarily, members of the established church were taken to be only one-third of the population of the city, because this was found to be the proportion 'which conformists bore to the rest of the inhabitants in St Michan's parish on viewing and comparing them together in 1723, and because this parish corresponds to the rest of the city ... in the proportion which Conformists, Dissenters and Papists bear to each other'.[76] The conformist populations of the different parishes were then computed by simply taking one-third of the population of each parish as computed by the method mentioned above, a computation which, as we have seen, was itself bizarre.

The figures given in this survey for the populations of parishes, as well as the

74 Monck Mason, H., op. cit., part 3, p. 153.   75 Ibid., p. 155.   76 Ibid.

figures for the established church in those parishes, are in the majority of cases quite incorrect and the survey cannot be relied on at all in either of these respects. Indeed, the only part of the survey which can be taken at all seriously is the number of inhabited houses for each parish, which adds up to a total of 11,718 for the city as a whole.

VARIOUS ESTIMATES, 1740S TO 1760S

From the 1740s to the 1760s there were a number of enumerations, often contradictory, of the houses in Dublin and of estimates of the population of the city. In 1740, according to Warburton,[77] the supervisors of the hearth tax returned the number of protestant housekeepers in Dublin city and county as 7,065, a figure which is obviously too low. An enumeration made in 1745 for the lord mayor showed 5,639 protestant families and 3,575 catholic ones in the city,[78] i.e. a total of 9,214 but here as in other surveys of the period, for families we can presumably read houses. Since the enumeration was made for the lord mayor, it seems safe to assume that the liberties of the earl of Meath, the dean of St Patrick's and the archbishop were not included, but even on that assumption the figure of 9,214 houses appears too low when compared with figures of the total number of houses for 1744 and 1745 in note 3 above.

On the basis of the number of burials in Dublin in 1753, John Rutty MD estimated the population of the city in that year as 62,500, but he rejected this in favour of a figure of 128,570, calculated by taking the hearth tax figure of 12,857 houses for 1753 and multiplying by an average of ten persons per house.[79] It is of interest that, when Rutty was writing in the early 1770s, he could discern a decrease in the birth-rate, the cause of which he put down to increased consumption of spirituous liquors.

Thomas Newenham, writing in the early years of the nineteenth century, recalled that Dublin city furnished 11,772 protestants for a militia in 1756.[80] The occasion was the outbreak of the Seven Years' War and the threat of a French invasion of Ireland. Using a rule-of-thumb (already mentioned) prevalent at the time that men capable of bearing arms were equivalent to at least one-fifth of the population, he arrived at a total protestant population of the city of 58,860 (say, 59,000). The preciseness of the figure of 11,772 indicates that it was the result of an enumeration of some sort, but whether it covered the earl of Meath's and the archbishop's liberties is not entirely clear. Newenham took it as applying to the entire city, and the figure of 59,000 protestants (plus 3,000 for the garrison) for the mid-1750s should be accepted, I suggest, as a reasonably dependable rough estimate. It compares with an estimated total population, including garrison &c.,

77 Warburton, J. et al., op. cit., vol. 2, p. 847.   78 Short, T., op. cit., p. 229.   79 Rutty, J., op. cit., p. 17.   80 Newenham, Thomas, *A view of Ireland*, London 1809, p. 182.

of 135,000 for 1756, divided 54 per cent catholic and 46 per cent protestant and this would mean that catholics achieved a majority for the first time in the 1750s.

According to *Watson's Dublin Almanac* the following were the number of houses, as disclosed by the hearth tax returns, in Dublin city in the years mentioned: 1749:12,407; 1752: 12,575; 1753:12,857; 1760: 13,461.[81] As already conjectured these figures appear to be in respect of inhabited houses. A comparison of the figure for 1753 with a figure of 11,645 houses produced by a count by me of the houses in Rocque's map (drawn in 1754–5),[82] shows that the hearth tax figure for 1753 is reasonably close to actuality, given that the count mentioned necessarily does not include Donnybrook parish (about 550 houses) nor the extremities of several other parishes.

It is, however, appropriate at this point to review the figure for the average number of people per house. It is important to remember that there are two sets of figures to be considered – the average number of persons for inhabited houses and the average number of people where all houses, including waste or uninhabited houses, are taken into account. The first of these increased from 9.2 in South's survey of 1695 to 11.2 in Whitelaw's census of 1798, while the second increased from 7.8 in 1695 (South) to 10.4 in 1798 (Whitelaw). From the late 1720s onwards an average of ten, presumably per inhabited house, gained wide acceptance among eighteenth century commentators. Whitelaw's average of 11.2 would gradually have been building up in the decades prior to the 1790s and, on the basis of an average of about ten in the 1730s, it is reasonably safe to assume an average of 10.5 persons per house in the 1760s. On the basis of a city of 13,461 houses there would thus have been a population, including garrison &c., of 145,300 in 1760. As already argued, after 1760 the number of houses in the city, as disclosed in the hearth tax returns published in *Watson's Dublin Almanac*, should be regarded as increasingly unreliable as a basis for estimating population.

THE RELIGIOUS CENSUS OF 1766

This census was authorized by a resolution of the Irish house of lords dated 5 March 1766 which stated:

> Resolved that the several archbishops and bishops of this kingdom shall be and are hereby desired to direct the parish ministers in their respective dioceses to return a list of the several families in their parishes to this house on the first Monday after the recess, distinguishing which are protestants and which are Papists, also a list of the several reputed Popish priests and friars residing in their parishes.[83]

81 See *Watson's Dublin Almanac* for 1752, 1753, 1755, 1761 and 1767 respectively.   82 See note 8 in regard to the number of houses shown in Rocque's map.   83 *Journal of the Irish house of lords*, vol. 4, p. 370.

No set form as to how the census was to be returned was laid down by their lordships or by the prelates who coordinated it. Consequently, the returns varied considerably in content. Some merely gave the number of families of each religion in the parish. Some gave lists of heads of families, with an indication as to religious persuasion. Some gave the total number of persons of each religion. The original returns were destroyed in the fire in the Public Record Office in 1922, and the information in the returns is now available only in cases where details had been abstracted prior to the date of the fire.

In the case of the city of Dublin it appears that the original returns were themselves quite unsatisfactory.[84] Donnelly, in his *Short histories of Dublin parishes*, written in the early years of the present century, included figures from the census for some parishes – he may indeed have presented all the information that was available. In some cases the figures given by Donnelly are evidently the number of families, while in other cases they are apparently the entire catholic and protestant populations of the parish.

For the purposes of the census we can divide the city into a western sector and an eastern one, the western sector, north and south of the city being predominantly catholic, and the eastern sector, both north and south, solidly protestant, with the exception of a few catholic areas. Strangely, all the information (except in the case of St Bridget's and Donnybrook) given by Donnelly relates to the catholic western sector of the city, but even this is far from complete. However, it is possible to make the following reasonably reliable estimate of the total population of this sector of the city, and the numbers of each persuasion, estimated figures being inserted where necessary.

Civil parish	Number of catholics	Number of protestants
St Luke's (a)	4,953	2,908
St Audoen's (a)	4,900	2,000
St Michael's ⎤		
St John's ⎥ (b)	6,379	5,357
St Werburgh's ⎥		
St Nicholas's Within ⎦		
St James's (c)	7,375	3,995
St Nicholas's Without (d)	9,000	2,000
St Catherine's (e)	16,000	3,000
St Michan's (f)	15,250	5,780
St Paul's (g)	5,800	2,200
TOTAL	69,657	27,240

84 The situation was not, however, as bad as Warburton makes out when he states: 'The [return] was so imperfect that of 209 parishes in the diocese of Dublin ninety only was returned' (Warburton, J. et al., op. cit., vol. 2, p. 847). The number of operational parishes in the diocese was about ninety not 209. Edward Wakefield (op. cit., vol. 2, p. 587) seems to imply that returns of some kind were made by all operational parishes.

(a) These are the figures given by Donnelly for St Luke's and St Audoen's.[85] They are evidently the total populations of catholics and protestants. It is interesting that St Luke's, which earlier in the century had a strong working-class protestant majority, had in 1766, according to these figures, a 63 per cent catholic majority.

(b) These four civil parishes together formed the catholic parish of SS Michael & John. It is likely that St Michael's and St John's had catholic majorities, while, according to Donnelly, St Werburgh's was predominantly protestant and St Nicholas's Within fifty-fifty. The figures, taken from Donnelly, are evidently the total populations of catholics and protestants.[86] Total combined populations in 1798 was 11,491.

(c) The figures given by Donnelly (1,475 catholics, 799 protestants) are apparently heads of families. As suggested by Donnelly and others, I have assumed an average of five persons per family in arriving at the figures above.[87] According to Whitelaw St James's parish had a population of only 6,104 in 1798, but this arose because he used the South Circular Road as the limit of the city and so understated the population of this parish by several thousand people, principally from around Kilmainham.

(d) To arrive at this estimated figure I have assumed a total population of 11,000 – in 1798 it was 12,300 – and apportioned it nine catholics to two protestants. Donnelly commented that the returns were 'not forthcoming but, if available, would be found to be preponderatingly catholic'.[88]

(e) To arrive at this estimated figure I have assumed a total population of 19,000 – it was 20,200 in 1798 – and apportioned it sixteen catholics to three protestants. In 1798 Whitelaw, who was minister of this parish, gave the then proportions as nine catholics to one protestant. There is evidence that the parish was built up early in the century; there were 1,361 houses in 1733 (Monck Mason) as against 1,481 (Whitelaw) in 1798.

(f) The figures given by Donnelly (3,051 catholics, 1,157 protestants) are evidently in respect of heads of families.[89] I have assumed an average of five per family in arriving at the figures above.

(g) To arrive at this estimated figure, I have assumed a population of 8,000 – it was 10,000 in 1798 – and split it in the same proportions of protestants and catholics as in the case of adjoining St Michan's.

It will be seen that there were then in these eleven parishes an estimated 69,600 catholics and 27,200 protestants, giving a total of 96,800, or nearly two-thirds of the population of the city, estimated at 149,000 (including garrison) in

85 Donnelly, Nicholas, *Short histories of Dublin parishes*, Dublin, issued in parts at various dates from 1907 to 1912, part 2, p. 55 (St Luke's) and p. 175 (St Audoen's). The son of a Dublin merchant, Donnelly (1837–1920) was auxiliary bishop of the Dublin diocese from 1883 to 1920.   86 Ibid., part 2, p. 194.   87 Ibid., part 2, p. 230.   88 Ibid., part 2, p. 56.   89 Ibid., part 3, p. 58.

1766. These eleven parishes would therefore have been divided 72 per cent catholic to 28 per cent protestant.

Apart from St Bridget's and Donnybrook there is no information available from the 1766 census for the remaining parishes. Donnybrook, according to Donnelly, had a catholic majority, with 259 catholic and 174 protestant families,[90] but this looks like an under-estimate, since the parish is credited with 496 houses in 1718. Donnelly's figures could be translated into populations of 1,295 catholics and 870 protestants.

The figures of 430 catholics and 84 protestants presented by Donnelly in respect of St Bridget's are simply incredible, given that he commented that this parish was 'very protestant'.[91] It appears most likely that these figures have been transposed and that they should read 430 protestants and 84 catholics. It is also apparent that, even if the figures are intended to be heads of families only, they are quite incomplete since the total population of this parish in 1766, taking Whitelaw's 1798 census as a guideline, should have been around 8,000. The figures, as now adjusted, do bear out Donnelly's remark that the parish was 'very protestant', but hardly as protestant as these incomplete figures might suggest.

St Mark's parish had by the end of the century within its boundaries some of the most congested streets and lanes in the city and so could be presumed to have had a catholic majority at that date; it seems safe to assume a fifty-fifty situation in 1766. St Mary's was also in all probability divided fifty-fifty at this date; the catholic qualification rolls disclose that in the late 1770s there was a strong concentration of catholic merchants and manufacturers in this area.[92]

The remaining parishes of Saints Peter, Anne, Andrew and Thomas can be presumed to have had protestant majorities of varying degrees. But an important factor in these parishes was the number of servants employed (20 per cent in 1798) and the number in the lower class (44 per cent in 1798),[93] a significant number of whom would have been catholic in 1766. It seems reasonably safe to conclude, therefore, that in this eastern sector of the city (eight parishes) the protestant proportion was somewhere between 60 and 70 per cent. This would mean that, on the basis of a total population for the city of 149,000, the protestant proportion would be between 38 and 42 per cent and the catholic between 58 and 62 per cent.

In broad terms we seem to be talking about a city 60 per cent catholic and 40 per cent protestant in 1766. This would mean that in the thirty-three year period from 1733 to 1766 there was a complete turn-around in the proportions of protestants and catholics in the city, from a 60 per cent protestant and 40 per cent catholic situation in 1733 to a reverse of these proportions in 1766. Part of the reduction in protestant numbers was no doubt due to some movement of

90 Ibid., part 6, p. 55. **91** Ibid., part 1, p. 18. **92** Wall, Maureen, 'The catholic merchants, manufacturers and traders of Dublin 1778–1782' in *Reportorium Novum*, vol. 2, no.2, pp 298–323. **93** See Appendix 6, p. 52.

protestants from city parishes to outlying areas, in particular to Glasnevin[94] on the north side and to Blackrock on the south side.[95]

When Thomas Campbell, a noted divine, visited Dublin in 1775, he commented: 'According to some inaccurate returns the number of houses belonging to each denomination is nearly equal: yet it is generally thought that there are two Papists to one Protestant.'[96] This situation could be explained by the greater average number of persons per catholic house as well as by the number of catholic servants working in protestant houses. The population of Dublin in 1775 Campbell reckoned to be above 160,000, at twelve persons per house or six to a family. The average of twelve per house was manifestly too high having regard to the 11.2 per house emerging from Whitelaw's comprehensive census in 1798.[97] Data from a municipal tax on houses in Dublin in 1778, to provide additional funds for poor relief, suggest a population of 151,000 (including garrison) at that date on the basis of 14,000 houses and an average of 10.5 persons per house.

In 1789 Gervaise Bush published his *Essay towards ascertaining the population of Ireland.*[98] While this was a critical analysis for the entire country of the 1788 house returns under the hearth tax, it did not give separate figures for Dublin city – there is a composite figure for city and county – and is therefore of little interest for our purposes. In 1791 refined and detailed house returns based on the hearth tax were presented to the Irish house of commons and published in the journal of that body, but again they are not germane to our purposes since a composite figure appears for Dublin city and county. These are the last hearth tax house figures of any demographic value since the sweeping exemptions from the tax made in 1793 and 1795 meant that the house numbers as disclosed by the hearth tax returns henceforth represented only an indeterminate fraction of the total number of houses.[99]

Beaufort in his *Memoir of a map of Ireland*, published in 1792, gives a figure of 14,327 houses for Dublin city, which at an average of ten persons per house, resulted in a population of 144,000.[100] But in the light of Whitelaw's census of 1798, dealt with below, this estimate of population can be disregarded.

WHITELAW'S CENSUS, 1798

James Whitelaw, a native of County Leitrim, was church of Ireland minister of St Catherine's parish for over thirty years. With the aid of several assistants he carried out during the months of May to September 1798 a very detailed survey of

94 Donnelly, N., op. cit., part 4, p. 22.   95 Mac Cóil, Liam, *The book of Blackrock*, Blackrock 1977, p. 29 et seq.   96 Campbell, Thomas, *A survey of the South of Ireland*, London 1777, p. 18.   97 Dickson, D., op. cit. in note 7, p. 179 and CARD, XII, pp 536–7.   98 Bush, Gervaise, 'Essay towards ascertaining the population of Ireland' in *Proceedings of the Royal Irish Academy*, vol. 3 (1789).   99 Dickson, D. & others, op. cit. in note 67, p. 127 and *Journal of the Irish house of commons*, vol. 15, Appendix p. ccii.   100 Beaufort, Daniel, *Memoir of a map of Ireland*, Dublin 1792, quoted in Edward Wakefield, op. cit., p. 686.

the city, street by street, giving (except where a house was let in tenements) the name of the occupant of each house and his occupation. This detailed survey was, however, available only in manuscript and does not appear to have survived.

At first sight it might appear that Whitelaw was unfortunate in the year in which he chose to carry out his census, but that was certainly not how he saw it. In fact he looked upon the rising in that year as far more of a help than a hindrance, in that, arising out of the troubled state of the country, the names of the inhabitants of each house were, on the orders of the lord mayor, required to be fixed on the door of the house. Such a requirement, if it were properly carried out, would obviously be of great benefit to the census enumerators. But Whitelaw was to discover that it was only in the more opulent districts that these lists were dependable. With regard to the lower class areas he was to complain:

> My assistants and I, undeterred by the dread of infectious diseases, undismayed by degrees of filth, stench and darkness, inconceivable by those who have not experienced them, explored in the burning months of the summer of 1798 every room of these wretched habitations, from the cellar to the garret, and on the spot ascertained their population.[101]

Whitelaw published the results of his census in a book entitled *An essay on the population of Dublin being the result of an actual survey taken in 1798*. He included in his book tables for the different parishes, showing the number of people in each street, lane, alley etc. broken down into three divisions, the upper and middle class, the servants of the foregoing and the lower class. These were further divided into males and females. The tables also showed the number of inhabited houses in each street lane, and so on, and the number of waste houses. The totals from these parish tables he brought together in a table for the city as a whole, which is reproduced here as Appendix 6 (p. 52 below). It is interesting that Whitelaw defined the lower class as 'the labouring poor, working manufacturers etc., not in the service of others'.[102]

Whitelaw did not concern himself with whether certain areas (i.e. the liberties of the earl of Meath and the archbishop) were designated as 'county' rather than as 'city'. He concerned himself instead with what to him logically constituted the city proper, that is the area encompassed by the circular roads and, nearer the Liffey, the two canals.[103] It is interesting to note, then, what Whitelaw saw as the extremities of the city – on the north side: Aughrim Street, Prussia

101 Whitelaw, James, op. cit. in note 2, p. 4.   102 Ibid., p. 10. There are a number of discrepancies in the figures, as presented by Whitelaw, in Appendix 6, but it is not possible to say whether these were due to errors in addition or to printers' errors. We can let the figures stand as they are, since the overall results are not greatly affected by the discrepancies.   103 Since some parishes extended beyond the circular roads and the canals, Whitelaw's decision arbitrarily to regard these as the outward limits of the city, has led, notably in the case of St James's parish, to a degree of incomparability with previous surveys and enumerations which appear to have been generally based on a city of entire parishes.

Street, Grangegorman Lane, Phibsborough Road, Dorset Street, Summerhill, North Strand – although as an afterthought he added to the latter the new housing area of Spring Garden, off North Strand but on the northern side of the Royal Canal. On the south side the extremities of the area covered by the census consisted of Kilmainham Road, Dolphin's Barn, Clanbrassil Street, Portobello, Charlemont Bridge and so by the line of the Grand Canal to the Liffey. This meant the exclusion of several populous suburbs contiguous to the perimeter of the city as defined by Whitelaw, such as Kilmainham, Harold's Cross (which latter then had a population of 1,200), Rathmines, Ranelagh and the parish of Donnybrook, which up to this had been included in surveys of the population of the city and comprised the areas of Ringsend, Irishtown, Ballsbridge and Sandymount. On the north side it meant the exclusion of the contiguous villages of Glasnevin, Drumcondra, Phibsborough and Ballybough.[104]

However, one can see the point in the exclusion of all of these except Donnybrook: in an exercise of this kind one has to draw the line somewhere. Donnybrook parish had always, for the reason already given, been included in previous surveys and enumerations, and, for the sake of comparison alone, it must be added to Whitelaw's. In 1813 Donnybrook parish had a population of 4,910 living in 684 houses.[105] It would be safe to assume a population of 4,000 in 1798. Also excluded from Whitelaw's figures, because of a disagreement with the residents, was Ormond Market, off Ormond Quay.

It will be seen from the appendix that on the basis of his census Whitelaw arrived at a population figure of 172,091, excluding certain institutions. To cover these institutions he made the following additions: garrison: 7,000;[106] Royal Hospital : 400; Foundling Hospital: 558; St Patrick's Hospital: 55; House of Industry: 1,637 and Trinity College: 529. He thus arrived at a total population for Dublin city in 1798 of 182,270. But according to Warburton's *History of Dublin*, Whitelaw omitted a second house of industry with about 1300 persons, hospitals, asylums and penitentiaries with 1700 persons and prisons (excluding Kilmainham) with 650 persons.[107] If, in addition, 4,500 is added in respect of Donnybrook parish and Ormond Market, a revised figure of 190,500 is arrived at as the population of the city in 1798.

On the basis of 15,199 inhabited houses the average number of persons per inhabited house for the city as a whole disclosed by this census must have ap-

104 A contemporary comment in this regard is worth recalling: 'Kilmainham (which is in fact the county town [of County Dublin]) is as much a part of Dublin as Dorset Street; the same may be said of Dolphin's Barn, Harold's Cross, Rathmines &c.; also Grangegorman, Glasmanoge [Constitution Hill approx.], Phibsboro' &c. on the north side; they are all one uninterrupted continuation of the suburbs, except where intersected by the Circular Road' (Warburton, J. et al., op. cit., vol. 2, appendix XI, p. lxxiv). The comment is probably that of Robert Walsh, the only one of the collaborators in this history of Dublin to live to see it published.   105 Warburton, J. et al., op. cit., vol. 2, appendix XI, p. lxxiv.   106 According to Warburton (op. cit., vol. 2, appendix XI, p. lxxv) there were six military barracks in Dublin at this time.   107 Ibid.

peared somewhat high at 11.2 seeing that since the 1720s an average of about ten persons per house was the figure generally favoured.[108] Whitelaw was to find that the average number per house varied greatly from parish to parish – from a high of almost sixteen persons average per house in the poor, working-class parishes of St Luke and St Michael to a low of 8.7 persons per house in the fashionable, wealthy and protestant parish of St George on the north-east of the city.

As regards the different classes into which Whitelaw divided the population, it must have been difficult at times to decide whether a particular person belonged to the lower class or to the upper and middle class and no doubt some quite arbitrary decisions had often to be made. Nevertheless, the division into classes presumably is broadly correct. St Luke's heads the list of poor, working-class parishes with 94.4 per cent of the population in the lower class, and is followed closely by St Nicholas's Without with 92.6 per cent. Other parishes with high percentages of lower-class people were St Michael's (88.8 per cent), St Catherine's (85.7), St James's (83.5), St John's (80.4), St Mark's (79.6), St Michan's (78.6) and St Paul's (75.6).

At the other end of the scale St Anne's had only 27.7 per cent in the lower class, but had 44.6 per cent in the upper and middle class. St George's had 30.7 per cent in the lower class and 35.9 per cent in the upper and middle class. St Thomas's had 45.4 per cent lower class and 34.3 per cent upper and middle class. Other parishes with rather high percentages of upper and middle class were St Andrew's (37.4 per cent), St Bridget's (34.1), St Peter's (33), St Werburgh's (32) and St Nicholas's Within (28.2).

The percentage of the population who were servants averaged 10.7 per cent for the city as a whole, but the percentage varied a great deal from parish to parish – from 33.4 per cent of the population (or an average of 2.9 servants per house) in the case of St George's to only 1.4 per cent of the population (or an average of one servant to every four houses) in the case of St Luke's and St Nicholas's Without. Other parishes with more than an average of two servants per house were St Anne's (2.8) and St Peter's (2.1).

The general picture which emerges is of a city with a western half, north and south of the Liffey, predominantly lower-class, and an eastern half, north and south, peopled mainly by the upper and middle class and their many servants. The only exceptions to this east-west divide were St Mark's, a mainly working-class parish in the eastern half, and St Audoen's in the western half, which was decidedly a cut above the rest in that half with 21.2 per cent of the population in the upper and middle class.

---

108 To arrive at the average of 11.2 persons I have included the parish of Donnybrook and the Ormond Market. This average is in respect of inhabited houses. If waste houses were included, the number of houses would be 17,001 (including Donnybrook and Ormond Market) and the average number of persons per house 10.4.

PROPORTIONS OF CATHOLICS AND PROTESTANTS IN 1798

Whitelaw gave some serious consideration to whether he and his assistants should ascertain the religious persuasions of persons surveyed but he finally abandoned the idea, remarking: 'I found it a subject of extreme delicacy; the temper of the times seemed to discourage inquiry, and I was obliged, though with reluctance, to abandon the idea.'[109] For his own parish of St Catherine, however, he tells us that the total population could be broken down into 18,000 catholics and 2,000 protestants.[110]

Varying estimates of the proportions of catholics and protestants around the turn of the nineteenth century have been given by different writers. Wakefield in his *An account of Ireland*, published in 1812, gave the proportions as one protestant to six catholics in the city *and* county of Dublin.[111] Warburton's *History of the city of Dublin*, published in 1816, 'could not even form an opinion on the subject', but remarked that 'in a letter published in 1814 by the guardians of the Methodist's societies, the protestant population of the metropolis is stated at 60,200, giving a ratio to catholics of about one to two'.[112] In a population of 190,500 a protestant share of 60,200 would amount to 31.6 per cent, a reasonably credible estimate. Newenham, writing before 1809, was quite close to this estimate when he concluded that the protestant population of the city was something short of 59,000.[113]

The catholic archbishop, Troy, reporting to Rome in his *Relatio status* in 1802 claimed that in the nine catholic parishes of the city of Dublin there were about 200,000 catholics.[114] This is a very round number indeed and round numbers should normally be treated with a degree of suspicion. It has to be taken into account, of course, that some of these catholic parishes extended far out into the country. On the north side they extended out to Finglas whence they followed the line of the Tolka river to the sea. On the south side St Nicholas's Without extended out to Donnybrook and took in Ranelagh, Rathmines, Rathgar and Harold's Cross, while St James's included Dolphin's Barn, Kilmainham and Islandbridge and bordered on Chapelizod.[115] But even when this factor is taken into account, the figure of 200,000 leaves very little for other denominations and can be nothing other than a gross exaggeration.

In arriving at the likely proportions of catholics and protestants as the century came to a close, we, unlike the on-the-spot commentators, have the benefit of surveys and censuses carried out in the nineteenth century, in particular the report on religious public instruction in Ireland (1835), the statistics in which relate to 1831. This report, subject to the revision I have made in regard to St Catherine's, shows that in a population of 250,245 for Dublin city in that year,

109 Whitelaw, J., op. cit., p. 6.   110 Warburton, J. et al., vol. 2, p. 847.   111 Wakefield, E., op. cit., vol. 2, p. 606.   112 Warburton, J. et al., op. cit., vol. 2, p. 847.   113 Newenham, T., op. cit., in note 81, p. 182.   114 *Reportorium Novum*, vol. 2, no. 2, p. 382.   115 See *Catholic Directory for 1821* reprinted in *Reportorium Novum*, vol. 2, no. 2.

there were 183,931 catholics (73.4 per cent), 62,782 members of the established church (25 per cent) and 3,249 for other persuasions (1.4 per cent), i.e. 26.4 per cent for all protestants.[116]

However, this 1735 report covers some areas, then largely protestant, outside the 1798 census area (e.g. Harold's Cross, Rathmines and Ranelagh), and the protestant proportion for the area covered by the 1798 census, would accordingly in 1831 be some percentage points less than the 26.4 per cent mentioned, say 22 per cent. This figure of 22 per cent in 1831 can be seen as a point in the gradual, unrelenting decline of the protestant proportion of the city for more than one hundred years. We have seen that in 1766 the protestant proportion was estimated at around 40 per cent, and on the basis that 1798 represents the mid-point between 1766 and 1831, the protestant proportion of the population of Dublin city in 1798 emerges as somewhere in the region of 30 per cent.

CONCLUSIONS

1   The following are the estimated population figures for the city of Dublin at different dates which emerge from the foregoing:

Year	Estimated population	Notes
1695	51,000	(average number per inhabited house: 9.2) Based on John South's population figures, with additions in respect of the garrison and the liberties of the earl of Meath, the archbishop of Dublin and the dean of St Patrick's, which, it is demonstrated, are not covered by South's figures.

116 *Report of the Commission on religious public instruction in Ireland 1834*, vol. 1, p. 116b. This is not the most accurate of surveys. As to how they obtained particulars of religious persuasion, the commissioners state in their report (p. 2): '...we determined upon making the population figures for 1831 the basis of our operation ... by referring them back to the original enumerators in order that they might distinguish the religious persuasion of the several persons therein mentioned'. But the commissioners were not bound by the enumerators' figures. They sometimes accepted in preference the estimate of the local vicar or curate, as in the case of St Catherine's where I have reinstated the enumerator's figure as being more in line with Whitelaw's estimate of 1798. The commission's figures are particularly untrustworthy in relation to dissenters, several thousands of whom in Dublin appear to have been returned as members of the established church. As compared with the 1.4 per cent returned by the commission for 'other persuasions/dissenters', the figures in the 1861 and 1871 censuses were 3.4 per cent and 4.6 per cent respectively, while according to statistics in Warburton, J. et al., op. cit., vol. 2, 848, dissenters accounted for around 4 per cent of Dublin's population in the early years of the nineteenth century. However, the commission's figure for all protestants of 26 per cent in 1831 appears credible when viewed against 22.7 per cent for all protestants in 1861 and 20.8 per cent in 1871.

Year	Estimated population	Notes
1716	93,000	(average number per inhabited house: 9.8) Figure extrapolated from the Archbishop King abstract of men capable of bearing arms, and 4,000 added in respect of garrison and institutions; 5 per cent of houses deemed to be waste.
1733	127,000	(assumed average number per inhabited house: 10) This is based on the mean of two separate houses figures for 1733 – 12,942 (David Bindon attrib.) and 11,718 (Monck Mason) multiplied by an average of ten persons per house, with 4,000 added in respect of garrison and institutions.
1760	145,000	(assumed average number per inhabited house: 10.5) Based on the figure from the hearth tax returns for 1760 of 13,461 houses with an average of 10.5 persons per house, and 4,000 added in respect of garrison and institutions.
1798	191,000	(average per inhabited house: 11.2) Whitelaw's census figure of 182,370 with additions in respect of Donnybrook, the Ormond Market and certain institutions, all omitted by Whitelaw.

2   Dublin at the beginning of the eighteenth century can be envisaged as an island of protestantism surrounded by a sea of catholicism. Since Dublin only began to achieve a surplus of births over deaths in the last quarter of the nineteenth century,[117] it must follow that the increase in the city's population from 1700 up to then was provided predominantly by migration from the provinces, in particular from the counties of Leinster (all catholic strongholds) which, according to the 1841 census, accounted at that date for almost 60 per cent of the city's migrant population.[118] Given this scenario, it was inevitable that the quadrupling of the population of the city between 1700 and 1800 would be accompanied by a change in the religious profile of Dublin from being strongly protestant at the beginning of the century to being strongly catholic at the end.

3   Appendix 5, p. 51 is a graph showing for the period 1695–1798 the total population of the city of Dublin, as well as the numbers of catholics and protestants. It will be seen that the total population increased from about 51,000 in 1695 to 191,000 in 1798. While the number of protestants increased from about 60,000 in 1716 to about 75,000 in 1733, there was a steady decline after that, levelling off at

117 Dickson, D., op. cit. in note 7, p. 185.   118 Ibid., p. 184.

about 59,000 in 1766, and ending the century at about the same figure. The protestant proportion of the total population shows a continuous downward trend
from about 65 per cent in 1716 to about 30 per cent in 1798. The catholic population, on the other hand, shows a steady increase from about 32,000 in 1716 to
about 133,000 in 1798, or in proportional terms an increase from 35 per cent in
1716 to 70 per cent in 1798. The graph shows that numbers-wise the catholics
overtook the protestants in the 1750s. In addition to migration of catholics from
the provinces, the catholic increase was due to some extent to a higher fertility
rate among catholics.

4   Although by the end of the century protestants had been reduced to a minority of about 30 per cent of Dublin's population, they remained in complete control of the administration of the city. The 1793 catholic relief act did indeed provide for the admission of catholics as freemen of the guilds, but very few in fact
were successful in gaining admission. Since the common council of Dublin corporation was composed of so many representatives from each guild, catholics
continued to be effectively debarred from membership of the corporation, which
was indeed quite barefaced in their assertion of protestant ascendancy:

> We tell them [the catholics] that the Protestants of Ireland would not be
> compelled by any authority whatever to abandon that political situation
> which their forefathers won with their swords and is therefore their birth-
> right. That no doubt may remain of what we understand by Protestant
> ascendancy ... we consider the Protestant ascendancy to consist of a Prot-
> estant king in Ireland, a Protestant parliament, a Protestant hierarchy,
> Protestant electors and government, the benches of justice, the army and
> revenue, through all their branches and details, Protestant. And this sys-
> tem supported by a connection with the Protestant realm of Britain.[119]

This wholesale gerrymander was to continue for the first four decades of the
nineteenth century until the Municipal Reform Act of 1840 enabled catholics to
take their place in the corporation and Daniel O'Connell to be elected lord mayor
of Dublin.

5   Some of the loss of protestant population was due to the movement of
protestants to more prestigious and salubrious areas on the outskirts of the city,
such as Glasnevin, Drumcondra, Sandymount, Ranelagh and Blackrock. It is
true that as Dublin city became more catholic, Dublin county became more protestant. According to Bindon's 1732–3 survey, Dublin county had 1,928 protestant and 6336 catholic houses/families, which, after taking account of the larger
size of catholic families, would mean that the county was about 80 per cent catholic
and 20 per cent protestant at that date. In contrast to this, the proportions in 1831

119 Letter of 11 September 1792 from Dublin Corporation to the protestants of Ireland; NLI
microfilm copy in Pos. 3142.

were about 70 per cent catholic and 30 per cent protestant.[120] However, it has to be said that protestant gains in the county in no way compensated for their losses in the city.

6   While in the second half of the century some movement of population to outlying suburbs had begun, there were areas in the city proper which had not yet been built on. For example, some areas in the poor, unfashionable south-west of the city (Fairbrother's Field and the district known today as Maryland, for instance), were not built upon until the early decades of the twentieth century. In any consideration of the population of Dublin in the eighteenth century, ideally the growth of the outer suburbs should also be looked at, but unfortunately there is little in the way of statistics of population of these areas available until official censuses began to be taken in 1821.

7   The trend in Dublin's population in the early nineteenth century is also of interest. It might be thought that the Union would have had a stagnating effect, and undoubtedly it did result in large numbers of the nobility and gentry forsaking their town houses, with the consequent loss of the gaiety and glitter of the winter season. However, there was a population explosion taking place throughout the country in the first four decades of the nineteenth century, resulting in a doubling of the population in that period. While the increase in Dublin city was nothing like that in the country generally, there was nevertheless quite a substantial increase of 40,000 in the city's population between 1798 and 1821.[121] The figures for 1821 are directly comparable since they are for precisely the same area as those for 1798 – the area bounded by the circular roads and the canals, as appropriate. The growth of the city, then, in the post-Union period, when one might have expected a degree of stagnation, was far greater than during the period of Grattan's Parliament, generally hailed as a time of great progress.

8   Developments in the nineteenth century in the suburbs of the city, which legally formed part of the county, are worthy of mention. In 1861 the area from Sandymount across to Kilmainham and from Clontarf across to Grangegorman, with a population of 50,500, was 41 per cent protestant, and in terms of house and property ownership the protestant proportion was far higher than this. This situation continued, with little reduction in the protestant proportion, down to the end of the nineteenth century. We can see the legacy today of this protestant proprietorship in the spacious houses, avenues, parks and squares and the many very fine churches of all (protestant) denominations, in particular in the area from Sandymount across to Harold's Cross, that is, the former townships of Pembroke and Rathmines. Indeed, the paucity and, in some cases, the ordinariness of catholic churches in the area as compared with protestant ones, even today is remarkable. The severely functional catholic church of the Three Patrons in Rathgar, built in the 1860s mainly by the catholic poor, sits tightly on its

120 *Report of the commission on religious public instruction in Ireland, 1835*. These percentages have been arrived at by adding together the totals for the various parishes concerned in Co. Dublin.   121 *Census of Ireland 1821*, p. xxii.

rood of ground, while up the road the presbyterian church lords it from a height, looking for all the world like a mini-cathedral. The decline of the protestant denominations in the area to the present level of probably not much more than 5 per cent can be attributed to a number of factors – the end of the British regime, the loss of protestant males in the Great War, the papal decree *Ne temere* – but probably the principal reason was Partition, which effectively cut off the oxygen of protestant migration into Dublin from the six north-eastern counties. Had Dublin continued as the capital, with all the attendant implications, of a thirty-two county Ireland, the protestant denominations in the area, and in the city generally, would be in a much healthier condition than they are today.

APPENDIX 1

*Map showing the locations of the different parishes in Dublin
in the eighteenth century*

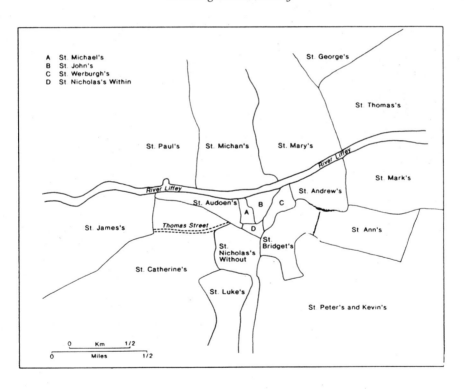

APPENDIX 2

Enumeration of houses and hearths in Dublin 1695–6 by John South

Parish	\multicolumn{14}{c}{No. of Hearths}														Total Hearths	Houses
	1	2	3	4	5	6	7	8	9	10	11	12	13	14		
St Audoen	28	31	40	20	30	30	20	24	13	10	9	5	3	13	1573	276
St Michael	1	7	16	24	14	25	12	14	9	10	5	1	2	7	969	147
Christ Church Yard	3	5	3	3	6	7	2	–	1	1	2	–	–	–	161	83
St John	14	21	40	35	33	49	28	22	17	14	5	5	3	15	1839	301
St Werburgh	8	19	50	42	45	26	40	29	24	9	11	9	3	13	2049	328
St Andrew	38	117	141	90	70	65	48	22	25	16	13	5	–	13	3111	663
St Nicholas Within	1	2	13	8	11	7	13	13	3	7	4	8	1	4	678	95
St Nicholas Without	88	248	234	150	93	92	45	28	25	11	7	8	1	5	4041	1035
St Peter & Kevin	42	60	89	47	52	43	17	25	14	10	3	4	5	14	2050	425
St Bridget	15	56	62	81	54	64	43	21	12	6	6	2	1	2	2068	425
Donnybrook	122	68	15	12	4	2	1	1	1	1	–	1	–	1	443	229
St Michan	94	137	143	124	78	116	134	93	65	39	14	21	8	35	6135	1101
Christ Church Liberty	82	24	5	9	1	–	–	1	–	–	–	1	–	–	206	123
St Catherine & James	95	163	147	104	67	90	52	40	19	9	4	4	7	17	3598	818
TOTAL															28921	5999
The College															144	
Blue Coat School															25	
Kilmainham Hospital															120	
Bridewell															8	
Newgate															2	

Note: The total number of houses should add up to 6,049, not 5,999. However, we do not know whether this is due to an error in the number of houses for one of the parishes or to an error in addition. Since the difference of 50 is not large, it seems best to let the figures stand as they are.

APPENDIX 3

Enumeration of population of Dublin 1695–6 by John South

Parishes	Men	Women	Children		Servants		Total		Totals
			Male	Female	Male	Female	Males	Females	
St Audeon's	675	919	422	480	194	312	1291	1711	3002
St Michael's	435	420	268	306	113	183	816	909	1725
Christ Church Yard	43	43	18	28	11	22	72	93	165
St John's	686	769	391	440	180	273	1257	1482	2739
St Werburgh	551	563	266	336	286	345	1103	1244	2347
St Andrew's	906	1095	575	623	313	345	1794	2063	3857
St Nicholas's Within	260	234	130	145	78	122	468	501	969
St Nicholas's Without	904	1438	515	551	261	268	1680	2257	3937
St Peter's & Kevin's	493	674	296	356	213	297	1002	1327	2329
St Bridget's	568	657	312	342	181	283	1061	1282	2343
Donnybrook	240	259	208	172	68	79	516	510	1026
St Michan's	2163	2697	1179	1369	589	897	3931	4963	8894
Christ Church Liberties	42	43	18	27	11	22	71	92	163
St Catherine's & James's	1662	1943	849	893	487	448	2998	3284	6282
The College	230	–	–	–	24	4	254	4	258
Blue Coat Hospital	–	–	70	–	–	–	70	–	70
Kilmainham Hospital	310	–	–	–	10	10	320	10	330
Bridewell	8	8	–	–	–	–	8	8	16
Newgate	50	6	–	–	–	–	50	6	56
TOTAL	10226	11768	5517	6068	3019	3910	18762	21746	40508

APPENDIX 4

Archbishop King's abstract of the numbers of protestants and papists able to bear arms in the City of Dublin and liberties thereof

Parishes		Protestants	Total of protestants	Papists	Total of papists
St Werburgh	Housekeepers	774		182	
	Inmates & Lodgers	385		89	
	Servants	122	1281	53	324
St John	Housekeepers	211		51	
	Inmates & Lodgers	422		195	
	Servants	103	736	33	279
St Andrew	Housekeepers	696		73	
	Inmates & Lodgers	898		207	
	Servants	370	1964	79	359
St Michan	Housekeepers	605		311	
	Inmates & Lodgers	607		418	
	Servants	220	1432	131	860
St Mary (a)	Housekeepers	536		166	
	Inmates & Lodgers	473		141	
	Servants	505	1514	93	400
St Nicholas Without	Housekeepers	277		147	
	Inmates & Lodgers	565		524	
	Servants	67	909	78	749
Donnybrook & Ring's End &c	Housekeepers	154		147	
	Inmates & Lodgers	105		44	
	Servants	36	295	33	224
St Peter	Housekeepers	251		27	
	Inmates & Lodgers	183		45	
	Servants	168	602	15	87
St Nicholas Within	Housekeepers	72		13	
	Inmates & Lodgers	192		76	
	Servants	80	344	22	111
St Catherine	Housekeepers	175		178	
	Inmates & Lodgers	174		386	
	Servants	24	373	59	623

Appendix 4 (contd)

Parishes		Protestants	Total of protestants	Papists	Total of papists
St Paul	Housekeepers	159		90	
	Inmates & Lodgers	89		74	
	Servants	130	378	91	255
St Bridget	Housekeepers	466		65	
	Inmates & Lodgers	488		155	
	Servants	235	1189	53	273
St Audoen	Housekeepers	136		99	
	Inmates & Lodgers	231		503	
	Servants	103	470	44	646
St Michael	Housekeepers	84		84	
	Inmates & Lodgers	147		150	
	Servants	43	274	36	270
St James	Housekeepers	97		45	
	Inmates & Lodgers	145		94	
	Servants	45	287	62	201
	TOTALS:		12048		5661

(a) In St Mary's parish there were 26 servants of unknown religion and four Jews.

APPENDIX 5

Thousands

Population of Dublin 1695–1798

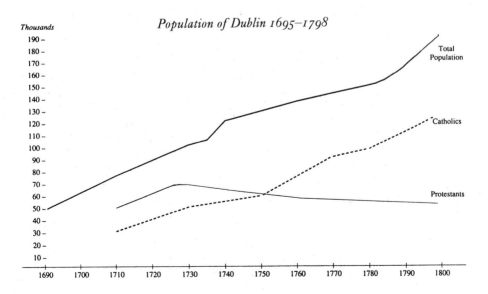

APPENDIX 6

General table of the population of Dublin in 1798, as divided into its nineteen parishes and two deaneries

Names of Parishes, &c.	Upper / Middle Classes			Servants of Ditto			Lower Class			TOTAL Males	TOTAL Females	GRAND TOTAL	No. of houses		Average to a house
	Males	Females	Total	Males	Females	Total	Males	Females	Total				Inhabited	Waste	
St James's	342	367	709	97	201	298	2432	2665	5097	2871	3233	6104	538	32	11.34
St Catherine's	991	846	1837	378	660	1038	7008	9693	17301	8977	11199	20176	1481	140	13.62
St Luke's	150	148	298	32	75	107	2846	3990	6836	3028	4213	7241	454	41	15.95
St Nicholas's Without	347	347	694	50	169	219	4861	6532	11393	5258	7048	12306	950	55	12.95
St Nicholas's Within	163	153	316	45	92	137	306	362	668	514	607	1121	107	10	10.48
St Audeon's	585	513	1098	156	302	458	1612	2023	3635	2353	2838	5191	415	53	12.5
St Michael's	124	108	232	10	50	60	1064	1243	2307	1198	1401	2599	163	20	15.94
St John's	316	333	649	46	118	164	1577	1752	3329	1939	2203	4142	295	31	14.08
St Werburgh's	609	551	1160	98	253	351	941	1117	2118	1648	1981	3629	305	33	11.9
Deanery of Christ Church	25	10	35	3	4	7	80	111	191	108	125	233	23	2	10.1
Deanery of St Patrick	76	64	140	14	30	44	832	1065	1897	922	1159	2081	162	11	12.84
St Bridget's	1287	1445	2732	195	580	775	2054	2448	4502	3536	4473	8009	744	27	10.76
St Peter's	2283	3017	5300	1217	2048	3265	3390	4108	7498	6890	9173	16063	1512	116	10.61
St Ann's	1486	1737	3223	715	1286	2001	870	1134	2004	3071	4157	7228	711	36	10.17
St Andrew's	1489	1373	2862	289	661	950	1738	2132	3870	3516	4166	7682	709	63	10.83
St Mark's	599	684	1283	121	354	475	3127	3797	6924	3847	4845	8692	646	61	13.45
Total population on south side of river Liffey	10872	11695	22567	3466	6883	10349	35338	44232	79570	49676	62881	112497	9215	731	12.2
St Paul's	781	1002	1783	186	444	630	3321	4170	7491	4288	5616	9904	1050	116	9.45
St Michan's	1312	1409	2721	374	772	1146	6375	7850	14225	8061	10031	18092	1520	141	11.9
St Mary's	2452	3014	5466	979	1771	2750	3859	4579	8435	7290	9364	16654	1590	43	10.47
St Thomas's	1316	1624	2940	650	1087	1737	1787	2098	3885	3753	4809	8562	892	82	9.6
St George's	817	1011	1828	706	997	1703	688	877	1565	2211	2885	5096	587	89	8.68
Total Population on north side of river Liffey	6678	8060	14738	2895	5071	7966	16030	19574	35604	25603	32705	58308	5639	471	10.34

Note: As an afterthought to the above Whitelaw added Spring Garden, 'a suburb beyond the circular-road, omitted in the parishes of St Thomas and St George, taken from the return of the Conservators in 1804', involving a population of 1,286 in 345 houses, and resulting in a total population for the city of 172,091 in 15,199 houses.

2

The Irish catholic lobby in the first half of the eighteenth century

Since the activities of this lobby were concerned almost exclusively with anti-catholic measures proposed by the Irish parliament, it is useful first of all to set out briefly the procedure by which such measures were enacted into laws.

Under the act known as Poynings' Law, passed by the Irish parliament in Drogheda in 1495, it was for the king and privy council to determine when a parliament should be called in Ireland and what bills could be proposed to it. In addition the English parliament, as this law came to be interpreted, claimed, and occasionally exercised, the right of making laws for Ireland.[1] By the eighteenth century, however, it had become accepted procedure that the heads of bills should be initiated and passed in Ireland and then submitted to the English privy council for approval. Heads of a bill could originate in the Irish house of lords, the Irish house of commons or, infrequently, in the Irish privy council. The heads went through all stages in the house in which they were initiated and the agreement of the other house was not at that point required, although it was not unknown for, say, members of the commons to attend, as spectators, debates in the lords, when some particularly interesting measure was under discussion in the upper house.[2] During the Restoration period it was the practice for the originating house to send a copy of the heads of each bill to the other house for information only, and this practice was taken up occasionally after the revolution of 1688. When the practice was revived in 1733, however, the lord lieutenant, the duke of Dorset, moved quickly in the commons to put an end to it for the reason that 'it had the appearance of an Innovation and is disliked in England',[3] presumably because it was perceived as in some way a threat to Poynings' Law.

1 An example of this was section 8 of the English act, 3 William & Mary c. 2 of 1691, which provided that no person could sit in the Irish parliament, nor hold any government office, civil, military or ecclesiastical, nor practise law in Ireland until he had subscribed to the oath of allegiance, the new oath of supremacy and the declaration against Transubstantiation.   2 When in January 1756 heads of a bill for registering popish priests were being debated in the lords, it is recorded that the speaker and all the house of commons came into the lords' chamber to listen to the debate – see Fagan, Patrick, *Divided loyalties. The question of the oath for Irish catholics in the eighteenth century*, Dublin 1997, 94.   3 Letter dated Dublin Castle 10 January 1734 from Chief Secretary Walter Cary to Charles Delafaye in Irish state papers in the Public Record Office London: National Library of Ireland (NLI) microfilm Pos. 3835, f 17.

When a measure had passed all stages in the initiating house, that house ordered that the main promoter should attend the lord lieutenant with the heads
and desire that the same might be transmitted to Britain in due form. However,
before the lord lieutenant transmitted the heads to the English privy council in
London, they were put before the Irish privy council, over which the lord lieutenant presided, for approval. The Irish privy council did, on occasion, make
changes in the heads, as in the case of the infamous castration bill in 1719,[4] or,
quite exceptionally, it might reject the measure altogether, as in the case of the
registry of priests bill 1757.[5] Although it was the practice to refer to heads, as
approved by the Irish privy council, as a bill, strictly speaking in accordance with
Poynings' Law, heads were not entitled to be called a bill until they had been
approved by the English privy council.

To help a bill on its way through the English privy council the lord lieutenant
and the administration in Dublin had their own representative in London, whose
duty it was to bring pressure to bear in the appropriate quarters to have bills
approved. But there were often vested interests opposed to a particular bill and
these would seek to exert pressure on the privy council to have the bill amended
to their liking or rejected altogether. These vested interest groups could take
various forms, for example, Irish manufacturers lobbying against a duty on woollen yarn, dissenters lobbying against the Irish test act, merchants lobbying against
a bill for better securing and collecting his Majesty's revenue and, the one with
which we are concerned here, catholics lobbying against anti-catholic measures
proposed by the Irish parliament. Thus the English privy council often found
itself in the situation of being pressurized by two opposing sides, by the lord
lieutenant's representative, on the one hand, advocating the bill in question and,
on the other hand, by some vested interest opposing it. The council could ap-
prove, reject or amend a bill, which was then returned to Dublin. If approved by
the English privy council, the bill went through the various stages and was passed
in both houses of the Irish parliament, and later received the royal assent from
the lord lieutenant. If the English privy council proposed amendments to a bill,
the Irish parliament had the option of accepting the bill as amended or of not
proceeding further with it. If the English privy council rejected a bill, the Irish
parliament had no option but to accept that decision, but there was nothing to
stop it from passing and submitting similar heads of a bill in a subsequent session.

The first thing to be observed, then, about the Irish *ad hoc* catholic lobby is
that it was not the only pressure group the lord lieutenant and Irish administration had to contend with, although it was arguably the best established and most
enduring. Secondly, this lobby operated at three levels – (a) at home, by repre-

4 Burns, Robert E., *Irish parliamentary politics in the eighteenth century*, vol. 1, Washington
D.C., 1989, pp 91–2.   5 Fagan, P., op. cit., p. 111.

sentations to the administration and to the house concerned when heads of a bill were first mooted and during their passage through the house; (b) by representations to the English privy council, as already indicated, and (c) by persuading some European state, notably Austria, to bring pressure to bear on the British government to have a particular measure negatived. Thirdly, the *ad hoc* lobby was far more active and indeed more effective than the Catholic Committee established in 1756, at least in the first fifteen years of the latter's existence, but it has to be said that this was largely due to the differing roles of the two bodies. While it was the task of the *ad hoc* lobby to fight the introduction of a succession of anti-Catholic penal measures, the main aim of the Catholic Committee, coming into existence at a time when the enactment of further such measures had almost entirely ceased, was to repeal that great corpus of legislation collectively known as the Penal Laws, a large part of which was by then a dead letter. The lobby, then, can be seen as exercising an offensive and necessarily very active role, while the task of the Catholic Committee was less urgent, its pace being determined by how much progress it wished to make itself rather than by the stark imperative of pending anti-catholic bills.

The catholic lobby was greatly assisted by (a) the procedure, outlined above, under which heads of bills processed in Dublin required the approval of the English privy council before being formally passed by both houses of the Irish parliament, and (b) by the fact that from the late seventeenth century until the beginning of the Seven Years' War in 1756 Britain's main ally in her European wars was the catholic emperor of Austria, who naturally came to be perceived by Irish Catholics as a powerful intermediary with the British government for the quashing of anti-catholic measures proposed by the Irish parliament. For the first fifty years of the eighteenth century, in addition to the direct lobbying already mentioned, we find the emperor, or his ambassador in London, being appealed to again and again to exercise this intermediary role, and with some degree of success. Other catholic powers – Spain, Portugal and even France, when she was at peace with Britain – were also on occasion requested to use their good offices in London on behalf of Irish catholics.

As to actual instances of this *ad hoc* catholic lobby in action, a start might be made with the Banishment Act of 1697. This act required all catholic regular clergy, bishops and secular clergy exercising ecclesiastical jurisdiction to depart the country before 1 May 1698 under pain of high treason. It passed through its various stages with such speed, attended by a degree of subterfuge, that it may have taken the catholic body by surprise. It appears that the measure was brought to the attention of the Vatican authorities (by whom it is not clear) and that the Vatican instructed the internuncio in Brussels to make representations to Count Auersperg, the imperial ambassador in London. Auersperg informed the internuncio on 9 May 1698 that the Irish lord chancellor, Lord Methuen, had confirmed that the banishment act would not be fully enforced and that some regular clergy would be allowed to stay, especially those who were too old to be sent away.[6] The internuncio must have received a further dispatch from Auersperg for on 4 July 1698 the internuncio wrote to Cardinal Secretary of State Spada in Rome that Auersperg had informed him that Methuen had been shown a letter written by Lord Galway, one of the lords justices, giving assurances that moderation would be used in dealing with catholics, and that it was not intended to make any further changes in Irish ecclesiastical affairs apart from the expulsion of the regular clergy, a measure which was being taken for grave reasons of state.[7]

The assurances stated to have been given by the lord chancellor were quite misleading as far as bishops were concerned, for their expulsion was enforced so fully that by 1703 there were only two or three bishops at large in Ireland.[8] However, Austrian intervention may have had some effect in staying the hand of the Irish authorities for the regulars soon began to filter back to such an extent that by the 1720s they were believed to be as numerous as at any time since Charles II's reign, and a start was made by Rome in 1707 to appoint some bishops who were able covertly to exercise their functions.

The act of 1704 to prevent the further growth of popery was unusual in that the original proposals were drafted by the Irish privy council (with Ormonde, the lord lieutenant, presiding) and sent over to the English privy council for approval without being put before one of the Irish houses of parliament as heads of a bill. Although unusual for the eighteenth century, this procedure was strictly in accordance with Poynings' Law. When Irish catholics got wind of what was before the English council, a petition was presented to the queen by Lord Fitzwilliam of Merrion and Lord Bellew of Duleek on behalf of themselves and other beneficiaries of the Articles of Limerick. The queen ordered that a copy of the draft bill be given to the petitioners and that they be heard by the English law officers. At this stage the measure was limited to preventing protestants being seduced into turning catholic, to preventing catholics from acquiring protestant estates and to putting a limit on the number of catholics who might reside in the cities of Limerick and Galway.[9]

Ormonde's secretary, Edward Southwell, pointed out that if the measure was not put before parliament as heads of bill under the usual procedure, the Irish commons would itself frame such a measure in the form of heads of a bill, and this was in fact what eventually happened. Because of delays by the law officers the Irish parliament had no measure of the kind in question before it when it met in September 1703 and the commons, after further consultation with London, went ahead with preparing heads of a bill with much wider aims, and in particular much more inimical to catholic possession of landed estates than that originally proposed. When passed, the heads were considered of such importance that they were presented to the lord lieutenant by the speaker accompanied by

6 Giblin, Cathaldus, 'Catalogue of material of Irish interest in the collection Nunziatura di Fiandra, Vatican Archives' in *Collectanea Hibernica*, no. 4 (1961), p. 72.   7 Ibid., p. 66.   8 Wall, Maureen, *Catholic Ireland in the eighteenth century*, Dublin 1989, p. 12.   9 Simms, J.G., 'The making of a penal law 1703–4' in *Irish Historical Studies*, vol. 12 (1960), p. 106.

the whole house. In a speech the speaker referred to the efforts of papists to oppose the bill and to the great sums of money they had raised for that purpose.[10] The bill was sent over to London on 7 December 1703. Through their solicitor in London, Mulloney, the catholic lobby submitted a petition against the bill and also against the bill for registering popish priests (see below) which was being put through at the same time. In addition the earl of Antrim joined with Lord Fitzwilliam of Merrion in a protest against the major bill on the grounds that it was a violation of the Articles of Limerick.[11]

Although catholics for a time had hopes that the bill would be turned down by the English council, the final outcome was that the bill was rendered even more penal in the council by the inclusion of a clause, aimed at dissenters, barring from certain employments and offices anyone who had not received the Sacrament according to the rites of the established church and according to the Test Act.

There are differing views as to the reason for this unexpected behaviour by the English council. According to Bishop Burnet there was strong opposition to the bill from those in the council who had 'a mind to have a share in the presents' offered for opposing it by the Irish catholic lobby, and that the additional clause was introduced in the hope that it would prove so unpalatable to the Irish parliament that they would reject it, with the result that the entire bill would fail.[12] There is another view that the dissenter clause was introduced to appease certain Irish bishops in the house of lords, like Archbishop King, who had opposed previous anti-catholic bills and had scruples about infringing the Articles of Limerick.[13] But without assigning any such deep, Machiavellian motives to the British authorities, the inclusion of the clause can be seen simply as an exercise in even-handedness in dealing with catholics and protestant dissenters which might come in useful in controverting any representations by the imperial ambassador against the bill. The harsh terms of the original bill, with their implications for the treatment of protestants in the Austrian Empire and other catholic countries, could be a deep embarrassment to the queen in her dealings with the emperor, her very catholic ally in the War of the Spanish Succession then raging; but if protestants as well as catholics were seen to be penalized under the bill, that would to an extent serve to spike the guns of Austrian objectors.

On return of the bill to Ireland there was a last ditch effort by catholic interests to oppose it in both the commons and the lords. Nicholas Viscount Kingsland, Richard Lord Bellew, Col. John Brown, Col. Thomas Burke, Col. Robert Nugent, Capt. Arthur French prayed to be heard by counsel both before the commons

---

10 Ibid., p. 110.   **11** Ibid., p. 113. This may be the Moloney who came to the attention of the benchers of Lincoln's Inn in November 1717 for having 'appeared frequently in the Hall in a Barr gown, though on enquiry it does not appear to them [benchers] he was ever called to the bar'. Moloney was required to appear at the next council of the benchers but there is no further reference to him. See *The black books of Lincoln's Inn*, London 1899, vol. 3, p. 251.   **12** Ibid., p. 115.   **13** Ibid.

and the lords and this was agreed to.[14] The three advocates who appeared at the bar of the house of commons to put the catholic case were Sir Theobald Butler, Counsellor Edmund Malone and Sir Stephen Rice. In a lengthy and passionate speech, Butler, in addition to appealing against the many clauses in the bill inimical to catholics, also spoke against the clause affecting dissenters.[15] But all his eloquence was to no avail. Not a single member showed himself in any way influenced by Butler's pleading. The same counsel were heard by the lord chancellor on behalf of the house of lords with results which were equally fruitless. Apart from some lengthy discussion on the dissenter clause, the bill had an easy passage through both houses and received the royal assent on 4 March 1704.

The registry of priests bill 1704, as presented to the English privy council, contained a clause requiring priests registering to take the oath of abjuration.[16] It also apparently contained a clause (which can only be guessed at) in regard to popish solicitors against which there were petitions from Oliver Weston and Edward Byrne. Both these clauses were removed by the English privy council, perhaps as a sop to the catholic lobby which had failed so comprehensively in their representations against the bill to prevent the further growth of popery. As we have seen above, catholic lobbying against the latter bill, when it was before the English council, covered also the registry bill.

Although the Irish parliament accepted the registry of priests bill as amended, they were not prepared to let go on the requirement that registered priests should take the oath of abjuration. Accordingly, in August 1707 the Irish house of commons put rapidly through all stages heads of a bill which provided that registered priests should take the oath and which eliminated loopholes perceived in the 1704 act to prevent the further growth of popery. For information as to how the catholic lobby came into action to defeat this bill we are indebted to a report sent by someone in London to the Brussels internuncio, who transmitted it to Rome.[17] After setting out the salient points in the bill, the report goes on to state that when the bill was sent to London for approval, Irish Catholics dispatched a delegation there to implore the queen to withhold her consent, and also to make it clear that it was impossible for catholic priests to take the oath contained in the bill. The delegation also enlisted the help of the envoys in London of the various catholic powers. The delegation's efforts were so successful that certain changes were made in the bill before it was returned to Dublin. These changes the Irish parliament was not prepared to accept and accordingly the bill failed.

14 *Lords Journal Ireland*, vol. 2, p. 71.   15 Mitchel, John, *The history of Ireland from the treaty of Limerick to the present time*, London c.1867, vol. 1, pp 33–8.   16 Simms, J.G., *War and politics in Ireland*, London 1986, p. 22. Oliver Weston 'inasmuch as he had taken the oath of abjuration', requested a saving in his favour in the clause in regard to popish solicitors, and Edward Byrne, described as 'an Articleman', made a similar request – see *Commons Journal Ireland*, vol. 2, part 1, p. 431.   17 Giblin, C., op. cit., no. 15 (1972), 12–13.

However, the Irish parliament was not prepared to let the matter rest and in the next 1709–10 session what appears to have been heads of a bill similar to the 1707 bill passed all stages in the commons and were sent to London for approval in June 1709. The catholic lobby swung into action on two fronts, firstly, by mustering the support of the ambassadors of the catholic powers in London with a view to having the bill negatived by the English privy council, and, secondly, by dispatching a priest from Dublin to Louvain to get the opinion of the strict faculty of that university on the propriety of Irish catholic priests and laymen taking the oath of abjuration, and to bring the oath and indeed the other provisions of the bill to the attention of the Brussels internuncio, Grimaldi.[18] A later commons address to the lord lieutenant mentions that the bill had been returned unamended to Dublin by the privy council 'notwithstanding the strong efforts made against it by the Irish Papists in Great Britain'.[19] From this we gather that the Irish lobby tried to have the bill negatived in London but failed to achieve that end.

Meanwhile, Internuncio Grimaldi had initiated a diplomatic intervention in London by the imperial ambassador, Gallas, but by the time the latter had got around to making the necessary representations the bill had already been approved by the privy council on 31 July 1709.[20] Presumably Gallas concentrated on the other lengthy provisions of the bill apart from the oath of abjuration, for it is difficult to see how the imperial ambassador could be expected to work up much enthusiasm against an oath abjuring James Stuart, considering that the latter was busily engaged in plotting against the Anglo-Austrian alliance and indeed had served with Austria's enemy, the French, at Oudenarde and Malplaquet.

Although it appeared to be the opinion of the strict faculty of Louvain that the oath of abjuration was such as could be taken by Irish catholics, the decision of Pope Clement XI was that the oath was not acceptable.[21] But despite the papal pronouncement some thirty-three priests are said to have taken the oath, most of them admittedly after being presented by grand juries. Country-wide efforts over the next five years by the authorities to force compliance failed to make much impression on clergy or laity and eventually fizzled out.

It is necessary now to revert to the year 1707 when the heads of a popish solicitors bill were brought into the lords, the aim of which was to require solicitors, in addition to the oaths and declaration against transubstantiation prescribed by the 1698 solicitors act, to take the oath of abjuration. Following a petition from Francis Glascock, Robert Ridge and Peter Daly and a separate petition from Oliver Weston, the house agreed to insert a saver in the heads in respect of common solicitors, managers or agents covered by the Articles of Limerick, who had been practising in the courts in King Charles's time and had taken the oath of abjuration before 1 July 1707.[22]

What has come to be called the castration bill of 1719 was in part a reaction to

---

18 Ibid., p. 115.   19 *Dublin Intelligence*, 6 September 1709.   20 Giblin, C., op. cit., no. 15 (1972), p. 117.   21 Giblin, C., ibid., passim.   22 *Lords Journal Ireland*, vol. 2, p. 503.

the abortive Jacobite expedition to Britain of that year. In an effort to stop the entry of illegal priests into the country, the bill proposed, *inter alia*, branding on the cheek with the letter P all priests illegally in the country and their subsequent deportation.[23] The Irish privy council did not, however, consider this an adequate deterrent and inserted in the bill instead the penalty of castration.

The lord lieutenant, the duke of Bolton, was embarrassed by the castration clause and actively canvassed the English privy council to have it struck from the bill. This the council agreed to and the bill was returned to Dublin amended accordingly. The bill, as amended, was passed by the Irish house of commons but was turned down by the lords.[24] This meant that the bill had failed.

Although Archbishop King maintained the reason for rejection in the lords was that most of the lords were of opinion that 'we should execute more of the acts we already had against popery before we ask for more',[25] the lords journals show that the failure of the bill in that house was due to successful lobbying by a group of catholics (Festus Burk, George Aylmer, Richard Blake and Michael Nugent) in regard to a clause in the bill on reversionary leases.[26] This group in a petition pointed out that they and several other Catholics would be 'greatly prejudiced' if the clause should pass and they prayed that they be heard by their counsel. The house on 30 October 1719 agreed to this and counsel for the petitioners was heard the following day. The lords were apparently so impressed that they sought the opinion of the judges on the clause in question and the upshot was that the clause was voted upon by the house and rejected.[27] The entire bill accordingly failed. A contemporary account of what transpired in the house on this occasion is enlightening:

> I believe you will this post have several accounts how the Popery Bill was thrown out, after the hottest dispute and the longest debate that was ever known in this Kingdom. My Lord Molesworth spoke for two hours as fine as it was possible for man to speak against the bill, and with such weight that he had a great influence not only on the Audience in general but on many of the opposite Lords; and he spoke with so much tenderness and compassion of the unfortunate Papists and the miseries they laboured under, that it was very moving. My Lord Chancellor was very violent against it on Saturday; but by Monday it might be plainly seen how long he was in

23 Burns, R.E., op. cit., vol. 1, pp 91–3. The bill was entitled 'an act for securing the Protestant interest by further amending the several acts of parliament made against Papists and to prevent the growth of popery'. The penalty of castration was not new. Castration of priests had been discussed in the English parliament in 1674; see S.J. Connolly, *Religion, law and power: the making of protestant Ireland 1660–1760*, Oxford 1992, p. 281. John Whalley in his *Humble address to the Irish houses of parliament*, proposed in the 1690s that authors of catholic pamphlets 'if of the clergy, be g--t [gelt] and banished'. 24 *Lords Journal Ireland*, vol. 2, pp 675 et seqq. 25 Letter dated 12 November 1719 from Archbishop King to Edward Southwell quoted in Burns, R.E., op. cit., vol. 1, p. 92. 26 *Lords Journal Ireland*, vol. 2, pp 675 et seqq. 27 Ibid. under date 2 November 1719.

the Duke of Botton's closet, but he notwithstanding gave his vote against it. It was carried by a majority of one disputed vote, the house divided four or five times in the debate, and with [word or words missing] the clause was rejected ... I must tell you the whole success of the matter is due entirely to Counsellor Patrick Browne, a young Popish lawyer, who drew the case, many of the arguments and managed it entirely.[28]

This account shows that there were members in the house of Lords, such as Lord Molesworth, who were prepared even at this dark period to champion the cause of the catholics, and that the lord lieutenant was also favourably disposed to catholics and was prepared to use his influence in their favour. It has not been discovered whether the Counsellor Patrick Browne mentioned was the counsel who presented the case before the house or whether he performed merely a subsidiary, back-room role.

The popery bill of 1723 was a further attempt by the Irish parliament to require registered priests to take the oath of abjuration. It also provided that all regulars, unregistered priests and bishops should depart the country by 25 March 1725 on pain of high treason. In an effort to stop the bill while it was still in its preliminary stages, the catholic lobby was active on several fronts. At home the noted controversialist and writer, Fr Cornelius Nary, penned a trenchant pamphlet, *The case of the Roman Catholics of Ireland*, in which he made a compelling case against the bill in general and against the oath of abjuration in particular.[29] The bill was also brought to the attention of the Vatican, via the Brussels internuncio. The pope then wrote with all speed to the different catholic rulers with a view to their making representations to the British government.[30] As a further initiative, the Franciscan, Fr Sylvester Lloyd, departed for France with the intention of securing the support of the French authorities for the withdrawal of the bill, this being one of those rare periods when France and Britain were at peace and enjoying amicable relations.[31] But any meaningful role by Lloyd in the matter of French intervention has been disputed by Sir Patrick Lawless, the Irish-born Spanish envoy in France, who claimed that the bill was shelved following his persuading the Spanish diplomat, de Pozzobueno, to make representations in London.[32] No doubt as a result of these combined efforts, the bill was rejected by the English privy council when it came before that body.

Following the execution of a number of protestants at Thorn in the catholic kingdom of Poland, there were rumours that, as a reprisal, the bill would be

28 Letter dated 3 November 1719 from John Brown to James Cotter in *Cork Historical and Archaeological Journal*, vol. 68, p. 85.   29 Nary, Cornelius, *The case of the Roman Catholics of Ireland*, included in Hugh Reily's *Genuine History of Ireland*, 1762 edition, pp 112–32. The earliest publication of Nary's pamphlet so far discovered is in the 1742 edition of Reily's history.   30 Giblin, C., op. cit., no. 14 (1971), p. 3.   31 Fagan, Patrick, *An Irish bishop in penal times: the chequered career of Sylvester Lloyd* OFM *1680–1747*, Dublin 1993, pp 49–53.   32 Fagan, Patrick (ed.), *Ireland in the Stuart papers*, vol. 1, p. 58.

revived in the following 1725–6 session of parliament. Four members of the Irish hierarchy, Hugh MacMahon of Armagh, Edmund Murphy of Dublin, Christopher Butler of Cashel and Bernard Dunne of Kildare, accordingly met in Dublin and decided that the Franciscan, Ambrose O'Callaghan, should go to Vienna to solicit the intervention of the emperor. This mission O'Callaghan carried out in September-October 1725.[33] Fr Sylvester Lloyd paid a second visit to France for the same purpose, but once again the efficacy of his efforts was disputed, this time by Abbé James Dunne, later bishop of Ossory, who claimed that the possibility of the bill being introduced was staved off, on Dunne's initiative, by the intervention of first minister de Fleury with Horace Walpole, British ambassador in Paris and brother of the British prime minister.[34]

On the succession of George II to the throne in June 1727 some catholics felt that an address of loyalty to him might prove beneficial to catholic interests, more particularly as the king was known to be well-disposed to catholics prior to his succession. The address was drawn up by Thomas Nugent, earl of Westmeath, but generally known as the Lord Delvin and was said to have been signed by some sixty catholic nobles and gentry about Dublin. Delvin brought the address to London where he delivered it to the lord lieutenant for presenting to the king. The latter received the address very graciously and commanded the lord lieutenant to assure the Lord Delvin that his Majesty desired nothing more than to make all his subjects easy and happy under his government. Such an address was of course anathema to the Jacobites, who, led by Fr Sylvester Lloyd, mounted a vigorous campaign against it, addressing a pamphlet in the form of queries to the promoters of the address.[35]

However, the promoters were so emboldened by the reception the address had received from the king that they are said to have petitioned the Irish house of commons for leave to take long leases and mortgages of lands; the petition was not only rejected but, to the great confusion of the petitioners, hissed with indignation out of the house.[36] Later in the summer of 1728 Delvin was very active in London, where he was received by the king and was considering handing in a petition in the name of Irish catholics requesting that they might have leave to purchase land and to take long leases. In return for these concessions they were prepared, in addition to the recent address of loyalty, to give the government all such further security for their fidelity and allegiance as should be thought necessary.[37]

In the summer of 1728 a congress of European states was convened at Soissons, an old cathedral town on the Aisne in north-east France, the general aim of which was the resolution of differences between the various states, and for a time there was an expectation that the question of religious toleration might figure in the agenda. The primate, Hugh MacMahon, selected Bishop Dunne of Kildare to

33 Ibid., pp 59–60.   34 Ibid., pp 57–8.   35 Fagan, P., op. cit., note 31, p. 89. Since there is some confusion about the identity of 'Lord Delvin', an extended note in the matter will be found in Appendix 7, pp 74–6.   36 Ibid., pp 91–2.   37 Ibid., p. 95.

represent the Irish catholic interest at Soissons, but Dunne, ardent Jacobite that he was, declined to make any move without the nod from the Pretender. Sylvester Lloyd had no such doubts as to what he should do, when he was selected by the Irish regular clergy to perform a similar function. Lloyd proceeded to London where he was to find marked differences between English catholics as to the line to be taken, but in the event all his efforts proved abortive when it became clear that religious toleration would not be on the agenda of the congress.[38]

The Lord Delvin, Lloyd's old enemy, also turned up on the fringes of the Congress in the autumn of 1728, still intent on advocating that catholics should take an oath of loyalty to the king, but he must have soon realized that it was vain to hope for any action from the congress in the matter of religious toleration.[39]

The next occasion on which a catholic lobby was to manifest itself was in 1731–2 when five bills, inimical to catholic interests, were initiated by the Irish house of lords, viz. (a) a bill closing loopholes in the law on the holding of arms by catholics, (b) an amendment of the law in relation to popish solicitors, (c) a bill for registering the popish clergy, (d) a bill for better putting in execution the laws banishing popish regulars and (e) a bill to annul and make void marriages between protestants and papists celebrated by popish priests and friars.

The report of a lords committee, established to inspect and report on original papers seized by the authorities in the homes of Bishop Thaddeus MacCarthy of Cork and of Joseph Nagle of Cork, a catholic solicitor, contains some valuable information on the activities of the catholic lobby on this occasion.[40] The decision to seize the papers of the persons mentioned derived from an information sworn by John Hennessy, dissident parish priest of Doneraile, that the collection of money for the use of the Pretender had been organized by certain Munster bishops. No documentary evidence of this allegation appears to have been found, because, it was claimed, Nagle had timely warning and had disposed of incriminating documents.

However, documents were discovered in Nagle's home in regard to a collection made throughout the country in 1731–2 for the purpose of opposing certain of the bills set out above when they came before the English privy council. The collection was organized from Dublin by Thomas Woulfe, a catholic merchant in St Audoen's parish. In the course of a letter dated 11 December 1731 to Nagle, Woulfe stated:

> There is a bill brought into the House of Lords, whereby the R. Catholics of this kingdom are to be grievously affected, and Leave is given to bring in some other bills against us, and the Clergy, destructive of our religion, which will soon be transmitted to the Council in England. Our friends

38 Ibid., chapter 6. 39 Fagan, P., op, cit, in note 32, vol. 1, pp 122–3. 40 *A Report from the committee appointed to inspect the original papers seized in the houses or lodgings of one MacCarthy alias Rabah, a reputed titular popish bishop, and Joseph Nagle, a reputed popish solicitor, both of the city of Corke*, 19 December 1733, passim.

here have agreed to make opposition to them in a legal way, at every stage as they pass through, in order to hinder them from being passed into laws. As it will be requisite to have some money to defray the expenses thereof, I am ordered by our friends here to desire you to speak to your friends in an earnest manner to contribute, as we here in Dublin have already done, and remit the money forthwith to Mr Miles Reilly, merchant in Dublin, who is appointed to receive the same.[41]

It is not possible to say which bill Woulfe had in mind in the opening line above, but the report of the lords committee states that Catholics were especially interested in two of the bills, one for disarming papists and the other in relation to popish solicitors.[42] In a further letter dated 25 December 1731 Woulfe chided Nagle on account of the sparseness of the collection made in Cork city, a mere £100 as compared with over £120 collected 'in the little parish of St Audians [*sic*]' in Dublin. Apparently Nagle had also suggested that there was 'a former fund', the outstanding balance of which might be used 'to defray our present expense in England'. Woulfe also made a distinction between bills directed against the catholic laity (i.e. (a) and (b) above) and the three bills directed specifically against the catholic clergy when he speaks of making it 'our duty to preserve them [the clergy], in taking care to avert their penal bills as our own'.[43]

Woulfe expressed the view that action in England against the bills would be much more fruitful than action at home on return of the bills, and that 'therefore our greatest efforts must be to put a stop to them on that side, for which, and many more reasons, this is the place to have what money which is needful for the occasion'.[44] It also emerges from the documents discovered by the lords committee that the catholic merchants were concerned with a bill for better securing and collecting his Majesty's revenue and that Nagle suggested their joining with protestants to petition against it 'especially in the House of Lords, which is the likeliest place to hope for redress'.[45]

There are several references in other state papers of the time to the activities in London of catholic agents against the bill regarding the holding of arms by papists and the bill in regard to popish solicitors. In relation to the first bill Primate Boulter commented that 'the Papists here [Dublin] declare publicly that they have imployed agents on the other side of the water to have the bill sunk there',[46] but he was assured from London that 'whatever endeavours the Papists may have used to obstruct the bills being approved here in Council, who have sent over an agent to solicit against it [*sic*], they have been very unsuccessful and you may be persuaded that any application from that quarter would be of little weight here'.[47] Boulter was glad to hear the Papists met with so little encourage-

41 Ibid., p. 7.   42 Ibid., p. 2.   43 Ibid., p. 8.   44 Ibid., p. 8.   45 Ibid., p. 9.   46 Letter dated 4 December 1731 from Primate Boulter to duke of Newcastle, Irish State Papers on NLI microfilm Pos. 3651, f. 131 (1731).   47 Letter dated 6 January 1732 from unidentified person to Primate Boulter in ibid. f. 1 (1732).

ment on this occasion, 'the rather because we think here that they have been guilty of a great rudeness to my Lord Lieutenant and the Privy Council at least, in not preferring a petition here against it, if they had anything reasonable to object; and if they had been rejected here, it had then been time enough to apply on the other side'.[48]

Chief Secretary Walter Cary expressed the view that, while the catholics lobbied against both bills, they regarded the bill in relation to popish solicitors as by far the more serious from their point of view. He argued that the great pains taken to defeat this bill were so many proofs of its consequence. He continued:

> Some are of opinion that the opposition already given to the disarming bill was only to gain time and strengthen the attack against this [the solicitors bill]. It is certain that my Lords Carlingford and Westmeath, though they have frequently waited on my Lord Lieutenant, never opened their lips against the disarming bill, while it was depending in the House of Lords, tho' their names are to the petition against it in England.[49]

When the solicitors bill had been returned approved by the privy council and it was being put formally through the commons, a petition against the bill was lodged on 1 April 1734 by six catholics (Sir Edmond Butler, William Purcell Esq. of Crumlin, John Reilly, Dublin merchant, Francis Lynch, Dublin merchant, Augustus Clarke, Dublin merchant and Richard Mathews, Dublin brewer), praying that they be heard by their counsel, but the petition was rejected by the house on the same day.[50]

Later, when the same bill was in the lords, a petition was lodged on 9 April by Edmund, Viscount Mountgarrett, Thomas, Lord Cahir and four of those concerned with the petition on 1 April in the commons, viz. Purcell, Reilly, Lynch and Clarke. They stated that they were advised, and that they apprehended, that they would be greatly affected by the bill and requested to be heard by their counsel. The house thereupon ordered that counsel for the petitioners be heard before the house in committee, but there is no further mention of the matter in the *Lords Journals*.[51] Presumably the house went through the motions of hearing counsel and then ignored what the latter had to say, for no change was made in the bill.

The solicitors bill passed into law later that year, but the arms bill did not become law until 1739.

---

48 Letter dated 15 January 1732 from Primate Boulter to duke of Newcastle in ibid. f. 6 (1732). 49 Letter dated 2 January 1732 from Walter Cary to Charles Delafaye in ibid., f. 14 (1732) Carlingford's and Westmeath's complacent attitude to the arms bill was no doubt due to the expectation that they personally had little to fear since they could expect to be licensed to carry arms under the licensing provision in the bill. 50 *Commons Journal Ireland*, vol. 4, part 1, p. 137. 51 *Lords Journals Ireland*, vol. 3, p. 282.

Action against the five bills, or at least against some of them, also took the form of representations to the Brussels nuncio and to the Austrian emperor. The agent in this case was Ambrose O'Callaghan, now bishop of Ferns. Whether he undertook this mission at the behest of the other members of the hierarchy, or off his own bat, is not clear. Certainly, O'Callaghan was a man who loved travel and lobbying against the bills would have furnished him with an excellent excuse for an extended sojourn in Europe.[52] In any event June 1731 found him in Brussels where no doubt he informed the nunciature of the proposed bills. From there he went to Vienna whence on 4 August 1731 he was able to report to the Stuart court that he had arrived there about a fortnight previously and

> had the best success imaginable so as to be now almost ready to go back with the emperor's commands to Count Kinski so that he may act in his Imperial Majesty's name to hinder any new grievances which the Irish parliament may propose or invent against the Roman Catholics. Before I left home some of the whiggish members told us they'd not be muzzled at next sitting. I hope to be at London before my Lord Dorset [lord lieutenant] sets out for Ireland.[53]

On 9 August 1731 O'Callaghan reported that he had had an audience the day before with the emperor who told him that 'he [emperor] should be very forward upon all occasions of a like nature to interpose in our favour, but bid me tell the people they should do nothing that may displease the king or government'. O'Callaghan proposed to leave the following day for London, where he would confer with Kinski, the imperial ambassador.[54] The intention apparently was that Kinski would have a word with Dorset about the proposed bills before the latter set out for Dublin about 4 September to open the new session of parliament. Any overtures Kinski may have made at this stage to Dorset were not successful in stopping the heads of the bills in their progress through the Irish lords, but no doubt he continued to make representations against the bills when they came before the English privy council early in 1732.

It seems highly likely that O'Callaghan concerned himself exclusively with the three bills aimed specifically at the catholic clergy, while it is quite clear that the agent employed in London by the catholic laity was under orders to confine himself to the disarming bill and the popish solicitors bill. We can discern in this a rift between the aims of the laity and those of the clergy, a rift which had manifested itself a few years earlier on the occasion of the catholic address to the king in July 1727 and was to surface on many occasions thereafter before the catholic relief acts.

It is also significant that the three bills which apparently were the subject of

---

52 Nuncio Spinelli once jokingly cited O'Callaghan as an example of perpetual motion.   53 Fagan, P., op. cit in note 32, vol. 1, p. 168.   54 Ibid., p. 169.

representations by the imperial ambassador were turned down by the privy council, while the two lobbied against by the catholic agent in London were approved
by the council. In turning down the three bills the council proffered the rather
lame excuse that they 'were of an extraordinary nature and very different from
the laws of England against Papists'.[55] It was unlikely the council would have
admitted to what was probably the real reason for turning down the bills, that is,
that they had succumbed to pressure from a foreign catholic state. We may de-
duce from the foregoing that representations by the Austrian emperor or possibly other catholic states against anti-catholic measures were likely to be more
effective than those of catholic agents in London employed by a Dublin lobby.

In relation to the bill above for registering the popish clergy, it is possible that
catholic lobbying also took the form of proffering to the administration a form of
oath prepared by Fr Cornelius Nary when the heads of that bill were going through
the lords.[56] While no copy of this bill has been discovered, according to one source
it included an oath of abjuration (of the Stuarts) and of loyalty to the king, to be
taken by priests registering. This would mean that Nary's oath, which did not
include an abjuration of the Stuarts, had not, if proffered, been accepted.

Nary's oath surfaced many years later when it was included by James Hamilton, earl of Clanbrassill, in his registry of priests bill 1756. This matter is gone
into in some detail in my book *Divided loyalties: the question of the oath for Irish
Catholics in the eighteenth century*. When writing that book I was unaware of a
letter dated 18 August 1757 from Hamilton to the lord lieutenant, the duke of
Bedford, in which Hamilton stated:

> In the bill I offered in the last session, I had inserted an oath drawn up by
> the late archbishop of Tuam [Synge], but upon conversing with some lead-
> ing men among the Papists, I found they had scruples about taking it. I
> therefore inserted, in lieu of it, the oath as it now stands, which was drawn
> up by Father Nary several years ago, who was greatly esteemed both by
> Protestants and Papists. This oath he declared himself ready to take and
> said that all honest men of his profession [religion] would do the same. He
> has been long dead, but his authority is still of great weight, and I really
> believe that most of the priests in Ireland will be influenced by it.[57]

Although this letter serves to confirm the conclusions arrived at in *Divided
loyalties*, in regard to the part played by Nary's oath in the registry of priests bills
1756 and 1757, it does not shed much light on the occasion or purpose for which
that oath was originally drafted. Since the oath refers to George II it seems that it
was drafted some time after that monarch's accession to the throne in 1727 and

55 Irish State Papers in NLI microfilm Pos. 365 1, f. 74 (1732).   **56** For Nary's form of oath see
Fagan P., op. cit. in note 2, p. 68.   **57** Malcomson, A.P.W., *Eighteenth-century Irish official
papers in Great Britain*, Belfast 1990, p. 168.

some time before March 1738 when Nary died. It is clear from the words in the extract above – 'this oath he declared himself ready to take ...' – that Nary made his form of oath public at some stage. Perhaps the most likely such occasion would have been when the 1731 heads of bill for registering the popish clergy were being debated in the lords, although it is possible that his oath saw the light earlier when the Lord Delvin, following on from the address to the king in July 1727, was engaged in further representations in London in 1728 involving a form of oath to the king.[58]

Piqued no doubt by the rejection of the three bills aimed at the catholic clergy, the Irish house of lords passed a resolution in their next 1733–4 session requiring the magistrates to put the existing laws against popery into execution. This resulted in what amounted to a persecution of the catholic clergy in the first half of 1734. The fact that the ambassadors in London of the catholic states all maintained chapels in their embassies there and that many of the chaplains in these chapels were Irish priests, was a further important facet of the Irish catholic lobby in London, since these priests were in excellent positions to influence the ambassadors concerned. Thus when Stephen Dowdall, chaplain at the Austrian embassy chapel in London, was appointed bishop of Kildare early in 1734, he remained on in London for some time for the purpose of persuading the various ambassadors to take up with the British government the persecution being then pursued in Ireland. In a letter to the Stuart court Dowdall said he had recourse to all the ambassadors 'but especially to those of France and Spain who exerted themselves with a zeal becoming them, and they assured me we shall be connived at as hitherto', in other words, that a blind eye would be turned to the requirements of the law.[59]

Around the same time Archbishop Christopher Butler of Cashel wrote a long letter to the Brussels nuncio outlining the extent of the persecution. In May 1734 the nuncio forwarded to Cardinal Firrao in Rome a copy of Butler's letter, but commented that the fury of the persecution appeared to have abated somewhat and that he hoped the former quiet would be restored shortly. In fact the persecution does not appear to have lasted more than six months.[60]

In 1738 an act was passed by the Irish parliament to control enlistment of Irishmen in foreign services. It is of interest to find on that occasion Sylvester Lloyd, then bishop of Killaloe, writing to Col. Daniel O'Brien, the Jacobite agent in Paris, in the following terms.

The above is an exact copy of the bill lately passed by the House of Commons and now returned with the approbation of the English Privy Coun-

58 Fagan, P., op. cit. in note 31, p. 95.   59 Fagan, P., op. cit. in note 32, vol. 1, p. 197. The fact that Dowdall found the ambassadors of France and Spain apparently more accommodating than that of Austria, may have been due to a coolness at this time between Austria and Britain, resulting from the latter's decision to remain neutral, despite Austrian pressure, in the War of the Polish Succession 1733–5.   60 Giblin, C., op. cit., no. 9 (1966), p. 40.

cil. It has not yet gone through the [Irish] House of Lords but will in all probability this week. I likewise send you a copy of some reflections made by a friend of yours upon some clauses in the bill. I was in hopes they might have been insisted upon and enlarged by some of the Lords but we cannot find one who will venture to speak in favour of your friends in foreign service. It is not doubted here but that the bill will soon put an end to the Irish regiments. It is not my fault that this bill was not opposed properly and in due time but alas we have heads[?] and very divided ones, not to say worse[?], but I must not venture to speak my sentiments.[61]

This letter is an indication of the easy relations existing at the time in question between the catholic side, including the bishops, and some members of the house of lords, although there was a limit to the circumstances in which these lords could be expected to come to the aid of the catholic side, and sponsoring catholic-inspired amendments to a bill regarding recruitment to foreign services, such as the French, was definitely beyond the pale. The fact that the bill was 'not opposed properly and in due time' presumably by lobbying against it when it was before the English privy council, Lloyd puts down to divisions among the Catholics. It has to be said that Lloyd was himself a prime cause of such divisions. In his capacity as an ardent Jacobite, he had, as noted already, mounted a virulent campaign against the address to the king promoted by the Lord Delvin and other catholic nobility and gentry in 1727 and was to continue his opposition for many years thereafter to any accommodation with the government in the matter of an oath for catholics.[62]

A proclamation in February 1744 reactivating the laws against catholic clergy had its origin in the impending war between Britain and France and French plans to invade Britain with Jacobite help. The ensuing persecution was claimed to be the worst since Queen Anne's time, but it also turned out to be the last general persecution in Ireland.

Catholic reaction to the proclamation took various forms. In Madrid Fr John Lacy, with hopes of advancement to an Irish bishopric, translated the proclamation into different languages and dispatched copies to the Vatican and the catholic courts of Europe, 'in order. that they should not only take compassion on my poor nation but that at the same time they should together join for to drive away the tyrannous usurper and place our lawful king on the throne of his ancestors'.[63] This latter sentiment ignored the reality that protestant Britain was about to enter the War of the Austrian Succession on the side of catholic Austria and against protestant Prussia. Lacy also reported that his initiative had been well received at the Spanish court and that orders had been given at all Spanish seaports 'to receive well and harbour' all such as came from Ireland.[64]

61 Fagan, P., op. cit., in note 32, vol. 1, p. 276.   62 Fagan, P., op. cit., in note 31, chapters 5 & 6, passim.   63 Fagan, P., op. cit., in note 32, vol. 2, pp 14–15, letter dated 30 August 1744 from Lacy to the Stuart court.   64 Ibid., p. 15.

Somewhat belatedly about 20 August 1744 Archbishop Linegar of Dublin reported to Cardinal Corsini, protector of Ireland, that Ireland was grievously afflicted by misfortunes and persecutions and because of this he was compelled to have recourse to Corsini, who was such a vigilant and sympathetic protector.[65] But whether the Vatican took any action arising out of this has not been discovered.

Austrian intervention on this occasion took the form of representations by one of her greatest generals, Count Nicholas Taaffe, a native of Sligo. Taaffe, on a visit to Dublin in the summer of 1744, had personal experience of the persecution through being unable to attend Mass, because all the chapels in the city were closed by government order.[66] The representations which he subsequently made to George II, whom he knew personally from campaigning together on the continent, were instrumental in bringing about some easement of the repressive measures in the Autumn of 1744 and must also have influenced the benign policies towards catholics followed by the earl of Chesterfield, who was appointed lord lieutenant in January 1745 and came over to Ireland in August 1745.

The Jesuit, Fr Bernard Rothe's little-known mission to Austria in October-November 1748 had its origin in a meeting of a number of catholics in London 'privately commissioned by most of the gentry and prime persons of the Catholic clergy at home'. This London meeting came to the conclusion that the Treaty of Aix-la-Chapelle, which brought to an end the War of the Austrian Succession, represented 'a favourable circumstance for obtaining some relaxation of the rigour of the laws, amaking and apreparing every day against them'. They considered that the most efficacious remedy would be to apply to the court of Vienna for a strong recommendation in favour of the catholics of Ireland. They discounted any approach to either France or Spain because the notoriety of the Spanish Inquisition and French usage of the Huguenots 'hindered the recommendation of both these powers from being agreeable to the British nation'. Since there was a great regard for Jesuits at the Austrian court, it was believed that a Jesuit was the fittest person to undertake the mission to Vienna, and Fr Rothe was accordingly selected.[67]

Fr Rothe was born in Kilkenny in 1693 and was educated at the Jesuit College at Poitiers in France, where he was later a professor. He joined the *Journal de Trevoux* in Paris in 1743 and was a prolific writer.[68] He was at first hesitant about undertaking the Austrian mission, but, following pressure from the papal nuncio in Paris, he set out for Vienna and arrived there on 6 October 1748. After meeting with some initial discouragement, arising out of 'the actual misintelligence between the Court of Vienna and the present British Government', he at last obtained from the emperor and his chief ministers the most positive assurances

65 Giblin, C., op. cit., no. 10 (1967), p. 99.   66 Moran, Patrick, *The Roman catholics of Ireland under the penal laws of the eighteenth century*, London 1900, p. 54.   67 Fagan, P., op. cit. in note 32, vol. 2, pp 99–100, letter dated 23 December 1748 from Rothe to Stuart court.   68 Hayes, Richard, *Biographical dictionary of Irishmen in France*, Dublin 1949.

that as soon as the situation of affairs could allow, 'they would interpose the most earnest intercession in favour of the Irish Catholics'.[69]

It will be noted that Rothe gives a very general reason for his mission to Vienna at this time. However, the Augustinian, Fr James MacKenna, claims that the catholic lobby in London in the early months of 1748 had a very specific aim. Writing from Dublin to the Stuart court on 13 February 1748, MacKenna mentions a bill in regard to protestant guardians for wealthy orphaned catholic children, which he claimed had been sent to the English privy council for approval. Some money, he said, had been collected for the purpose of contesting the bill in London and Count Taaffe had gone over there for that purpose.[70]

I can find no evidence in the Lords or Commons journals of such a bill in the 1747–8 session. However, there was a bill that session for making more effectual the act to restrain foreign education of catholics, which was presented in the lords by the bishop of Meath and may have contained some ancillary provisions in regard to guardians. The heads of this bill were passed by the lords on 13 January 1748 and were sent to the lord lieutenant for transmission to London.[71] Apparently, following its return as an approved bill, a petition was presented on 30 March 1748 by Lord Mountgarrett, John Nugent, Robert French and Nicholas Weldon on behalf of themselves and other catholics against the bill 'whereby petitioners apprehend they will be greatly affected'. The lords agreed to hear counsel for the petitioners and they were so impressed by the case made that the judges were required to prepare heads of a revised bill.[72] This had the effect of side-lining the bill and nothing further appears to have been heard of it.

Rothe's mission to Vienna was the last attempt to use the emperor's influence with the British government towards having anti-catholic measures by the Irish parliament quashed. With the outbreak of the Seven Years' War in 1756 Austria and Britain severed their long association as allies, and contested that long and bitter war on opposing sides. It also has to be said in any event that the era of penal legislation had come to a close and there would be little occasion henceforth for engaging the services of foreign governments towards having anti-catholic measures negatived by the English privy council.

CONCLUSIONS

It will be seen then that the *ad hoc* catholic lobby in the first half of the eighteenth century was continuous, persistent, disparate and quite often successful. There was hardly an anti-catholic measure sponsored by the Irish parliament in that

---

69 Fagan, P., op. cit. in note 32, vol. 2, p. 100. 70 Ibid., p. 87. 71 *Lords Journal Ireland*, vol. 3 under date mentioned. Since MacKenna goes into some detail in regard to a bill about guardians, it seems unlikely that he was mistaken. Like many other negatived bills of the Irish parliament, no copy of this foreign education bill can be traced. 72 *Lords Journal Ireland*, vol. 3, under dates 30 March, 2 & 5 April 1748.

period which was not opposed in some fashion by the catholic interests concerned. Such opposition could be manifested by individuals affected petitioning one of the houses of parliament, or by a case being made by counsel at the bar of the house, or by representations to the English privy council when the heads of a bill came before that body for decision. Quite often, too, opposition took the form of requesting Austria or some other catholic power to intervene with the British government.

There were also some rare instances where catholics took the initiative in making positive proposals to the authorities. Into this category falls Fr Cornelius Nary's intervention, anonymously, by pamphlet in 1727 in a controversy between Edward Synge *fils* and Stephen Radcliffe, vicar of Naas, concerning Synge's proposal to bring catholics in from the cold by way of a special oath for them.[73] Also in this category is the form of oath for catholics proposed later by Nary himself. The Lord Delvin's advocacy of an address of loyalty to the new king, George II, in July 1727 and his subsequent proposals for an oath for catholics in return for certain concessions is another example of a positive initiative. That none of these initiatives came to anything was due in part at least to opposition to them from within the catholic body itself.

This brings us to the inevitable divisions and varying objectives and *modi operandi* of the various constituents of the catholic body. Firstly, there was the division between clergy and laity. The laity seldom displayed much concern about bills which affected the clergy only, nor were the clergy much concerned about bills which affected only the laity. As a case in point, would the laity have bothered opposing (with such good results) the castration bill in 1719 if it had not contained a clause in regard to reversionary leases affecting wealthier catholics? As to the *modi operandi* used, it will be seen that the clergy almost invariably pinned their hopes of quashing unwanted measures on the intervention of Austria, or some other catholic power, with the British, or (rarely) Irish authorities. The laity, on the other hand, relied almost exclusively on direct petitions or representations to the Irish parliament, or by representations by their agent in London to the English privy council.

Secondly, the catholic body for most of the period was riven by differences between Jacobites and what might be called loyalists. This rift can first be seen in 1709 and the following years when catholics took sides over the oath of abjuration of the Stuarts in the popery act of that year. In the 1720s the Lord Delvin's and Fr Nary's proposals mentioned above were strenuously, not to say virulently, opposed by the Jacobite faction, led by Fr Sylvester Lloyd. That such bickering had necessarily to take place largely *sub rosa,* did not detract from its baneful effect on the possibilities of concessions to catholics, who instead had to content themselves with the *cul de sac* of toleration by connivance.

---

73 Fagan, P., *Dublin's turbulent priest: Cornelius Nary 1658–1738*, Dublin 1991, chapter 10, passim.

While the lobby lacked a permanent structure, there was in the catholic hierarchy a permanent organization in a position secretly to organize and direct representations against measures affecting the catholic clergy. Action by the laity against measures affecting them was to an extent haphazard and often a matter of a few individuals coming together and deciding that something should be done, although there is a suggestion by Joseph Nagle, the Cork solicitor, in 1731 that funds remaining over from one campaign might be used on a subsequent one.

The catholic nobility and gentry were still relatively strong in the opening decades of the century and those who were protected by the Articles of Limerick were in a position to make measured, if somewhat muted, protests. It is revealing to find that catholic Lords Carlingford and Westmeath had 'frequently waited upon' the lord lieutenant in the early 1730s. Strangely, noble families which were to be prominent in catholic affairs in the second half of the century – Trimleston, Fingall, Kenmare and Gormanston – figure hardly at all in the first half.

Portentously, by the mid-century many of those families which had been vocal in the catholic cause earlier, had gone over to the established church, for example, Lord Fitzwilliam of Merrion in 1710, Lord Mountgarrett in 1749 and the earl of Westmeath in 1756.[74] Of the counsellors who appeared at the bars of the houses of parliament in 1704 in a fruitless appeal against the popery bill of that year (Sir Toby Butler, Sir Stephen Rice and Edmond Malone), Butler's son, if not Butler himself, defected to the established church, as well as some of Rice's and Malone's relations. Such defections were, however, more than compensated for as the century wore on by the vast advances made by catholics in trade and industry in the cities and larger towns.

Lastly, it has to be said that Poynings' Law was a blessing in disguise as far as the catholics were concerned in the first half of the century. The operation of that law meant in effect that the Irish parliament was a parliament without teeth. Heads of bills passed there could be, and often were, turned down by the English privy council. Such rejection came about principally from the fact that the operation of the principle of the balance of power in Europe dictated that until the Seven Years' War (1756–63), protestant Britain should be the ally of the very catholic emperor of Austria. Anti-catholic proposals by the Irish parliament were in these circumstances often an embarrassment to the British government, which, in the face of pressure from the emperor or his ambassador, felt constrained to turn down such proposals, or, where anti-catholic laws were in fact enacted, to ensure that they remained little more than dead letters on the face of the statute book.

74 O'Byrne, Eileen (ed.), *The convert rolls*, Dublin 1981.

APPENDIX 7

THE IDENTITY OF 'LORD DELVIN'

There is some confusion about the identity of the Lord Delvin who was involved in the Catholic Address to the king in 1727 and subsequent events. Throughout the eighteenth century, the earl of Westmeath was generally, but not exclusively, known as Lord Delvin or *the* Lord Delvin. Why this was so may have to do with, at least in the early eighteenth century, the fairly recent (1642) creation of the earldom; the title of Lord or Baron Delvin was of such antiquity that it took some time for the new title to stick. Unfortunately, however, Lord Delvin was also a courtesy title accorded to the eldest son and heir of the earl of Westmeath.[75] Two people sporting what appeared to be the same title was of course a recipe for confusion.

At the time we are concerned with here the earl of Westmeath, or the Lord Delvin, was Thomas Nugent. He had been a colonel in the Jacobite army in Limerick during the siege, and so, although a catholic, was enabled to hold on to his estates in accordance with the Articles of Limerick. Thomas's eldest son and heir, Christopher, was, as noted, also entitled to be styled Lord Delvin.

When writing previously on this subject I had little difficulty in concluding that it was Thomas Nugent, the earl, and not his son, who played such a prominent part in the address to the king in 1727 and in subsequent events. The later discovery in the National Library of Ireland of a letter dated 20 September 1755, presumed to be from William Henry, dean of Killaloe, to the archbishop of Canterbury caused me to take a fresh look at the question of the identity of Lord Delvin.[76] This letter is concerned chiefly with the extent to which Catholics enjoyed the free practice of their religion in the early 1750s, but in a reference to the Catholic Address to the king in 1727 Henry says that the Lord Delvin in question was 'a son of the earl of Westmeath', in other words, that he was Christopher and not Thomas Nugent. The writer goes on to state that

> Lord Delvin and his associates were on this account solemnly excommunicated at Rome. In consequence of which his Lordship and the others submitted to penance. He afterwards ceased from all public intercourse and continued the remainder of his life a bigoted papist.

William Henry, who died in 1768, would have been a fairly near contemporary of the events in question and was probably a young man at the time of the address to the king in 1727. His disclosure, therefore, cannot be dismissed lightly and it is useful to set out some of the pertinent points in the case.

Thomas Nugent, who died in 1752 aged ninety-six, would have been aged about seventy-one in 1727. While in the normal course a man aged seventy-one

75 *Burke's peerage*, 105th edition, p. 2794.   76 National Library of Ireland microfilm Pos. 4.

in the eighteenth century would not be likely to be very active, the fact that Thomas lived to such a great age could mean that he was a very active man into his seventies. Thomas Prior, in his list of absentees published in 1729, lists Lord Delvin with the earls and credits him with an income of only £400 a year.[77] Prior, therefore, apparently believed that Thomas, the earl, rather than Christopher, his son, was the absentee. It is possible he was mistaken for the income of £400 sounds more like that of the son than of the father.

Sylvester Lloyd, later successively bishop of Killaloe and of Waterford & Lismore, makes reference to *the* Lord Delvin in four of his letters to Col. O'Brien, the Jacobite agent in Paris, between 15 July 1727 and 1 August 1728, in regard to the Catholic Address to the king.[78] Indeed, in one of these letters he styles the man in question as the Right Honourable the Lord Delvin. The use here of the definite article and of the style 'The Right Honourable' may be highly significant. The fiction is that the earl of Westmeath loans the title of Lord Delvin to his eldest son and heir, but the earl remains *the* Lord Delvin, and the eldest son is only entitled to style himself Lord Delvin, without the definite article. Furthermore, the style 'The Right Honourable', as far as the peerage is concerned, should be extended only to peers below the rank of marquis, that is, earls, viscounts and barons. It should not be applied to the holder of a mere courtesy title. These are niceties with which Sylvester Lloyd, a convert from the established church and indeed a parson's son, would be likely to be familiar, and they provide a solid basis for believing that Thomas Nugent was the person involved in the address to the king and subsequently.

It is pertinent to mention that, while Lloyd in his letter of 15 July to Col. O'Brien uses the title 'the Lord Delvin' elsewhere in that letter, when he comes to mention some of the signatories of the address he uses the title 'Earl of Westmeath', no doubt because that is how the document was signed. It has to be asked why didn't Lloyd use the title 'Earl of Westmeath' in the rest of the letter, and the answer presumably is that Thomas Nugent was better known as the Lord Delvin than as Earl of Westmeath. We cannot be sure whether Christopher Nugent was also a signatory of the address; the name of one of the signatories mentioned by Lloyd is illegible through blotting, but it is a short name and it may be Delvin, although it is perhaps more likely that it is Bellew.

It should also be mentioned that the lord lieutenant, in correspondence he had with Lord Delvin at the time in question, makes reference to 'his Lordship and the other catholic peers' and that the *Dublin Journal* extracted the lord lieutenant's letter under the heading 'extract of a letter from his Excellency, Lord Carteret, to a noble peer'.[79] Again, it is apparent from this that Thomas Nugent was the peer in question.

---

77 [Prior, Thomas], *A list of absentees of Ireland*, Dublin 1729.   78 Fagan, P., op. cit. in note 32, vol. 1, pp 95–119 passim. In fact in a letter by Lloyd, at page 119 of the work cited, 'Lord Delvin' appears without the definite article, but on checking back with Lloyd's original letter, I find that this also should have read 'the Lord Delvin'.   79 Fagan, P., op. cit. in note 31, p. 89.

Thomas Nugent continued to be active politically into the 1730s at least. It will be seen above that the chief secretary, Walter Cary, in a letter dated 2 January 1732 mentions that Lords Carlingford and Westmeath had frequently waited on the lord lieutenant. The earl must have remained mentally active right into his nineties, for John Ferrar in his *History of Limerick* reproduces a letter from him dated Clounine, 22 August 1749 in regard to the trial of Col. Luttrell and other matters relating to the siege of Limerick.[80] He would have been then aged about ninety-three.

Thomas Nugent died on 30 June 1752 while Christopher died at Bath on 12 April in the same year. Since the latter predeceased his father, he never succeeded to the earldom. That honour went briefly to Thomas's brother, John, formerly an officer in Nugent's Regiment, and after that in 1756 to John's son, another Thomas, who severed the family's ties with catholicism by conforming to the established church.[81]

To conclude, the weight of the available evidence is that Thomas Nugent, earl of Westmeath was the person involved in the address to the king and subsequent events, and that William Henry was mistaken when he attributed involvement in these events to Christopher Nugent, Lord Delvin, eldest son of Thomas.

---

80 Ferrar, John, *History of Limerick*, Limerick 1787, p. 354. Clounine is Clonyn Castle, the family seat of the earls of Westmeath, near the village of Delvin in that county.   81 Burke's peerage, 105th edition, p. 2794.

3

The catholic presence in medicine

When an eighteenth-century protestant gentleman looked around for career out-
lets for his sons, there were in the main five possibilities to choose from – the
established church, the government service, the army, the law and medicine. A
catholic gentleman in the same situation would find that his sons, as far as employment at home in Ireland was concerned, were barred from the first three of
these occupations, that they could have practised the fourth, law, in some limited
degree, and that the fifth, medicine, was the only one which remained fully open
to catholics throughout the entire period of the penal laws and offered the possibility of a professional career befitting a gentleman. Of the three branches of
medicine, physic, surgery and pharmacy, physic was the more attractive from the
points of view of both prestige and emoluments.

I

The physician profession

A catholic bent on a career as a physician had perforce to attend a medical school
abroad to acquire the necessary degree, for the body charged with the control
and development of physic in Ireland, the College of Physicians, did not until
rather late in the century admit catholics to its licentiateships. That college was
originally set up by royal charter in 1667. In 1692 it was granted a new charter
purporting to arm it with powers of an extraordinary and extensive nature, which,
if confirmed by act of parliament, would have vested in it a monopoly in the
control of the practice of physic in Dublin, since one of the provisions of the
charter stated that 'no physician or other person should be allowed to practise
physic in the city of Dublin or its liberties without the licence of the college'. But
the charter's provisions never acquired any legal validity because they were never
confirmed by act of parliament, although the college several times solicited such
confirmation.[1]

It is true that early in the century the college was inclined to agonize over

---

1 Widdess, J.D.H., *History of the Royal College of Physicians in Ireland* (RCPI), Edinburgh &
London 1963, passim.

whether its licentiateships might be conferred on catholics. In 1700 the question was raised as to how fellows of the college should behave towards papist physicians. In 1732 a committee was appointed to consider what was proper to be done in regard to popish physicians in Dublin and it was subsequently ordered that the president and treasurer should obtain the opinion in writing of the recorder of Dublin as to whether the college had a power of licensing popish physicians. But on neither of these occasions was any conclusion recorded.[2]

Denys Scully in his *Statement of the penal laws*, published in 1812, maintained that over the years the college had projected an anti-catholic bias. He pointed out that when the Catholic Relief Act of 1793 opened trades and professions generally to catholics, and even provided specifically that catholics should be capable of being appointed professors or fellows of the college, the college authorities thought fit to counteract the effect of the statute by passing a by-law requiring a catholic to take a BA degree in Trinity College, Dublin as a qualification towards acquiring a fellowship (as distinct from a licentiateship) in the College of Physicians. Scully noted that this by-law had the effect of completely excluding from fellowships the older class of catholic physician, who had been educated at such places as Edinburgh, Paris, Leyden and Rheims, and of excluding to a great extent the younger class of catholic physician, since it would be some time before any appreciable number of catholics could acquire the necessary BA degree from TCD following the opening up of that college to them in 1793, and could have accumulated the necessary experience to be considered for fellowships.[3]

Scully went on to state that, though not expressly disqualified by statute, catholic physicians, as well as surgeons and apothecaries, 'not inferior in learning, skill or character to those of other persuasions' were virtually excluded from medical honours and public situations. He maintained that catholics, qualified for medical situations, considerably outnumbered the protestants, and yet they were so entirely overlooked where public appointments were concerned, that a stranger might well imagine that there existed no catholic physicians, surgeons or apothecaries in Ireland.[4]

While Scully had a point concerning the non-appointment of catholic professors or fellows in the college – the first catholic professor, Martin O'Tuomy, was not appointed until 1812 – he is a bit economical with the truth by failing to mention that long before the Relief Act of 1793, the college had been admitting catholics to licentiateships. The college records show that a catholic, John Fergus, was admitted as a licentiate as early as 1735, but he may later have been removed from the register since his name never appeared in the list of licentiates published in *Watson's Almanac* or *Wilson's Dublin Directory*. However, from the early 1770s there appears to have been an active policy of admitting well-known catholic physicians as licentiates – John Purcell on 4 November 1771, John Michael

2 Ibid., passim.   3 Scully, Denys, *Statement of the penal laws*, Dublin 1812, p. 289.   4 Ibid., p. 295.

Daly on 2 June 1772 and Patrick Maguire on 7 February 1785. John Kelly and Gerard (Garret) Hussey, who in all probability were catholics, were admitted as licentiates on 4 November 1771 and 27 January 1772 respectively.[5]

It can also be said in the college's favour that they contributed £30 towards the release of a catholic physician, Francis Duany, from a debtors' prison in 1793. As to their action to circumvent the provisions of the Catholic Relief Act of 1793,[6] it can be said that their behaviour, while highly reprehensible, was no worse than that of the Dublin trades guilds generally, as only a handful of catholics were admitted free brothers of guilds in that city, despite the provisions in that regard in the 1793 act.

Scully appears to have been quite inaccurate when he stated that catholics, qualified for medical situations, considerably outnumbered protestants. The 1861 census (the first to include such information) shows that in the country as a whole at that time only 34 per cent of physicians and 30 per cent of surgeons were catholics,[7] and the probability is that the proportions of catholics in those professions were even lower when Scully published the book in question in 1812.

However, it must be pointed out that the likelihood is that catholics did not suffer any great disadvantage in being deprived of licentiateships by the College of Physicians for the greater part of the century. It is a fact that until the passing of the School of Physics Act of 1785, licentiateships conferred by the college were apparently so little valued that some protestant physicians were in no hurry to acquire one. From 1761 onwards *Watson's Almanac* or *Wilson's Directory* published each year lists of the names and addresses of physicians practising in Dublin, indicating those who were either fellows or licentiates of the college. In the list for 1762 we find that out of 49 physicians listed, some 26 were neither fellows nor licentiates of the college, and of these 26 about half were protestants.[8] The truth is that in the first half of the century, to cut any kind of figure medically in Dublin, a degree from Leyden in the Netherlands (where the great Boerhaave held court until his death in 1738) or from a French university was a *sine qua non* for the ambitious physician. In the second half of the century a degree from Edinburgh, where the medical school was modeled on Leyden, became the desired accolade. It was only towards the end of the century that home-produced degrees, whether from the College of Physicians or from the newly-established College of Surgeons, began to acquire a standing comparable with those of foreign medical schools.

---

5 Belcher, T.W. (ed.), *Records of the King's and Queen's College of Physicians in Ireland*, Dublin 1866, passim.   6 Widdess, J.D.H., op. cit., passim.   7 *Census of Ireland 1861*, part IV. The figures for all Ireland have been arrived at by adding the figures for the four provinces in Part IV.   8 *Wilson's Dublin Directory, 1762*, part 2, p. 38. It should be mentioned, however, that the RCPI did not normally confer licentiates on physicians who practised midwifery. There were also a few protestants, who were not licentiates of the RCPI but who held MD degrees from Trinity College, Dublin.

Catholic physicians in Dublin, 1700–60

Since a comprehensive list of physicians for Dublin is not available until 1761 (in *Watson's Almanac* for 1761 and in *Wilson's Dublin Directory* thereafter), it follows that it is not possible to make even an educated guess as to the number and propor-tion of catholic physicians in the city before that date, because of the paucity of information available on catholic physicians and in the absence of a figure for the total number of physicians. For the period up to 1761, then, we have to content ourselves with information to be found in a variety of sources.

The government report on the number of catholic priests in Dublin city in 1697 tells us that Fr Netterville, a Jesuit, was then lodging on the quay (i.e. Arran Quay) in Dr Cruise's house.[9] There are references to a Dr Valentine Cruise in the records of the Dominican convent, Channel Row (now Brunswick Street) for the 1720s and the 1730s.[10] Valentine was probably a son of the Dr Cruise who lived in Arran Quay in the 1690s and who died *c.*1709. When some of the more notable catholics in the city were rounded up by the authorities in 1708, on the occasion of a Jacobite invasion scare, two catholic doctors, Wogan and Fitzpatrick, ap-peared in the list published in the press.[11] The Dr Fitzpatrick mentioned was Patrick Fitzpatrick.[12] In the parish register of St Michan's Catholic Church we find the name of another Dr Fitzpatrick, Dr John, cited as one of the witnesses to the marriage of Heckball, styled king of the beggars, to one Alice Lynch on 17 August 1731.[13]

Dr James Brenan, who practised in Dublin in the 1720s and 1730s, was in all probability a catholic, since he was stated to be the father or brother of the catho-lic surgeon, Peter Brenan. When the catholic Lord Kingsland was re-elected grand master of the Irish Freemasons for a second year in May 1734, it is of interest that he chose Dr Brenan as deputy grand master.[14]

A postulation dated 27 August 1729, supporting Bishop Stephen Mac Egan of Meath as a candidate for the archbishopric of Dublin, provides the names of what appear to be seven catholic physicians practising in the city at that date, viz. John Fitzpatrick and Val Cruise (already mentioned), James Dillon, Edmund Barry, Michael Loghlin, John Fergus and John Howard.[15] There may have been other catholic physicians (e.g. James Brenan) who did not sign this postulation, for there was another postulation in respect of a rival candidate. Considering that out of a total population of about 120,000 in Dublin city at that time, only about

9 List printed in *Irish Builder*, vol. 34 (1892), p. 174 et seq, from a manuscript in Marsh's Library, Dublin. The Dr Cruise mentioned here appears to be Christopher Cruise who died *c.*1709; see Arthur Vicar's *Index of prerogative wills*. Christopher's eldest son, Walter, was marked out for a legal career, entering Gray's Inn, London in 1705; see Joseph Foster (ed.), *Register of admissions to Gray's Inn*, London 1887. NLI microfilm Pos. 3787.   11 Brady, John, *Catholics and catholicism in the eighteenth century press*, Maynooth 1965, p. 9.   12 *Irish Ecclesiastical Record*, vol. 25 (1909), p. 507.   13 NLI microfilm pos. 8829.   14 *Faulkner's Dublin Journal*, 25–29 June 1734.   15 Fagan, Patrick (ed.), *Ireland in the Stuart papers*, Dublin 1995, vol. 1, p. 151.

40 per cent (48,000) were catholics,[16] a complement of at least eight catholic physicians in the city was not at all unreasonable.

James Dillon, above, was probably the Dr Dillon of whom Charles O'Conor of Belanagare, in a letter to Dr John Curry in March 1763, apparently on the death of Dr Dillon, wrote: 'Dr Dillon I knew. He thrived well by his profession in this country. He was a little singular in his manners and was charged with no small share of *astutia medica* [medical cunning]. On the whole he was a good man.'[17]

Edmund Barry, above, was a nephew of Edmund Byrne, archbishop of Dublin from 1707 to 1724. In his will[18] the archbishop left Dr Barry the residue of his estate. The names of Drs Michael Loghlin and John Howard, above, figure as witnesses and in other capacities in wills of the period.[19]

John Fergus, above, was an Irish language enthusiast who hailed from north Connacht and practised as a physician in the city from the 1720s to the 1760s. He is first mentioned as one of the physicians attending the Charitable Infirmary in *Watson's Almanac* for 1737 but he may have held that position prior to that date. He continued to attend that hospital without fee or reward until his death *c.*1761. He was succeeded in the practice by his son, Magrath Fergus, who survived his father by only a few years.[20]

From the 1740s onwards two further catholic physicians appear on the Dublin scene – John Curry and Richard Reddy.

John Curry was born in Dublin about 1710. He studied in the medical schools at Paris and Rheims universities and, equipped with a medical degree, returned to Dublin where he practised for many years in Cow Lane (now Greek Street). He interested himself in improving the lot of his fellow catholics, and in 1756 was instrumental, with his friend, Charles O'Conor, in setting up the Catholic Committee, which until the 1790s was foremost in the campaign for the repeal of the penal laws. A busy pamphleteer, his best known work was *An historical and critical review of the civil wars in Ireland.*[21]

Like Curry, Richard Reddy was born about 1710, and is presumably the Richard Reddy who matriculated from Leyden university in 1743 and took an MD degree there in 1745.[22] He practised in Dublin in Cow Lane from the late 1740s onwards. He too was a friend of Charles O'Conor, who credited Reddy with having encouraged him to undertake his Irish historical writings. He was still alive in 1774 when Gilborne wrote his doggerel verses about physicians, surgeons and apothecaries practising in Dublin at that time, where a passing reference is made to 'famed Richard Reddy'.[23]

16 See chapter 1 for further information on this point.   17 Ward, Robert E. & Ward, Catherine C. (eds), *The letters of Charles O'Conor of Belanagare*, Ann Arbor, Mich. 1980, p. 145.   18 *Archivium Hibernicum*, vol. 4 (1915), p. 68.   19 Twenty-sixth Report of the Deputy Keeper of the Public Records – *Index to the act or grant books and the original wills of the diocese of Dublin.*   20 Royal Irish Academy ms 23.D.20, p. 90.   21 *Dictionary of national biography*, London 1895.   22 Innes Smith, R.W. (ed.), *English-speaking students of medicine at the university of Leyden*, Edinburgh & London 1932, alphabetical list.   23 Gilborne, John, *The medical review, a poem*, Dublin 1775, p. 29.

Catholic physicians in Dublin, 1760–1800

From 1761 onwards, as already stated, lists were published each year (i.e. names and addresses) of physicians practising in Dublin city. How to identify catholic and protestant physicians on these lists presents a considerable problem more particularly during the 1760s and 1770s, but there are the following pointers.

Firstly, in the years prior to 1771 we can safely assume to have been protestants all physicians who are described as fellows or licentiates of the College of Physicians.

Secondly, for the last two decades of the century a reliable method for identifying catholic physicians emerges in the index to the Catholic Qualification Rolls (CQR).[24] The rolls arose out of the Catholic Relief Acts of 1778, 1782 and 1793 and are the lists of those who took the oath required of catholics who wished to avail of the reliefs under those acts. All physicians appearing in the CQR index can, then, be assumed to be catholics. It can also be assumed, in view of the property reliefs contained in the acts mentioned, that there were few catholic physicians in Dublin who did not enrol. Physicians missed out could include young unpropertied men who did not deem it necessary to enrol and physicians who enrolled in the provinces before moving to a new practice in Dublin.

Thirdly, parish registers, in particular marriage registers, are of some limited assistance in identifying religious persuasion.

Fourthly, several physicians, whose names occur in the lists of subscribers to various catholic books published in the period in question, can be assumed to be catholics.

List of physicians for 1762 [25]

There are 23 physicians on this list who are designated as fellows or licentiates of the College of Physicians and who can therefore be assumed to have been protestants. Of the remainder the following seven can be assumed to have been protestants for the reasons stated: Oliver Athey, since it appears from *Alumni Dublinenses* that he was for a period a student in Trinity College, Dublin; William Broughton, since his father, Thomas Broughton, merchant appears on a list of freemen of Dublin for 1761; Thomas Ellis (MD from TCD); Charles Lucas (well

24 The original Catholic Qualification Rolls (CQR) were destroyed in the fire in the Public Record Office in 1922, but there is in the National Archives an incomplete index to the rolls, that for Dublin ending in 1796. They become less useful as a source in the 1790s – see note 89 following. It should be mentioned that the special oath for catholics was originally contained in a 1774 act. Some ninety-five catholics from Dublin, including a few physicians and surgeons and one apothecary, took the oath in 1775 when there was nothing to be gained from doing so, and before the CQR came into effect following the 1778 relief act.   25 Although lists of physicians practising in Dublin were first published in *Watson's Almanac* for 1761, the list in the almanac for 1762 has been selected because the 1761 list contains the names of a father and son, John and Magrath Fergus, obviously operating as a single practice, and the inclusion of both would accordingly distort the figures. The year 1799 has been selected as the last year of the period under review and 1780 as the mid-point between 1762 and 1799.

known member of the Irish house of commons); John Moor (on list of freemen of Dublin for 1761); Sir Fielding Ould (master of the Rotunda Hospital and well-known to be a protestant).

With regard to catholic physicians on this 1762 list, we have already identified John Curry, Magrath Fergus and Richard Reddy as such. Since they appeared on a list of catholic gentry, merchants and citizens of Dublin who signed an address of loyalty presented to the lord lieutenant in November 1759, Edmund Netterville and Hanley Wale must also be accepted as catholics.[26]

The following six were also apparently catholics for the reasons stated:

(a) John Daly, on the assumption that he was the same man as the John Michael Daly who appears on the CQR index and who, as already stated, was admitted a licentiate of the College of Physicians on 2 June 1772.

(b) Charles Farrell appears to have been a brother or other near relation of Francis Ferrall (Farrell) whose name appears on the CQR index. Gilborne bracketed the two together to imply that they were related when he wrote: 'Two Ferralls, Francis, Charles, benign as day,/indulge the poor and make the rich to pay'.[27] Charles O'Conor in a letter to Dr Curry dated 1 October 1777 commented: 'I am sorry to hear of the sudden end of Doctor Charles Ferrall'.[28]

(c) The name Edward Jennings MD appears on a list of subscribers to a catholic catechism, *The real principles of Catholics*, published in 1750. He was a founder of St Nicholas's (Catholic) Hospital.[29]

(d) The name Constantine Geoghegan MD appears on the list of subscribers to a pro-catholic book entitled *Historical collections concerning the change of religion and the strange confusions following*, published in 1758. He was presumably one and the same as Constantine Geoghegan, Doctor of Physic, who appears on the CQR index with an address at Kells, County Meath.

(e) The name Edward McGowran MD appears on a list of subscribers to a catholic publication, *A Christian directory*, published in 1753.

(f) John Kelly was a founder of St Catherine's (Catholic) Hospital, which after a few years was amalgamated with St Nicholas's Hospital, in which Kelly was one of the physicians. Charles O'Conor makes a number of references to him in his correspondence[30] – yet another indication that he was a catholic. It is also of some significance that he became a licentiate of the College of Physicians on the same date, 4 November 1771, as the catholic John Purcell. Kelly died in 1774 and so could not have appeared on the CQR index.

One physician who is not listed in *Wilson's Directory* but is known to have had a large Dublin practice was Robert Barnewall, 12th Baron Trimleston. When he retired, his practice was taken over by the catholic Charles O'Brien.[31] Trimleston's inclusion would bring the number of Dublin physicians in 1762 to fifty.

26 *Dublin Gazette*, 15 December 1759.   27 Gilborne, J., op. cit., p. 29.   28 Ward & Ward, op. cit., p. 350.   29 Cameron, R.C., *History of the Royal College of Surgeons in Ireland*, Dublin 1886, p. 368.   30 Ward & Ward, op. cit., passim.   31 Gilborne, J., op. cit., p. 28. Gilborne also

There then remain seven physicians on this 1762 list where I have been unable to find any evidence of religious persuasion viz. John Donaldson, Lewis Ker, William Patten, Cornelius Sheridan, Thomas Southwell, Charles Smith and Michael White. While on a proportional basis at least one of these could be reckoned to be a catholic, it is best not to make such an assumption, since the sample is so small.

In summary, then, it could be concluded that of fifty physicians practising in Dublin in 1762, some twelve, or 24 per cent, were catholics.

List of physicians for 1780

From 1778 onwards there can, as noted above, have been few catholic physicians in Dublin who do not appear in the CQR index. In our examination of the 1780 and 1799 lists, then, it is scarcely necessary to identify individually the protestant physicians appearing on those lists. It is rather a matter of making a list of those (catholic) physicians who appear in both Wilson's list and the CQR index and of adding to these the few others who appear for one reason or another to have been catholics. It can then be assumed that the remainder were protestants.

In *Wilson's Directory* for 1780 a total of 48 physicians are listed as practising in the city. One catholic physician who does not appear in this 1780 list but who had enrolled in the CQR in 1778 was Francis Duany. His inclusion would bring the total on the list to 49. I have not included Arthur Lynch MD who enrolled in the CQR in 1786 since he may not have been practising in Dublin in 1780.

Of the physicians practising in Dublin in 1780, then, the following ten, who appear on the CQR index, can be assumed to have been catholics: John Purcell, John Michael Daly, Andrew Blake, Charles Brett, John Curry, Francis Ferrall, Patrick Maguire, James Murray, Charles O'Brien and Francis Duany. It is probable that Garret Hussey, who held his MD degree from Paris university, was also a catholic. This would mean that 11 out of 49, or 22 per cent, were catholics. It should be mentioned that two of those appearing on the 1780 list had originally been catholic but had converted to the established church. Michael Quinan converted in 1765 when he was practising in Sligo,[32] and Walter Wade, son of the catholic John Wade, chemist, Capel Street, in 1781. As well as being a physician, Wade was a distinguished botanist.[33]

listed the catholic Matthew Dowdall among the Dublin physicians, although he resided in Mullingar, Co. Westmeath.   32 O'Byrne, Eileen (ed.), *The convert rolls*, Dublin 1981, p. 236.   33 He was probably the Walter Wade, 'gent' of Donnybrook, Dublin who, according to *The convert rolls* (p. 273), converted to the estabished church in 1781. Later that year he married the quaker, Mary Chambers. In later life he described himself as 'a loyal protestant'. See E. Charles Nelson & Eileen McCracken, *The brightest jewel: a history of the National Botanic Gardens*, Kilkenny 1987, passim. For Wade's connection with the Free Masons see chapter 5.

List of physicians in 1799

A total of 59 physicians appear in *Wilson's Directory* list for 1799, but there was one further catholic physician, John Brenan, living in Abbey Street in 1799, who is not included.[34] His inclusion would bring the total number to 60, and of these the following eleven, who appear on the CQR index, can be assumed to have been catholics: John Purcell, John Michael Daly, Patrick Maguire, James Murray, Andrew Blake, Charles Brett, Andrew Daly, Francis Duany, Charles Teeling, Paul Johnson and John Brenan. In addition there were three others on Wilson's list who appear to have been catholics viz. Thomas Egan, Richard Kiernan and Anthony O'Donel. Thomas Egan can be identified as a signatory of the Catholic Petition of 1805, which was prefaced 'the humble petition of the Roman Catholics of Ireland, whose names are hereunto subscribed ...'[35] All who signed the petition can therefore be assumed to have been catholics. Egan was later to be physician to Maynooth college. Anthony O'Donel was another of the signatories of the Catholic Petition of 1805 and so can be assumed to have been a catholic.[36] The Richard Kiernan on the 1799 list was a member of the Catholic Committee and so in all probability a catholic. This gives a complement of 14 catholics among the total of 60 physicians in Dublin in 1799, or a catholic proportion of 23 per cent. It should be added that the John Bourke and William O'Dwyer, who appear on the 1799 list, were originally catholics who conformed to the established church, Bourke in 1783 and O'Dwyer in 1781.[37]

II

The surgeon profession

Originally the barbers and surgeons of Dublin belonged to the same guild, that of Saint Mary Magdalen, which was granted a charter in 1447 by Henry IV.[38] However, as the skills of the surgeons developed they tended to grow apart from the barbers, whom they learned to look down on as an inferior occupation, and so by Elizabethan times there had emerged in Dublin 'a society or community of men who took it upon themselves to practise or exercise the said (surgeon) art, and assumed the name and appellation of surgeon'.[39] Although the two trades were again incorporated into one guild in 1576, they once more proved uneasy bedfellows, to such an extent that we find the guild complaining in 1703 that 'several surgeons of the guild and several foreigners [i.e. non-members, mostly from the provinces] have combined together and printed a case to the present parliament endeavouring to obstruct all the brothers of the said guild who were

34 R.R. Madden ms in Gilbert Library, Dublin.   35 Mac Dermot, Brian (ed.), *The Irish catholic petition of 1805*, Dublin 1992, p. 148.   36 Ibid., p. 149.   37 O'Byrne, Eileen, op. cit., pp 19 & 294.   38 Webb, John J., *The guilds of Dublin*, re-issued London/New York 1970, passim. The apothecaries were brought into the guild at a much later date.   39 TCD ms 1447/8/2 – address dated 14 December 1781 to the lord lieutenant by the Guild of Barber-Surgeons.

not educated or bred surgeons from practising surgery.'[40] The seceding surgeons complained that they were always outvoted in the guild since the barbers out-numbered them ten to one and that the guild was 'a refuge for Empiricks, impu-dent quacks, women and other idle persons'.[41]

Over the next forty years the guild did its best to bring all surgeons into its fold.[42] For example, in 1729 it was arranged that for the future the position of master of the guild should be held in successive years by a surgeon, an apoth-ecary and a barber-perukemaker,[43] but the arrangement was soon rescinded. In 1741 the guild came to an elaborate arrangement with the College of Physicians (who hoped no doubt to keep thereby the surgeons in their place) under which admission to the professions of surgeon and apothecary was to be by open exami-nation presided over by the College of Physicians.[44] But despite the efforts of the guild, the majority of surgeons continued to practise independent of it, had their own association, and, while right up to the 1790s there were members of the guild who called themselves surgeons, it appears that any surgeon with preten-sions to a high degree of competence was not a member of the guild. As to how these independent surgeons learned their craft, it appears that the prospective surgeon was taken on as an apprentice by an established surgeon and trained in both the latter's home and in the hospitals. Many surgeons practised also as man-midwives, later in the century known more grandly as *accoucheurs*.

The fact of the matter was that a guild surgeon was an inferior surgeon and indeed was scarcely recognized as a surgeon at all. A comparison of a list of free brothers of the guild published in connection with the 1761 parliamentary elec-tion[45] in Dublin with the list of Dublin surgeons published in *Watson's Almanac* for 1761, shows that only two names, John Neale and Henry Lyster, are common to both lists. It is a truly damning comment on the general perception of the guild surgeon that only two of them were considered worthy to be included in the list of recognized surgeons published in *Watson's Almanac*. The two excep-tions mentioned may well have been members of the guild only for the purpose of availing of the privileges of free brothers, notably the right to vote in the elec-tion of members of parliament for the two Dublin city seats. This two-tier struc-ture of the surgeon profession was not unique to Ireland. We find the Dublin physician, Frederick Jebb, adverting to a similar situation in France in the eight-eenth century, where he claims the barber-surgeon was restricted to the minor

40 TCD ms 1447/8/1 – resolution of guild dated 30 September 1703.   41 See pamphlet in Thorpe collection in National Library of Ireland. This pamphlet is undated but it was evi-dently printed during Queen Anne's reign.   42 The guild is on record in 1716 and 1721 as seeking to persuade the surgeons to return to the guild. In 1729 the guild appointed a commit-tee to assist the master in his dealings with the surgeons; see ms 1447/8/1 passim. 43 TCD ms 1447/8/1 under date 21 June 1729.   44 Ibid.; resolution of guild dated 19 October 1741. The arrangements do not appear to have been implemented, but the fact that such arrangements were envisaged is an indication that there was still a significant number of surgeons in the guild at this time.   45 See list in National Library of Ireland.

tasks of blood-letting, tooth-drawing, the reducing of a fracture or the dressing of a simple wound.[46]

Any hope of a rapprochement between the guild and the independent surgeons was finally dashed in 1780 when the latter formed themselves into the Society of Dublin Surgeons. In 1781 this society submitted a petition to the lord lieutenant for a charter to set up a body to be known as the Royal College of Surgeons of Ireland on the lines of a similar body which had recently been set up in London. The petition was signed by thirteen of the most prominent surgeons in the city, including the catholic, William Dease, who was one of the prime movers in formulating the petition. The upshot was that the petition of the Society of Surgeons was successful, the charter requested was granted and the Royal College of Surgeons of Ireland was eventually set up in 1785. The College thus became the effective body for the regulation of the profession of surgery in Ireland.[47]

Catholic surgeons in Dublin, 1685–1760

The foregoing is a brief outline of the general developments in the surgeon profession in Dublin up to the end of the eighteenth century. To examine catholic involvement in the profession it is necessary to go back to the 1680s. During the brief period when catholics were in control of the administration generally of the country during the reign of James II, we find catholics in control of the barbers-surgeons guild, with a majority of catholics among the free brothers of the guild. The fact that protestants were allowed to remain on in the guild as free brothers during this period may have yielded later on some dividends in goodwill for catholics, accounting perhaps for the fact that for ten years after the defeat of the Jacobite cause, catholics continued to be listed as free brothers, although their numbers decreased from 37 in 1693 to 17 in 1702.

The list of 37 'Roman brothers' for 1693 included barbers, perukemakers and apothecaries as well as surgeons and indeed the latter must have been very much in the minority. Of the 37 it is possible to identify eight as surgeons viz. Patrick Archbold, Stephen Archbold Senior, Stephen Archbold Junior, Alexander Dowdall, John Dowdall, Dominick Hadson, Christopher Hussey and Thomas Bathe.[48] Patrick Archbold, Christopher Hussey and Thomas Bathe are described as surgeons in their wills published in 1695, 1702 and 1705 respectively. It can be assumed that Stephen Archbold Senior and Junior were surgeons because the records of the guild tell us that one Edward Johnston, surgeon, was admitted a free brother of the guild in 1733 on the basis of having served his apprenticeship to Stephen Archbold.[49] As to Alexander and John Dowdall, this family were well-known surgeons in Church Street and frequently advertised as such in the Dublin newspapers in the early decades of the eighteenth century.

46 Jebb, Frederick, *Physiological inquiry into the process of labour*, Dublin 1770, p. iv.   47 Cameron, C.A., op. cit., p. 187.   48 TCD ms 144/7.   49 TCD ms 1447/8/1.

Of the 17 'Roman brothers' listed for 1702 five can be identified as surgeons viz. John Dowdall, Stephen Archbold, Christopher Hussey, Dominick Hadson and Thomas Bathe.[50] The disappearance of 'Roman brothers' from the records of the guild after 1702 may have arisen from a tightening of the screw generally on catholics, but it has also to be kept in mind that, as already pointed out, by this date a large number of surgeons were operating outside the guild, and catholics would have been exercising that option as well as protestants. However, there is evidence that some catholics continued to follow the lowly trade of guild surgeon. In the guild's book of quarter brothers' bonds we find the following entries: John Archbold, surgeon (1728), William Ball, surgeon (1729), Jasper Delahide, surgeon (1733) and Denis Tynan, surgeon/apothecary (1736).[51] It should be explained that, while catholics were debarred from being freemen of guilds, they were, in the case of most guilds, admitted as what were known as quarter brothers, from the quarterly fee paid by such members.

The Charitable Infirmary, the institution later known as Jervis Street Hospital, was opened in Cook Street in 1718 and a few years later it moved to larger premises in Inns Quay. The surgeons who founded this hospital (George Duany, Francis Duany, Nathaniel Handson (Hadson?), Peter Brenan, John Dowdall and Patrick Kelly) are accepted by historians to have been catholics and the poor it was intended to serve were for the most part catholics.[52] It is of interest that a report on the infirmary in 1733[53] made special reference to the degree of cooperation achieved in the infirmary between the catholic surgeon families and the protestant surgeon families in the city, thus indicating that protestant as well as catholic surgeons were already attached to the infirmary at this early date.

There were at least four catholic surgeon families active in the city in the first half of the century – the Archbolds, the Dowdalls, the Duanys and the Brenans.

As regards the Archbolds, Stephen Junior, mentioned above, died about 1728 but the family continued in business as guild surgeons in the person of John Archbold who, as already noted, was admitted a quarter brother the same year.

We have seen that two Dowdalls, Alexander and John, figure in the list of catholic surgeons in Dublin in the 1690s and that John Dowdall was a founder of the Charitable Infirmary. In *Dublin Intelligence* for 16 September 1712 we find John Dowdall Junior, the Surgeons Arms, Church Street combining with G. Duany, the Surgeon's Arms, Strand Street to advertise their services. The indications are that the Dowdalls disappeared from the medical scene in Dublin around the 1720s.

A Mr Duany of Capel Street appears on a guild list of 'foreigners' dated 1710.[54] Within a short time there were three Duanys practising as surgeons in Dublin,

50 Ibid.   51 TCD ms 1447/9.   52 Evans, Ernest, 'The Charitable Infirmary' in *Irish Builder* vol. 39, pp 6–8 and Eoin O'Brien 'The Charitable Infirmary in Jervis Street, the first voluntary hospital in Great Britain or Ireland' in Eoin O'Brien (ed.), *The Charitable Infirmary, Jervis Street, 1718–1787*, Dublin 1988.   53 *Weekly Miscellany* of 28 December 1734.   54 TCD ms 144/7. See explanation of the term 'foreigners' at p. 26.

George, Gregory and Francis. Of these George and Francis have already been mentioned. We find Gregory Duany, surgeon, in January 1725 with an address opposite the Queen's Head in Charles Street, claiming to have 'for many years past cured many of the ruptures thought incurable by others ...'[55] Ernest Evans claims that these three Duanys were brothers, and more recent writers on the subject, O'Brien and Widdess, have accepted this view.[56] A Francis Duany appears on lists of visiting surgeons to the Charitable Infirmary in the 1750s.[57] Since he is described as Junior, it is likely that he was a son of the Francis Duany who was a founder of the infirmary. When Francis Duany Junior died in April 1757 his friend, Charles O'Conor of Belanagare, eulogized him in the *Dublin Journal* with these lines:

> He's gone, my loved companion, chosen friend!
> But self-lamenting strains I now forgo,
> And, for my private loss, those tears suspend
> Which rather for the public ought to flow.[58]

With the death of Francis Duany in 1757 the Duanys disappeared from the surgeon scene in Dublin. A Francis Duany practised as a physician in the city towards the end of the century but whether he was connected with the earlier Duanys is not clear.

With regard to the Brenans, a Pat Brenan, Church Street appears on a guild list of 'foreigners' for 1710,[59] while in an advertisement in the *Dublin Weekly Journal* of 11 March 1727 a Peter Brenan is recorded as performing the 'operative part' in a course of anatomy lectures to be given by James Brenan MD, Arran Quay. This Dr Brenan is variously described as the brother and the father of Peter. Peter Brenan, a surgeon, who died *c.*1767, was one of the founders in 1752 of the New Charitable Infirmary, later known as St Nicholas's Hospital. He left his surgical instruments to another catholic surgeon, Michael Keogh.[60] It seems unlikely, although possible, that he was the same Peter Brenan who was a founder of the Charitable Infirmary.

Another catholic surgeon who flourished early in the century was Hugh MacVeagh. That he was a catholic is confirmed by the following entry in St Michan's Church of Ireland parish register for 17 September 1712: 'Md. Hugh McVeagh, chirurgeon, and Mary Walsh spinster by a Roman priest'.[61] This appears to mean that the couple, following their marriage by a catholic priest, participated in a further ceremony in the established church, no doubt with a view to being on the safe side. Hugh McVeagh appears on the list of 'foreigners' for 1710 with an address in the Ormond Market.

55 *Dublin Postman* of 10 January 1725.   **56** O'Brien, Eoin, op. cit., passim.   **57** *Watson's Almanac* for 1757.   **58** *Dublin Journal,* 26–30 April 1757.   **59** TCD ms 144/7.   **60** Cameron, C.A., op. cit., p. 647.   **61** See register of St Michan's Church of Ireland parish as published by the Parish Register Society.

St Nicholas's Hospital was established in Cole Alley, off Meath Street, in 1752[62] This was a catholic hospital intended to serve the needs of the predominantly catholic parishes of St Nicholas Without and St Catherine. It moved to larger premises in Francis Street in 1753. *Watson's Almanac* first refers to the hospital in its 1758 edition, when the following were given as the visiting surgeons: Peter Brennan, Cusack Rooney, James Dillon, Barnaby Kelly and Michael Keogh. Four of these can definitely be said to have been catholics viz. Peter Brennan (see above); Cusack Rooney (who was a catholic and the originator of a minor dynasty of surgeons in that his son, grandson and great-grandson were all surgeons); James Dillon who is on record as taking the oath prescribed for catholics under the 1774 act and Michael Keogh who appears on the CQR index. In what was obviously a catholic hospital for catholic patients the probability is that the remaining surgeon, Barnaby Kelly, was also a catholic.

Another new catholic hospital, St Catherine's, was opened in Meath Street in 1758.[63] The visiting surgeons as given in *Watson's Almanac* for 1760 were Peter Brennan, Michael Keogh and James Ryan. The only new name here is James Ryan, who presumably was a catholic like the other two surgeons. St Catherine's Hospital was amalgamated with St Nicholas's in 1764.

Catholic surgeons, 1760–1800
The relative strength of the catholic surgeons in the city in the years 1762, 1780 and 1799 is examined below.[64]

Fifty-five surgeons, practising in Dublin, are listed in *Wilson's Directory* for 1762. One catholic surgeon not on this list was Cusack Rooney, already mentioned above. His inclusion would bring the total number to fifty-six. Of these no more than nine, or 16 per cent, appear to have been catholics. Of these nine, Peter Brennan, James Dillon, Michael Keogh we have already noted. There were three more attached to the catholic St Nicholas's Hospital who were probably catholics viz. Cormick O'Hara, James Ryan and Barnaby Kelly. Charles Reilly (d. 1764) was a surgeon in the Charitable Infirmary and may have been the Charles Reilly who was a signatory of the catholic address to the lord lieutenant in 1759 and of a postulation in respect of Stephen MacEgan as archbishop of Dublin in 1729. Evers Ryan was probably a brother or other near relation of James Ryan above. Gilborne in his doggerel about Dublin medics written in 1774 refers to 'three Ryans regular' as if they belonged to one surgeon family.[65]

Wilson lists a total of sixty-six surgeons in the 1780 directory. Of these, seven were definitely catholics since they appear either on the Catholic Qualification

62 Cameron, C.E., op. cit., p. 368, states that it was founded by Cusack Rooney in conjunction with Doctors Patrick Kelly, John Taaffe and Edward Jennings and Surgeons Peter Brenan, Thomas Mercer, James Dillon and Edward Walls. 63 *Watson's Almanac* for 1760. 64 The same years have been selected as in the case of the physicians; see note 25. 65 Gilborne, J., op. cit., p. 45. However, Cormick O'Hara may have been the person of that name who converted to the established church in 1761.

Rolls or in the list of those who took the oath prescribed for catholics under the 1774 act. These seven were: Gabriel Clarke, William Dease, James Dillon, John Doyle, Michael Keogh, Patrick Rooney and James Sullivan.[66] There are three further Dublin catholic surgeons who appear in the Catholic Qualification Rolls in 1778 but who do not appear in Watson's list viz. John O'Berne, John Esmond and Thomas Meyler. If we add these three to Watson's list, we can say that out of a total of sixty-nine surgeons in 1780, ten, or 14.5 per cent, were catholics.

Turning to Wilson's list of sixty-three Dublin surgeons for 1799, there are eight whom we know to have been definitely catholics viz. Michael Keogh, Francis McEvoy, James Rivers, Richard Dease, Patrick Rooney, John Doyle, John Adrien and Edward Geoghegan.[67] It seems safe to include also Richard Rorke who appears to have belonged to the same surgeon family as Mark Rorke, one of the surgeons attached to St Nicholas's Hospital. There would thus have been only nine catholic surgeons, or 14 per cent, in the total of sixty-three in Dublin in 1799.

III

The apothecary profession

The third component, or, as John Gilborne dubbed them, 'the Third Order',[68] of the medical profession in the eighteenth century and, dare one say, the Cinderella, was the apothecaries. Their functions corresponded roughly to those of the modern-day chemist or pharmacist, but there was less emphasis on dispensing the prescriptions of physicians and more on acting independently in prescribing medicines for patients and in putting on sale a variety of herbal remedies, cures, lotions, drugs, rubs &c. Considering the appalling depths of ignorance of the medical profession generally at that time, a good apothecary was likely at a time of illness to do one more good, or at all events, to do one less harm, than either a physician or a surgeon. Charles Lucas, an apothecary himself, had a proper sense of the importance of the craft when he pronounced:

> As pharmacy is the most useful and necessary art, nay, according to one of the fathers of physic, the most useful branch of medicine, when in a state of purity and perfection, so it is the most pernicious and destructive when it is not exercised with the utmost integrity, care, fidelity and understanding. No knave so vile, so dangerous to society as a bad apothecary.[69]

66 Of these, James Dillon took the oath in 1775; see note 24. The rest appear in the CQR which commenced in 1778.   67 Keogh, Doyle, Geoghegan and Rooney appear in the CQR. For McEvoy, Rivers and Dease see C.E. Cameron, op. cit., p. 187. For Adrien see J.D.H. Widdess, *An account of the schools of surgery*, Edinburgh 1949, p. 16. There must be some doubt as to McEvoy's continued affiliation to the Catholic Church in view of his marriage in 1786 in St Mary's Church, Dublin to Anne Fetherston, a member of a protestant gentry family from Westmeath. See St Mary's parish register as published by the Parish Register Society.   68 Gilborne, J., op. cit., p. 50.   69 Lucas, Charles, *Pharmacomastix*, Dublin 1741, p. 8.

Although British apothecaries were incorporated by royal charter in the reign of James I, Irish apothecaries belonged to the same guild as the barbers, surgeons and perukemakers until 1747. It is apparent, however, that the apothecaries were not included in this guild as originally incorporated in 1447 by Henry VI's charter, but that they gained admission at a much later date. How else can we explain a resolution in 1682 by the common council of Dublin Corporation deploring the practice of guilds admitting to membership trades which they were not under their charters intended to represent, and specifically mentioning as a case in point the barber-surgeons' admission to their fold of the apothecaries and the vintners'.[70] This may also be the reason why there are so few references to apothecaries in the records of this guild, and why apparently the apothecaries never carried much weight within the guild.

In 1741 in the lengthy pamphlet entitled *Pharmacomastix*, from which we have already quoted, Charles Lucas exposed the many shortcomings of the apothecaries:

> So, quacking being the principal business of the modern apothecary ... he, therefore, needs no judicious amanuensis, any raw boy being soon made capable of the ordinary business of the shop; for which reason, rather than pay journeymens' wages, apprentices are multiplied at any rate and at all hazards. Whence we come to have more apothecary shops than any city in Europe in proportion. We are within eight or ten equal in number to those of Paris, which I think is allowed to be six times as populous as Dublin.[71]

He goes on to refer to the deplorable standard of apprentices and of education generally among apothecaries and then sets out very elaborate proposals in regard to the admission of apprentices, the training and education of apothecaries and for the regulation of the trade and practice of the profession. His proposed reforms would be carried out under the aegis of the existing guild. Although he mentions in a footnote the other proposals, current at the time and already noted above, for a system of examinations for prospective apothecaries and surgeons, he did not offer any observations on those proposals.

While neither set of proposals was acted upon, they may have had some effect in the advancement of proposals for the incorporation of the apothecaries as a separate guild, an event which occurred in 1747. The new guild, which under its charter was entrusted with the regulation of the apothecary profession, was dedicated to St Luke, the evangelist, and it was accorded two seats on the common council of Dublin Corporation. It had the distinction of being the last of the Dublin guilds to be incorporated. In a list of freemen prepared on the occasion of a parliamentary election in Dublin in 1749, the apothecaries are credited with

70 Webb, J.J., op. cit., p. 195.   71 Lucas, C., op. cit., p. 26.

twenty-two free brothers, six being dissenters, one a quaker and fifteen established church.[72]

In 1750 the new guild restricted membership to practising apothecaries, but this was rescinded in 1777.[73] In the National Library of Ireland there is a copy of the oaths required to be taken by officers and freemen of the guild. These consisted of a simple oath of allegiance, followed by a renunciation of the pope's claim to have power to depose princes and a declaration, taken from the oath of supremacy, that no foreign prince, potentate etc. had any jurisdiction, ecclesiastical or spiritual, within the realm.[74]

There is some evidence of a less than liberal approach by the guild to catholics. In June 1750 Owen McDermott, Inns Quay, a catholic, was admitted a quarterbrother on paying £1. 9s. 3d. for intrusion and 5s. 5d. quarterage. In December 1753 Patrick Bride, stated to be a papist and a 'foreigner', agreed to pay £1. 10s. for intrusion and 5s. 5d. quarterage. However, some five years later Bride claimed that he had all the time been a protestant of the Church of England and was admitted a freeman of the guild by grace especial. He was later elected master of the guild.[75]

For the following thirty years the guild, if we are to judge by its minutes, ignored the catholic apothecaries, while the latter in turn were quite content to ignore the guild. The first evidence of a rapprochement between the two groups emerges in June 1783 when fifty-three named apothecaries, including several catholics, subscribed a resolution not to employ any person as a journeyman who had not served an apprenticeship of five years. In October of the same year the apothecaries of Dublin, 'reflecting on the divisions so long existing among them', agreed to transform themselves into a society to be called the Pharmacists Society, composed apparently of members of the guild and the other (i.e. catholic) apothecaries and druggists of Dublin, with the object of tackling the grievances of apothecaries generally. The guild records show that a leading light in the new society was the catholic apothecary, Anthony Thompson.[76]

All this paved the way for the act of 1791 (31 George III c. 34) by which the apothecaries were constituted as the Corporation of Apothecaries Hall, which is still in existence albeit with different functions. This was stated to be an act 'for more effectually preserving the health of His Majesty's subjects, for erecting an Apothecaries Hall in the city of Dublin and for regulating the profession of apothecary throughout the Kingdom of Ireland'. It was a major piece of enlightened legislation, far-seeing in its approach. As stated in the preamble, it had for its aim the elimination of frauds and abuses 'committed by the ignorance of divers persons pretending to the art and mystery of an apothecary, to the injury of the fair

72 Haliday pamphlet no. 214, Royal Irish Academy.   73 Cameron, C.E., op. cit., p. 88. The decision was not strictly adhered to. For example, Constantine Barber, a physician, was admitted a free brother of the guild in June 1755.   74 NLI ms 9000.   75 Records of the Apothecaries Guild on NLI microfilm Pos. 929 under dates mentioned.   76 Ibid. under dates mentioned.

trader, the disappointment of the physician and the imminent hazard of the lives of his Majesty's faithful subjects throughout the realm'. The Apothecaries Hall had the further very practical purpose of functioning as a store for the provision of drugs and medicines of a high standard to apothecaries.

Interestingly, the act was introduced at the request of the 'master, wardens and commonalty of the corporation of apothecaries and other apothecaries of the city of Dublin', an acknowledgment in itself that there were at this time many, predominantly catholic, apothecaries operating without reference to the guild. The fifteen prominent apothecaries who subscribed £100 each towards the erection of an Apothecaries Hall and who are named in the act, were by section 4 constituted a body corporate, with a protestant, Henry Hunt as the first governor and a catholic, Anthony Thompson, as deputy governor, each holding office for one year. In addition to Thompson, there were at least three other catholics – Richard Magan, James McLaughlin and Charles Ryan[77] – among the fifteen subscribers mentioned. There was provision for other Dublin apothecaries of seven years standing to become members of the Hall on payment of £100.

The act was notable for the number of oaths required to be taken by different people; (a) by the governor and deputy governor; (b) by the thirteen directors; (c) by the members; (d) by the agents and servants of the Hall and (e) by the examiners. But none of these oaths had any religious connotation whatever for catholics or for anyone else for that matter. They could be described as oaths of loyalty to the Hall and the profession, the oath for members including the additional undertaking not to take apprentices for a period of less than seven years and not knowingly to buy or retail contraband goods.

Sections 16 and 17 outlined the procedure for the sale, where required, of a member's business to another 'judicious apothecary'. Section 18 made provision for persons wishing to be apprentices, foremen and shopmen to be examined by the governors and directors in regard to education and qualifications and for the certifying of successful candidates. Section 22 provided that from 24 June 1791 no person should open an apothecary's shop 'or act in the art and mystery of an apothecary' until examined and approved by the governors and directors in regard to his qualifications and knowledge of the business. By section 25 apothecaries were debarred from taking apprentices for a period of less than seven years.

In effect, therefore, the act stripped the guild, at its own request, be it said, of its powers to regulate the profession and trade of apothecary. But the guild continued to have an existence as a vehicle for its free brothers to play a part in the affairs of Dublin Corporation and to have a vote in parliamentary elections for the two Dublin seats.

The guild, in its petition to parliament for the setting up of the Apothecaries Hall, had argued successfully against giving the physicians and surgeons any role in the new hall. They also secured the exclusion of druggists who, they said, were

77 The four, described as apothecaries, are to be found in the CQR index.

'dealers by wholesale and [since] few in number they could at any time establish a monopoly, create artificial scarcity and augment the price of most, if not all, of the necessary articles'.

To advert more specifically to the catholic presence throughout the century among the apothecaries, it is of interest that in the lists of catholic members of the barber-surgeons guild for 1694 (thirty-three names)[78] and for 1702 (seventeen names), only two, Richard Nugent and Phelix Reily, can be identified as, possibly, apothecaries, on the basis that 'Nugent the apothecary' and 'Reily the apothecary' figure in the records[79] of the Dominican Convent in Channel Row for the 1720s, although by that stage the Reily in question may have been Edmund Reily of Essex (Capel Street) Bridge, who appears on a list of prisoners in the Marshalsea for non-payment of debt in 1730–1.[80] There is the probability that either Robert White or Stephen Clinton, on the 1694 list, was an apothecary, since they were wardens in 1688 when catholics were in control of the guild and Patrick Archbold, a surgeon, was master, and by custom the two wardens would then be a barber and an apothecary.

Dominick Ryan, an apothecary in High Street, was one of two sureties for Fr Thomas Austin when he registered as parish priest of St Nicholas's Without in 1704.[81] Ryan's name again crops up as a witness to the will of Viscount Dillon in 1714[82] and he is presumably 'Ryan the apothecary' mentioned in the records of the Dominican convent in Channel Row in the 1720s.[83] It is not possible to identify any apothecaries in the 1710 list of 113 persons dubbed 'foreigners' by the guild, but in reality people from the provinces who had set themselves up in Dublin in the different crafts covered by the guild and in defiance of it.[84]

A difficulty in getting apothecaries to pay quarterage is mentioned in the records of the guild in November 1714.[85] Some or all of the culprits would have been catholics, but no names are mentioned. Robert Delahide and Redmond Wade whose quarterage payments were revised to 5s. 5d. (5 shillings sterling) in 1739 were in all probability catholic apothecaries since the names of Delahide and Wade figure among apothecaries in the index to the Catholic Qualification Rolls later in the century.[86] Denis Tynan, surgeon/apothecary, listed as a quarter brother in 1736 was probably also a catholic.[87]

There were apparently seven apothecaries on the list of catholic gentry, merchants and citizens of Dublin who signed an address to the lord lieutenant in December 1759 viz. Mathew Dease, Werburgh Street, Edward Dillon, Lr Ormond Quay, James Magan and Richard Magan, Skinner Row, Hugh Reily and Terence Reily, Thomas Street and Redmond Wade.[88] Four further names from around

78 Trinity College Dublin (TCD) ms 1447/8/1 under date mentioned.   79 NLI microfilm Pos. 3787 – Records of the Dominican Convent, Channel Row.   80 *Dublin Historical Record*, vol. 6, no. 2, p. 80.   81 *A list of names of popish parish priests*, Dublin 1705.   82 Eustace, P.B., *Registry of deeds. Dublin: abstract of wills*, Dublin 1956, vol. 1, no. 75.   83 NLI Pos. 3787.   84 TCD ms no. 144/7.   85 TCD ms 1447/8/1 under date mentioned.   86 Ibid.   87 Ibid.   88 *Dublin Gazette*, 15 December 1759.

this time have been found in other sources viz. Alex McMullin, Capel Street, Arthur Savage, Meath Street, Charles Ryan, Church Street and James McDonald, Hammond Lane.[89] Apothecaries who converted to the established church included Henry Hagan in 1752, Oliver Hely in 1753, Morgan O'Brien in 1760 and John McMahon in 1777.[90]

The real extent of the catholic presence in the apothecary profession only comes to light with the Catholic Qualification Rolls which we have already noted date from 1778. A total of seventeen apothecaries appear in the rolls, nearly all sworn in the months of October to December 1778.[91] There were a total of forty-nine apothecaries in the list of merchants and traders in *Wilson's Dublin Directory* for 1779. Some eight of the seventeen catholic apothecaries above are not to be found in the Wilson's directory list and must be added to that list, making a total of fifty-seven apothecaries. Relating, then, the seventeen catholic apothecaries to the total of fifty-seven, it can be concluded that about 30 per cent of apothecaries were catholic *c.*1779.

In 1801 William Drennan, the United Irishman, claimed that in Dublin 'the first apothecary', as well as the first merchant and the first physician, was a catholic.[92] As to the identity of this apothecary, the two most likely candidates are John Wade of Capel Street, described in *Wilson's Dublin Directory* as 'chemist appointed by parliament' and Charles Ryan, who was a prominent member of the Catholic Committee in the 1780s and 1790s.

The provision in section 7 of the 1793 relief act for the opening up of the guilds to catholics was of even less relevance to the apothecaries guild than to the other guilds, since, as we have seen, already in 1791 the newly-established Apothecaries Hall had taken over the power of the guild in regard to the supervision of members and the regulation of the apothecary trade, and the guild's only *raison d'être* was, as already noted, henceforth political. However, in 1793 two catholics were admitted as freemen of the corporation of apothecaries,[93] and, considering

89 All of these, except Charles Ryan, emerge from a comparison of names in the CQR with *Wilson's Directory* for 1762. The Ryan family had been apothecaries in the city from early in the century. Incidentally, Edmund Dillon was said to be the most expert player at hurling in the city – see John Gilbert, *History of Dublin*, vol. 1, p. 43.   90 O'Byrne, E. (ed.), op. cit. According to J. Brady, op. cit, p. 187, Oliver Hely was nearly related to Lord Donoughmore, whose family, Hely Hutchinson, had been catholic on the Hely side and presbyterian on the Hutchinson side.   91 NLI Pos. 1898. The names of the seventeen catholic apothecaries were: Robert Craly, Edmund Dillon, Patrick Dowell, Charles Drumgoole, Garrett Fitzgerald, John Geoghegan, James Loughlin, James McDonald, James McLouglin, Terence McMahon, Alexander McMullan, Richard Magan, Terence O'Reilly, Charles Ryan, Arthur Savage, Anthony Thompson and John Wade. It is not feasible, unlike in the case of physicians and surgeons, to make a list of catholic apothecaries for 1799; the index to the CQR is an unsatisfactory source for that year, because it is not available for the years 1790–2 and from 1796 onwards, and occupations are given only in a minority of cases for the period 1793–6.   92 Chart, D.A. (ed.), *The Drennan letters*, Belfast 1931, p. 311.   93 NLI Pos. 929, The two admitted, on payment of the usual fee, were Anthony Thompson and Thomas Dwyer. In fact four others also sought admission at the

catholic experience generally with the operation of section 7 of the act, these are likely to have been the only ones admitted.

CONCLUSIONS

1   Despite his lack of medical knowledge as compared with the medical practitioner of today, the physician in the eighteenth century was highly respected by all classes of the community. He was generally accorded the title of esquire, an honour which was not then bestowed indiscriminately on all-comers, as it is today. Many physicians, as they say, married well and those at the top of the profession earned very substantial incomes. For the occasional outstanding protestant physician in Dublin, such as Sir Fielding Ould and Sir Henry Jebb, there was the glittering possibility of a knighthood. Physicians enjoyed a far higher status than surgeons, although the more successful among the latter also earned substantial incomes, but surgeons were not esquires. On commencing practice as a physician in Newry, the young William Drennan, later a founder of the United Irishmen, was rather amused at the awe in which he was held by an experienced local surgeon.[94]

2   The best pickings, as far as the more ambitious physician was concerned, were to be found in Dublin city, where the wealth and fashion of the country were concentrated, and where the rich and great of the rest of the country maintained town houses. That competition among physicians in Dublin must have been considerable is evident from the high turnover in physicians practising there. For example of the 49 physicians in the *Wilson's Directory* list for 1762, only eleven, or 22.4 per cent, appeared in the 1780 list, and of 48 in the 1780 list, only 15, or 30.6 per cent, appeared in the 1799 list. It appears from this that some physicians, having gained experience in the provinces, moved into Dublin in their thirties or forties in pursuit of the better opportunities available there. The catholic presence in Dublin medicine has, then, to be viewed against a background of considerable competition, and it was to be expected that protestant physicians, having gained an ascendancy in this much-prized sector of the profession, were likely to give away as little as possible to the catholics.

3   The catholic population of Dublin increased from about 48,000 in 1730 to about 80,000 in 1760 and to about 130,000 in 1799. The protestant population of the city, on the other hand, declined from about 75,000 in 1730 to about 60,000 in 1799, although some, if not all, of this decline could be accounted for by a movement of protestants to the new suburbs of the city.[95] On the basis of the figures already arrived at of twelve catholic physicians in the city in 1762 and 14 in 1799,

same time, viz. Charles Ryan, Edmund Dillon, Richard Magan and James McLouglin, but these later withdrew their applications. Whether this was through pressure from the guild is not stated.   94 Chart, D.A. (ed.), op. cit., p. 10.   95 See Chapter 1.

it is clear that the increase in the catholic population in that period was not attended by a comparable increase in the number of catholic physicians. On the
other hand, the number of protestant physicians actually increased from 38 in
1762 to 46 in 1799.

4   Despite their minority position, some catholic physicians appear to have enjoyed a considerable reputation in the city. William Drennan claimed in 1801
that 'the first physician, the first apothecary and the first merchant in Dublin'
were catholics. The 'first physician' referred to here was in all probability John
Purcell (1744–1806), Lady Moira's doctor and regarded as the leading medical
practitioner in the city in the closing decades of the century.[96] Gilborne wrote of
him in 1775 when he was little more than thirty:

> Before John Purcell all disorders fly,
> no ailment can escape his piercing eye;
> the human microcosm he can unscrew,
> recesses the most hid expose to view;
> harangue on all with eloquence divine
> and the most learned of the learned outshine.[97]

5   As already mentioned, according to the 1861 census catholic physicians at
that date represented 33.6 per cent of the total number for the country as a whole.
In the case of Leinster 31.9 per cent of physicians were catholics.[98] While separate figure are not given for Dublin city, it is highly probable that as the most
protestant part of Leinster, the proportion of catholic physicians there was something less than 30 per cent (say, 28). Given that catholic physicians represented
around 23 per cent of the total number in Dublin in 1799, it appears that no great
progress was made by them in the period 1800–60, although this was a period of
great catholic resurgence in the country generally. In the censuses from 1871
onwards there is a composite figure for physicians and surgeons for Dublin city,
and these figures show a gradual percentage increase as follows: 30.5 in 1871,
35.5 in 1891, 42.2 in 1901 and 48.5 in 1911.[99] It is clear, then, that protestant
dominance in the medical profession in Dublin continued well into the twentieth century. Bearing in mind the growth of a large catholic middle class in Dublin and the rest of the country (apart from Ulster) in the nineteenth century, it is
difficult to explain this continued protestant dominance unless by the operation
of an 'Old Boy' network or a closed shop of some sort.

6   Turning specifically to surgeons, catholics were very much in a minority in
that profession in Dublin throughout the eighteenth century. Indeed, if anything,

96 Chart, D.A. (ed.), op. cit., p. 311. Three of the catholic physicians, Purcell, Egan and O'Donel,
had addresses in Sackville Street, then a premier residential quarter of the city; see *Wilson's
Dublin Directory* for 1799.   97 Gilborne, J., op. cit, p. 19. Purcell has a further claim to fame as
a grandfather of the poet, Edward ('Rubaiyat') Fitzgerald.   98 *Census of Ireland 1861*, Part IV,
p. 689.   99 See *Census of Ireland* for 1871, 1891, 1901 and 1911.

the situation dis-improved where catholics were concerned as the century advanced. This disimprovement probably derived from the founding of a large number of hospitals in the city, only two of which were catholic, in the first half of the century. The practice of surgery thus moved from the surgeon's home and became centred mainly in the hospitals. Catholic surgeons were to find themselves restricted to St Nicholas's Hospital and the Charitable Infirmary and it has to be said that in the case of the latter they enjoyed a far from monopoly position as the century advanced. Of the surgeons in the infirmary listed in *Watson's Almanac* for 1757, three appear to have been catholics (Francis Duany, Charles Reily and Jasper Delahoyd, the guild surgeon already mentioned) and three protestants (William Ruxton, Richard Houghton and Henry Lister). But when Duany died in that year he was replaced by the protestant John Neale, and for the remainder of the century catholic surgeons appear to have been a minority in the infirmary.

7   It has to be admitted, however, that from its foundation the Royal College of Surgeons of Ireland showed itself favourably disposed to catholic surgeons. It had its first catholic president in the person of William Dease as early as 1789. A president held office for one year only. In the first seventy-five years of the college's existence eleven of its presidents were catholics. In the earlier years three catholics, in addition to William Dease, were to hold the position – Francis McEvoy on three occasions (1791, 1804 and 1807), James Rivers in 1801 and Richard Dease, son of William, in 1809.[100]

8   Protestant dominance in the surgeon profession in Dublin was to continue in the nineteenth century and well into the twentieth century. The 1861 census showed that in Leinster 31.9 per cent of physicians and 29.4 per cent of surgeons were catholics.[101] The composite figures in the ensuing censuses for physicians and surgeons for Dublin city are given at paragraph 5 above. It will be seen that in Dublin in 1911 48.5 per cent of physicians and surgeons[102] were catholic, and on the basis that the surgeon profession continued to be more protestant than that of physician (as in the 1861 census for Leinster), it can be concluded that about 47 per cent of Dublin surgeons and near 50 per cent of Dublin physicians were catholics in 1911. As to the reasons for this continued dominance of protestants, the observations already made at paragraph 5 above in the case of physicians would appear to hold good also in the case of surgeons.

9   The apothecary profession emerges as the more catholic of the three medical professions in Dublin in the eighteenth century. As for the nineteenth century, the 1861 census disclosed that in Leinster nearly 50 per cent of apothecaries and assistants and 38 per cent of chemists and chemical students were catholic. There were no separate figures for Dublin city in that census. In 1871, however, figures

100 Catholics were also prominent in official positions in the college. For example in 1799 one of the three censors and three out of eleven in the court of assistants were catholics.   **101** *Census of Ireland 1861*, Part IV, p. 689.   **102** Ibid., 1911, General Report, p. 9.

are available for Dublin city and disclose that, out of a total of 233 chemists and druggists, eighty-eight, or 38 per cent were catholic.[103] But since these latter figures evidently refer to a wider grouping of occupations, they are of little value for comparison with the eighteenth-century situation.

103 Ibid., 1871, Dublin Tables, p. 135.

4

Catholics and the legal profession

The corner-stone of the legal profession in Ireland in the eighteenth century can be said to have been the Four Courts in Dublin, that is, the courts of exchequer, chancery, king's bench and common pleas. The first of these was presided over by a chief baron, the second by the lord chancellor and the remaining two by chief justices. Periodically, in their turn, the judges of these courts, including the chief baron and the chief justices, brought justice, such as it was, to the provinces when they went on circuit to preside over the assize courts and the courts of oyer and terminer in the county towns. Inferior to these were the courts of record with unlimited jurisdiction in personal actions and the quarter sessions courts with limited criminal and civil jurisdiction. More inferior still were the manor courts with a seneschal presiding, and with a jurisdiction somewhat similar to district courts today. There were also several specialized courts, including the prerogative, admiralty and consistory courts.

There were three main branches of the legal profession, barristers, attorneys and solicitors. Barristers, as well as giving legal opinions on cases put to them, held the monopoly, as they do today, of presenting and arguing cases in the superior courts, the attorneys and solicitors having done the ground-work. For most of the century entrance to the barrister profession in Ireland was through 'keeping terms' at one of the four inns of court in London, principally at the Middle Temple in the case of Irish students. It has been said that for most of the eighteenth century and before, the King's Inns in Dublin was not really a necessary institution.[1] Unnecessary it may have been, but it was there and it made its presence felt, in particular in the matter of making rules governing the barrister and attorney professions in Ireland, and in implementing legislation preventing catholics from practising as barristers. However, the Dublin inns were to become a more effective institution from 1782, when an act of that year required students intending, when qualified, to practise in Ireland, to become members of the Society of King's Inns before being admitted to one of the London inns.[2] Barris-

1 Nicholls, Kenneth, review of Colum Kenny, *King's Inns and the kingdom of Ireland*, in *Eighteenth-Century Ireland*, vol. 9 (1994), p. 156.   2 21 & 22 George III c. 32, an act to regulate the admission of barristers.

ters, as recipients of a degree, were regarded as far superior in status to attorneys and solicitors; all barristers were esquires, attorneys and solicitors at best mere 'gents'.

In the matter of attorneys and solicitors, the Judicature Act of 1873 abolished the term 'attorney' in England and Wales when it provided that 'all persons admitted as attorneys, solicitors or proctors[3] ... shall be called solicitors of the Supreme Court [of Judicature]'. A similar change was effected in Ireland by section 78 of the Supreme Court of Judicature (Ireland) Act 1877. These provisions imply that the functions of attorneys and solicitors had by then broadly converged, but it was a convergence which had evolved over time and was still in a process of evolution in the eighteenth century.

Of the two, the profession of attorney was by far the more ancient and, it has to be said, the more respectable. Attorneys had been the subject of regulation of various kinds under about thirty different statutes beginning with 5 Edward IV c. 2 in the fifteenth century. Entry to the profession had traditionally been through serving an apprenticeship to a practising attorney. A 1629 rule provided that no one was to be admitted an attorney in any of the courts of Dublin unless he had first been admitted to membership of the Society of King's Inns. This was confirmed by a 1794 rule which, in addition, set out the duration of apprenticeship, minimum age of admission thereto and for the provision of certificates of good behaviour by the master attorney on completion of apprenticeship.[4]

By contrast, the solicitor profession developed in a shadowy, haphazard, unsupervised fashion, having its origin in a species of advocate, called a *solliciteur* or petitioner, in the court of chancery, a court of equity for cases with no remedy in the common law courts; a court where, in theory at any rate, moral obligation and precedent, rather than common law or statute law, prevailed and where some lesser knowledge of these latter was required from practitioners. The solicitor could be seen as a sort of adjunct to the attorney, who was concerned with litigation in the common law courts, that is, the courts of exchequer, king's bench and common pleas. While it was claimed throughout the century that all attorneys were solicitors 'of course',[5] nevertheless the chancery court, as well as a small equity side of the exchequer court, remained the special preserve of solicitors, although it appears that for most of the century only a minority of solicitors were what was known as solicitors in chancery. Apart from acts in 1698, 1707 and 1727 aimed at preventing papists being solicitors, the profession remained untouched by statute and continued largely unregulated until the Solicitors Act of 1734.[6] This act, the penal anti-catholic aspects of which will be considered later, pro-

---

3 Proctors were advocates in the specialised courts mentioned.   4 Osborough, W.N., 'The regulation and admission of attorneys and solicitors in Ireland 1600–1866' in Daire Hogan & W.N. Osborough (eds), *Brehons, serjeants and attorneys*, Dublin 1990, p. 108.   5 See lists of attorneys in *Wilson's Dublin Directory* from 1762 onwards.   6 7 Geoge II c. 5. It is evident, however, that there was prior to this act a form of apprenticeship in operation for solicitors, since the act of 1707 barred solicitors from keeping catholic apprentices.

vided for the licensing of solicitors, as well as the swearing-in of barristers and attorneys, by the appropriate courts, and for a five-year apprenticeship for attorneys and solicitors. There must, however, certainly in the case of solicitors, be a serious doubt as to whether the act was implemented to any extent following an initial spurt of swearing-in or licensing the members of the three professions. It is evident, at any rate, that, following the licensing in 1734–5 of eighty-seven solicitors pursuant to the act, few, if any, further solicitors were licensed under it.[7]

As a rule, solicitors, unlike attorneys, were not admitted to membership of the Society of King's Inns. The only exception I can find to this is the eighty-seven solicitors who were licensed under the 1734 act and whose names were published in 1735. Why this particular group, and not others, was admitted to membership of the society may be due to their being the only ones to be so licensed.

A total of 573 attorneys and eighty-seven solicitors (as well as 190 barristers) were licensed in 1734–5 under the act mentioned. There was a gradual abandonment of the term 'solicitor' in the ensuing years, and by 1785 the two professions had coalesced to such an extent that the term 'solicitor' had almost disappeared from the lists published in *Wilson's Dublin Directory*, although it must still have continued to be used in respect of the many provincial solicitors. While about 800 attorneys were listed in *Wilson's Dublin Directory* for that year, only ten described as solicitors were listed, but again a note to the attorneys' list reminded us that all attorneys were solicitors 'of course'.[8] The converse of this was stated in a chancery rule of 1 January 1791 that 'no person shall presume to practise as a solicitor of the court of chancery, who shall not have been first duly sworn and admitted an attorney of his Majesty's courts of king's bench, common pleas or exchequer', such an attorney being required to obtain a certificate from the Chancery court that he was a fit and proper person to be admitted a solicitor of that court and that he had a fixed place of residence in Dublin.[9]

The stage had thus apparently been reached where every attorney was a solicitor 'of course' and every chancery solicitor was required to be an attorney, but

---

7 Lists of attorneys and solicitors first appeared in *Wilson's Dublin Directory* for 1762. In that year only twenty-two solicitors were listed as 'solicitors of the courts of Chancery and Exchequer sworn pursuant to act of Parliament' but these twenty-two all corresponded with names which had appeared in the 1735 list of solicitors licensed under the 1734 act. Again, in 1785 the names of only ten solicitors sworn under the act appeared in Wilson's list and these also corresponded with names in the 1735 list. It is evident that what was happening was that those, who had appeared in the 1735 list, were gradually dying out. It is possible that some few were licensed under the act subsequent to 1735 and had died or retired before 1762, but the more likely eventuality is that licensing of solicitors under the 1734 act was a once-off affair and that no further solicitors were licensed under the act after 1735.   8 Some forty-six of the attorneys on this list were not designated as belonging to any of the three common law courts, and the presumption must be that they practised as solicitors in the chancery court.   9 Osborough, W.N., op. cit., p. 132.

the preferred title was attorney. In fact no solicitors were listed as such in *Wilson's Directory* for 1797, but over 1400 attorneys were listed therein, and about half of these were stated to have been 'admitted solicitors in chancery pursuant to the order of that court of 1 January 1791'. The other half were attorneys attached to the courts of exchequer, common pleas and king's bench, a great many of them attached to two of these courts and some to all three. The huge increase in the number of attorneys as compared with 1785 must be attributed to the influx of some hundreds of solicitors to the ranks of the attorneys pursuant to the 1791 chancery rule.

The reluctance of attorneys practising as solicitors in the chancery court to describe themselves as solicitors continued well into the nineteenth century, and it was not till after the foundation of the Irish Law Society in 1830 that we find such persons being described as solicitors in the *Wilson's Directory* list.

But all of the foregoing was of somewhat academic interest to catholic law-yers, to whose varying fortunes in the seventeenth and eighteenth centuries we now turn.

Traditionally, the legal profession in Ireland was the special preserve of Old English families, in other words, the descendants of the Anglo-Norman invaders of the twelfth and thirteenth centuries. The English legal system in Ireland had its origins in the Pale, which was the first part of the country to be adequately colonised by Anglo-Norman families, and it is understandable that such families – to which must be added some Anglo-Norman families from outside the Pale – had the head-start on 'mere Irish' families in the administration of the law and the provision of lawyers, judges and court officials for that purpose. Thus from recorded times we find a preponderance of Old English names in the ranks of the lawyers and judges, names such as Aylmer, Luttrell, White, Barnewall, Dillon, D'arcy, Butler, Everard, Archer, Talbot, Verdon, Nugent, Fitzgerald, De Burgo, although with the passage of time some Celtic names begin to creep in.

The protestantization of the legal system could be said to have commenced in Henry VIII's time following the act of supremacy. A new oath of supremacy, required to be taken by judges, and the act of uniformity, with fines on those who failed to attend established church services , were instrumental during the reigns of Elizabeth and James I in making substantial inroads into the number of catholics in the profession. Although, as Bartholomew Duhigg, a protestant barrister writing *c*.1806, put it, 'the Statute of Supremacy affected [legal] practitioners only by an indirect and overstrained construction', catholics were nevertheless excluded from the profession by 'acts of state or Castle Chamber decrees'.[10] In any event, barris-ters and attorneys were too intimately involved in the machinery of the law not to feel a moral imperative to conform; the recusancy laws must have placed them in a particularly delicate and invidious position.

The effects of leniency towards catholics during Charles I's time were carried

10 Duhigg, Bartholemew, *History of the King's Inns*, Dublin 1806, p. 460.

over into the restoration period, although it appears that the number of catholic barristers and attorneys during that period was of no great significance in relation to the total number. In his *The case of the Roman catholics of Ireland* (see extract on p. 109) Fr Cornelius Nary (1658–1738), a doctor of civil and canon law of the University of Paris, mentions a figure of about one hundred catholic barristers and attorneys around that period, but if we relate this figure to a total figure of about 700, it appears that only about one-seventh of all barristers and attorneys were catholic. The figure of 700 has been computed by taking a bearing from the 763 barristers and attorneys sworn under the 1734 act plus a small number of catholics in these professions who declined at that time to conform. A rough approximation of how many did not conform can be obtained by deducting from Nary's figure of about 100 the seventy or so barristers and attorneys who emerge as having conformed in the period 1704–35.

It will be seen later from an examination of the lists of barristers, attorneys and solicitors sworn under the 1734 act, that around 84 per cent of barristers and 93 per cent of attorneys on those lists were protestant prior to 1704. If we factor into the equation something in respect of catholic barristers and attorneys who did not conform, it appears that about 80 per cent of barristers and about 90 per cent of attorneys were protestant in 1704, in other words, only 20 per cent of barristers and 10 per cent of attorneys were catholic at that time.

As further evidence on this point, as far as barristers are concerned, the number of Irish catholic students admitted to the inns of courts in London as compared with the total number of Irish students admitted, could be cited.[11] The alleged Popish Plot in 1678 occasioned a degree of paranoia on the government's part about the number and activities of catholics in London, and with a view to discovering the number of Irish catholic law students there, the four inns of court were required to furnish as at March 1679 the total number of Irish students registered with them, together with the number of these who were catholic. Lincoln's Inn claimed to have six Irish papists but did not state the period covered nor the total number of Irish students. The registers of this inn show that there was a total of twenty-nine admissions in the period 1667–79. In the Inner Temple there had been fifty-three Irishmen registered since the restoration but only five of these were catholic. Gray's Inn furnished a return of thirty-seven Irish students, of whom twelve were catholic. The period covered by these latter figures was not stated but from an examination of the Gray's Inn register, it appears that they relate to the seven years 1672–78. In the case of the Middle Temple a total of twenty-seven Irish students was returned and, again, an examination of the register suggests that the period covered was the four years 1675–8, but surprisingly none of the twenty-seven were returned as catholic.[12] Throughout the

11 Royal Commission on Historical Manuscripts report no. 11, appendix, part 2, p. 103, return of papists in the inns of courts dated 29 March 1679. 12 See Joseph Foster (ed.), *Register of admissions to Gray's Inn*, London 1887, and Henry F. MacGeagh (ed.), *Register of admissions to the Middle Temple*, London 1949, passim.

eighteenth century the number of catholics seeking admission to this inn of court was so high as to suggest that it was more favourably disposed to catholics than the other three inns. Making a nil return of catholic students in 1679 can be seen perhaps as an attempt to shield Irish catholic students there from the unwelcome attentions of government. An examination of the register of the Middle Temple for the years in question reveals that at least five of the Irish students came from catholic families. On the basis of the figures above it appears that only one-tenth of the Irish students in the Inner Temple were catholic, while around a third in Gray's Inn and near a fifth in the Middle Temple were catholic. Accepting, as they logically must, these figures as some kind of barometer of the position in the barrister profession in Ireland, the proportion of catholic barristers emerges as perhaps about a quarter of the total. This proportion is appreciably higher than the one-seventh arrived at for barristers and attorneys and again suggests that the attorney profession was significantly less catholic than the barrister profession.

With regard to solicitors, while I have uncovered no hard information on which to base a conclusion, it appears from comments made by the authorities on the occasion of the 1698, 1707 and 1734 acts (see below) that theirs was the most catholic of the three professions during the restoration period and thereafter.

As to the status of Irish catholic lawyers in the reign of Charles II, we have the evidence of Fr Nary, whose youth and early manhood in Ireland corresponded with that reign, that during that period catholic 'lawyers[barristers], attorneys and solicitors practised their respective callings with the same freedom and liberty as the Protestants'. He also states that during that period catholic gentlemen 'were in posts of honours, as sheriffs and justices of the peace and other posts of profit and trust'.[13] Further evidence of the liberty for catholic lawyers to practise in the courts in the reign of Charles II is to be found in Article 12 of the Articles of Galway (1691) which provided that 'all Catholic lawyers of the said town shall have the free liberty of practice that they had in King Charles II's time'.[14]

With the coming of the catholic James II to the throne in 1685, we can take it that catholic lawyers continued as formerly to practise but there was in addition an advancement of catholics to the highest judicial offices and the consequent sacking of protestants occupying those posts. Thus Sir Richard Nagle was appointed attorney-general, Sir Stephen Rice chief baron of the exchequer court, Sir Toby Butler solicitor-general and a commissioner of revenue, Denis Daly chief justice of the court of common pleas and Gerald (Garrett) Dillon prime serjeant.[15]

13 Nary, Cornelius, *The case of the Roman Catholics of Ireland* included in Hugh Reily, *Genuine history of Ireland*, 1762 edition, p. 115.   14 For Articles of Limerick and Galway see Thorpe collection of pamphlets in National Library of Ireland (NLI), vol. 9.   15 Moody, T.W. et al., *A new history of Ireland*, Oxford 1984, vol. 9, pp 514–23.

Following the defeat of the Jacobite cause in 1691, there was a complete *volte-face* with the return of protestants to all judicial positions, and a catholic was not to sit again on the bench in Ireland for nearly 150 years. With regard to lawyers, some limited degree of liberty to practise was provided in Article 2 of the Articles of Limerick which stated that 'all and every the said persons [that is, those living in the counties Limerick, Clare, Kerry, Cork and Mayo] of whatsoever profession, trade, calling soever they be, shall and may use, exercise and practise their several respective professions, trades and callings as freely ... as in the reign of King Charles II'. Since one of the main architects of the treaty on the Irish side was the Jacobite solicitor-general, Sir Toby Butler, it can be safely concluded that lawyers were regarded as included in the 'several respective professions'. As noted above, the Articles of Galway were quite specific on this point as far as Galway lawyers were concerned.

However, section 4 of the English act, 3 William & Mary c. 2, passed shortly after the signing of the treaty, required Irish barristers-at-law and attorneys to take the oath of allegiance, the new oath of supremacy and to make the declaration against transubstantiation 'from the first day of Hilary term next' (that is, January 1692), but there was a saver in section 8 of that act in respect of persons who on 3 October 1691 were in Irish garrisons and had submitted to the king. This, of course, represented a severe disimprovement in the position of catholic barristers and attorneys as compared with Charles II's time. Furthermore, it meant a virtual prohibition on catholics entering these professions in the future.

It will be noted that, for whatever reason, there was no mention of solicitors in this 1691 act. However, they were duly taken care of in a 1698 act (10 William III c. 13) 'to prevent Papists being solicitors', which required solicitors to take the same oaths and make the same declaration as barristers and attorneys. The preamble stated that in Ireland papist solicitors 'have been, and still are, the common disturbers of the peace and tranquillity of his Majesty's subjects in general'. It referred to the great number of papist solicitors and agents practising within the several courts of law and equity and the great mischiefs and inconveniences which were likely to ensue to the prejudice and disquiet of his Majesty's subjects.

This 1698 act provided for a penalty of £100 (to be paid to the informer) in the case of persons found guilty of not complying with the act, and solicitors so convicted were disabled to be executors or administrators, or to take any benefit by any legacy, gift, grant of any lands, tenements, goods or chattels etc. Section 2 required solicitors taking the oaths and making the declaration to educate their children as protestants. Section 4 provided a saver in respect of persons who were professed common solicitors, managers or agents in any of the courts in the reign of Charles II and who were adjudged to be comprehended by the Articles of Limerick.

Precisely what was meant by the term 'common solicitors', which, it will be seen, occurs in three further acts designed to exclude catholics from the legal profession, is not explained. It could be interpreted as marking a distinction between solicitors in chancery and other solicitors, but, if so, it would mean that solicitors working in the chancery court would be treated less favourably than attorneys in the three common law courts in the matter of the Articles of Limerick saver. An alternative interpretation might be that all solicitors were regarded as common as compared with attorneys.

The saver in respect of those comprehended by the Articles of Limerick must have been instrumental in allowing a large number to escape the restrictions imposed by the act, since there would have been, only thirteen years after the death of Charles II, large numbers of catholic solicitors who met the conditions specified, even if solicitors in chancery were excluded from the saver.

When, on the death of James II in 1701, Louis XIV recognized James's son as the rightful heir to the British throne as James III, the English parliament moved quickly to pass an act declaring 'the alterations in the oath appointed to be taken' (1 Anne c. 22 Eng.), and imposing a special oath, called the oath of abjuration, on state officials, expressly denying the right of the Stuart claimant to the throne. I note that Dr Simms states that the oath of abjuration was demanded from barristers from 1703,[16] and this was presumably on the basis that they were regarded as coming within the description 'state officials' in the act just mentioned.

Whether it was appropriate for catholic priests and laymen to take the oath of abjuration, was the subject of considerable controversy over a number of years. Although the oath was eventually condemned by the pope, this could be seen as a political decision deriving from the fact that the pope, having recognised James III as the rightful king, could scarcely have allowed Irish catholic clergy and laity to declare that they believed in their conscience that James had not any right or title whatsoever to the crown of England. It could be maintained that there was nothing in the oath contrary to catholic dogma; the rejection of the pope's deposing and dispensing powers, which was to be a feature of subsequent proposed oaths, did not figure in this the original oath of abjuration.

Barristers were next affected by the act to prevent the further growth of popery 1704 (2 Anne c. 6), for it appears that they were regarded as coming within the description 'every person or persons whatsoever ... who shall bear any office or offices, civil or military' in section 16 of that act. Such persons were required from Easter term 1704 to take the oath of supremacy, make the declaration against Transubstantiation and receive the Sacrament of the Lord's Supper according to the usage of the Church of Ireland. Evidence that barristers were included in the description is provided by an order made by the Society of King's Inns in May 1704 which stipulated that no person was to be admitted to the bar and practise as a barrister 'until he shall produce an authoritive certificate of his receiving the Sacrament according to the usage of the Church of Ireland ... the said admittance pursuant to the late act'.[17] There is a similar implication in the extract from Cornelius Nary's pamphlet The case of the *Roman Catholics of Ireland* repro-

16 Simms, J.G., *War and politics in Ireland 1649–1730*, London 1986, p. 216.   17 Duhigg, Bartholomew, op. cit., p. 258.

duced below. No saver was provided in respect of persons comprehended by the Articles of Limerick.

Reverting to solicitors, it was found that the penalty of £100 in the 1698 act for failing to take the oaths and make the declaration was not sufficient and that several known papists had frequently and openly practised as solicitors and agents. To remedy this situation a new act in 1707 increased the penalty to £200 and made it easier for catholic solicitors to be informed against. Furthermore, it was provided in section 4 that barristers and attorneys could not claim privilege in regard to giving testimony in a case brought against a papist solicitor. It was provided in section 1 that, in addition to the oaths and declaration required to be taken under the 1698 act, solicitors should take the oath of abjuration. Other sections barred catholics from serving on grand juries and prevented attorneys and solicitors from keeping papist apprentices. The saver in the 1698 act in regard to common solicitors comprehended by the Articles of Limerick was repeated although such persons were required to take the oath of abjuration before 1 July 1707. But the ban on papist apprentices was clearly meant to put a stop to catholics entering the profession in future.

The situation catholic lawyers found themselves in as a result of the foregoing pieces of legislation was summed up in Fr Nary's *The case of the Roman Catholics of Ireland* written in 1724:

> All Roman Catholic lawyers [barristers], attorneys and solicitors are disabled to practise their respective callings, except they take the Oath of Abjuration, the Oath of Supremacy and the Test, that is, become Protestants. So that of about an hundred Roman Catholic lawyers and attorneys, that attended the courts at Dublin, and in the country, not one of them is allowed to get a Morsel of Bread by those studies upon which they spent their youth and their time.[18]

It will be seen that Nary mentions only catholic barristers and attorneys as being deprived of earning a living from their profession and that he does not include solicitors under this head. The reason for this presumably was that, apart from the dwindling band of solicitors comprehended by the Articles of Limerick, a great deal of the work of all catholic solicitors consisted in instructing barristers, and in performing various legal functions which did not require an attendance in court.

Impeded from practising their profession and as a result faced with financial ruin, it is not surprising that of the relatively few catholic lawyers left, most of them conformed to the established church, but the sincerity of some of these conversions was questionable. Primate Boulter, in a letter dated 27 March 1728 to Lord Carteret, the lord lieutenant, then in London, complained that:

18 Nary, C., op, cit., p. 116.

The practice of the law from top to bottom is at present mostly in the hands of new converts, who give no further security of the reality of their conversion on this account than producing a certificate of their having received the Sacrament in the Church of England or Ireland, which several of them who were Papists at London obtain on the road hither, and demand to be admitted barristers in virtue of it at their arrival; and several of them have Popish wives, and mass said in their houses and breed up their children Papists. Things are at present so bad with us that if about six should be removed from the bar to the bench, there will not be a barrister of note left who is not a convert.[19]

To remedy the perceived evil, Boulter stated that a bill, 'of the last consequence to the Kingdom', had been sent over to London for approval by the privy council. To remove any ambiguity there may have been about barristers being covered by section 16 of the act to prevent the further growth of popery 1704, section 1 of the new act, 1 George II c. 20, provided that 'every person who from 1 August 1728 shall apply to be called to the bar, or to be admitted a six-clerk [an official of the chancery court] or attorney, or shall take upon him to practise as a solicitor' should take the oaths and subscribe the declaration in the 1704 act. Other sections required every convert lawyer, firstly, to prove that he had converted to the established church two years before his admission to the profession and, secondly, to bring up all his children protestants. It was also provided (section 4) that no one should be capable of acting as a sub-sheriff or sheriff's clerk who had not been a protestant for five years. There was a saver, for common solicitors only, in respect of persons comprehended by the Articles of Limerick who had practised in the courts in Charles II's time.

However, the authorities claimed that the activities of catholic solicitors in channeling business to convert barristers and attorneys continued even after the 1727 act to the detriment of barristers and attorneys who were protestant by birth. Dorset, the lord lieutenant, in a letter dated 17 January 1734 to the duke of Newcastle, secretary of state, pointed out that 'the influence of popish lawyers had been hitherto found so fatal that several acts had been passed since the Revolution to prohibit them from practising', but all had proved ineffectual 'by reason of the obloquy and danger of informing publicly against such offenders'. The protestant professors of the law, he complained, observed with concern the great share of business which was thrown by means of those (catholic) solicitors into the hands of the converts.[20]

One of the reasons why previous legislation in respect of catholic solicitors had proved ineffectual was that entry to the profession was unregulated, and

19 NLI microfilm Pos. 3650 f 35 (1728), letter from Primate Hugh Boulter to Lord Carteret, lord lieutenant, dated 7 March 1728. It will be seen below that Boulter's claims were very wide of the mark.   20 NLI microfilm Pos. 3835 f 23 (1734), letter from duke of Dorset to duke of Newcastle dated 17 January 1734. 'Popish lawyers' here appears to mean popish solicitors.

until a system of licensing by the appropriate courts was introduced, provisions aimed at debarring catholics from it would necessarily prove somewhat difficult to enforce. As already stated, the new 1734 act, therefore, sought to regulate for the first time the solicitor profession and to reinforce the existing regulation of attorneys.

The preamble to the act set out the reason for, and the aims of, the new legislation:

> Whereas the laws now in force against Popish solicitors have been found ineffectual by reason of the difficulty of convicting such solicitors, and the mischiefs thereby intended to be remedied remain, to the great prejudice of the Protestant interest in this Kingdom: and whereas by means of such Popish solicitors the acts against the growth of popery have been and daily are greatly eluded and evaded: for remedy whereof and for preventing obscure and ignorant persons from practising as attorneys and solicitors, be it enacted ...

The act went on to provide that barristers-at-law, attorneys and solicitors should take all the oaths and make the declaration 'required of persons to be admitted into offices of state by the statute made in the second year of the reign of Queen Anne', that is, the act to prevent the further growth of popery 1704. It further provided that no one could act as a solicitor in any of the Four Courts in Dublin, who was not thereunto licensed and authorised 'in the manner hereafter mentioned'.

Section 2 provided that no one was to be admitted an attorney or licensed to be a solicitor in any of the Four Courts who had not been a protestant from the age fourteen, or for two years before being admitted an apprentice, and who had not served an apprenticeship of five years at least to a six-clerk, an attorney of one of the said courts or a solicitor admitted and licensed in the manner set out in the act. Section 3 provided for registering of indentures of apprentices by their masters.

Section 4 required every barrister-at-law, attorney, certain court officers and every solicitor licensed under the act, to take a new oath to the effect that they would not suffer any barrister, attorney or solicitor, disqualified under the act [that is, of the catholic religion], to act in their name in any suit, cause or matter in any court of law or equity, nor employ as apprentice, clerk or solicitor anyone of the popish religion.

Section 18 provided that the act should not extend to any suits or prosecutions for any crimes whatsoever, which by the laws of the kingdom were to be punished by death; such persons might practise as solicitors in all such suits and prosecutions, as were allowed by law so to do before the making of the act.

There was the usual saver, for common solicitors only, in respect of persons comprehended by the Articles of Limerick.

It will be noted from chapter 2 that this act was strenuously opposed by the catholic lobby when, as a bill, it was before the English privy council. The degree of such opposition is a yardstick of its importance to the catholic community, and the extent to which catholic solicitors, in particular, had succeeded in evading previous acts aimed against them. Apart from its anti-catholic provisions, which primarily concern us here, the act is important to the extent that it sought to bring, though, as we have already seen, not very successfully, the solicitor profession under official regulation for the first time. But since the act brought within its licensing ambit only solicitors attached to the chancery and, minimally, the exchequer courts in Dublin, it appears to have left outside the net a large number of provincial solicitors, practising in inferior courts or engaged in extra-court work.

In 1735 lists were published of the names of the barristers, attorneys and solicitors who were sworn or licensed under the act.[21] As already noted, the list consisted of 190 barristers, 573 attorneys attached to the exchequer, common pleas and king's bench courts and 87 solicitors attached to the chancery and exchequer courts. The solicitors were divided eighty-four for the chancery court and fourteen for the exchequer court, but eleven of the latter appeared also on the chancery list, making a net total of eighty-seven. The eighty-seven solicitors listed can have been only a fraction of the total number of solicitors in the country at that time. Some idea of what the actual total was can be gleaned from the fact that in the 1790s, arising out of the 1791 chancery court rule requiring all solicitors desiring to practise in that court to be admitted as attorneys, about 600 solicitors appear as a result to have been reclassified as attorneys, and there would have been a further unquantifiable number who did not avail of that rule. However, the fact that so many solicitors remained outside the scope of the 1734 act in this respect was of no great benefit to catholic solicitors, who continued to be subject to the requirements in three previous acts (those of 1698, 1707 and 1727) with regard to the oaths to be taken and the declaration to be made before they could practise in any of the courts of law or equity. It sems likely that many catholic solicitors, rather than conform to the established church, remained outside the system altogether, occupying themselves with the many extra-court duties appropriate to solicitors, such as conveyancing, wills and agencies of different kinds.

Every person on these 1735 lists was by definition a protestant. It is of interest, then, to estimate, by means of a comparison with the Convert Rolls, how many, and what proportion, of these were converts from the catholic religion.[22] Any such comparison has to be preceded by the following caveats. Firstly, it does

---

21 Royal Irish Academy, Haliday collection, pamphlet no. 121, Dublin 1735.   22 O'Byrne, Eileen (ed.), *The convert rolls*, Dublin 1981. Rolls of people who converted to the established church were required to be kept by the court of chancery in accordance with the act to prevent the further growth of popery 1704.

not take account of persons who had converted to the established church prior to 1704, although there cannot have been many such still practising in 1734. Secondly, what is involved is a comparison of names, and while names on the two lists may be the same, the persons in some cases may have been different; in other words, the George Brown on the attorneys list may not be the same George Brown who appears in the Convert Rolls. Thirdly, no regard has been had to the unquantifiable, though small, number of catholics in the three professions who did not conform. The comparison, subject to these caveats, reveals that in the case of 190 barristers listed the names of only thirty, or 15.8 per cent, appear in the Convert Rolls. In the case of attorneys, out of 573 listed, the names of only forty, or 7 per cent, appear in the rolls, while in the case of solicitors, out of 87 listed, the names of only 19, that is 21.8 per cent, appear in the rolls. The net point emerging from this exercise is that already in 1704, when the convert rolls were introduced, about 80 per cent of barristers, about 90 per cent of attorneys and about 75 per cent of chancery solicitors were protestant. The exercise serves to completely demolish Primate Boulter's dire warning, quoted above, with regard to the number of converts in the legal profession in the late 1720s. It is difficult to understand why he could have been unaware that the legal profession in Ireland had been predominantly protestant for a very long time. It may have been the presence in the profession of so many with catholic-sounding names which induced him to arrive at such an erroneous conclusion.

The saver in the 1734 act in respect of solicitors comprehended by the Articles of Limerick can have meant very little in 1734 since, to qualify, a solicitor would need to have been practising in the courts some fifty years before in Charles II's time. Perhaps the last of the catholic solicitors to avail of this saver was Thady Dunne, who died in December 1748, aged eighty-four, and who was described as 'a gentleman of the Roman Catholic religion, a most upright and eminent agent and solicitor in Chancery, a sincere friend endued with every virtue'.[23] Town clerk of Cork in the reign of Charles II, he was comprehended by the Articles of Limerick and enjoyed the benefit of the Articles all his life.

As an 'Articles Man', Thady Dunne was enabled to carry on his profession, while no doubt staying on the right side of the government and keeping a low profile generally. But there were other catholic solicitors who were not so fortunate. It will be seen in Chapter 2 how the Cork solicitor, Joseph Nagle, was suspected to be part of a group collecting funds for the Pretender, but was found instead to be collecting money to fund representations in London against, principally, the 1734 solicitors bill. Nagle had previously, in 1725, been the subject of a house of lords enquiry into his activities as a solicitor. It has to be said to their credit that several lawyers with whom he had dealings tried in the course of the enquiry to protect or exonerate Nagle. Charles Powell, a six-clerk in chancery,

23 *Dublin Weekly Journal* of 24 December 1748.

instanced several legal cases where Nagle was involved, but he did not consider him (Nagle) a solicitor. A Maurice Roche deposed to the house that he had employed Nagle merely as a chamber-counsel. Lewis Pollard, clerk to Powell above, took Nagle to be a private counsel but not a solicitor. The house nevertheless resolved that the depositions of the foregoing were sufficient grounds for ordering a prosecution of Nagle for having acted as a solicitor, agent or manager.[24]

Mention should also be made at this point of the many catholic priests, especially those educated at the Irish College in Paris, who took degrees in civil and canon law from the University of Paris. Some of these held the degree of *doctor utriusque iuris*, or doctor of both kinds of law (i.e. civil and canon), but none of them sought to any extent to use their legal expertise in the public domain in Ireland apart from Fr Cornelius Nary, who for forty years, from 1698 to 1738, was parish priest of St Michan's in Dublin.

While in his many controversies on doctrinal matters with various worthies of the established church, notably with Edward Synge *père*, archbishop of Tuam, Nary adopted a quite uncompromising stance, he nevertheless succeeded in gaining the respect and forbearance of protestants generally because of his acceptance of the reality of the Hanoverian Succession and his Gallican proclivities in the matter of catholic doctrine. In his *The case of the Roman Catholics of Ireland* he made a trenchant case against the oath of abjuration and he later drafted an oath which he considered acceptable to catholics and which contained a rejection of the pope's deposing and dispensing powers. This was the oath which some twenty years after his death was incorporated by the Irish authorities in a registry of priests bill and received high praise for its legal adroitness from Charles O'Conor of Belanagare. Again, in an anonymous intervention in a controversy between Edward Synge *fils* and one Radcliffe, vicar of Naas, Nary, who claimed to be speaking for all the Roman Catholics of Ireland, once more rejected the pope's deposing and dispensing powers, and even advanced the proposition that, if Irish catholics were granted their civil rights by the government, they would fight against the pope himself 'should he come at the head of an army to invade their country or their civil rights'. It is surprising and illuminating that, given the precarious position of catholic priests at that time, the most prominent catholic apologist and activist in the first four decades of the century should have been a catholic priest.[25]

It might appear that, with the passing of the series of acts outlined above, catholic barristers, attorneys and solicitors had finally been consigned to the scrapheap. But, as it turned out, this was not quite the case. In regard to attorneys, there is evidence that some few declined to take the oath or to be licensed under the 1734 act. It is difficult otherwise to explain how the following could have been apparently catholic attorneys who conformed on the dates mentioned: Redmond

24 *Lords Journal Ireland*, vol. 2, p. 836.   25 Fagan, Patrick, *Dublin's turbulent priest: Cornelius Nary 1658–1738*, Dublin 1991, chapter 10, passim.

Kane, Dublin, attorney of the exchequer court (1762), John Kirwan, Ballygaddy, Tuam, Co. Galway, attorney of the common pleas and exchequer courts (1763), Charles Doyle, Bramblestown, Co. Kilkenny, attorney of the common pleas court (1762) and Matthias Reily, Dublin, attorney of the court of king's bench (1763).[26] It was felt at first that these might have been catholic apprentices who somehow slipped through the net, but an examination of the lists in *Wilson's Directory* suggests that they were all, by 1760, seasoned practitioners. Charles Doyle was so seasoned that his name does not appear on the lists after 1762. Matthias Reily had disappeared by 1770 and John Kirwan early in the 1770s. The one who lasted longest was Redmond Kane, who occupied the special position of clerk to Justice Scott of the king's bench and who was last listed in 1778. The fact that these four attorneys conformed apparently at a late stage prompts the question as to how many others did not do so but remained catholic to the bitter end.

A trawl of the convert rolls does not reveal any catholic solicitors who similarly conformed in the years subsequent to the 1734 act, but this does not mean that there were not some such solicitors who declined to conform. However, the ban on catholic apprentices was of course bound eventually to result in the total disappearance of catholic attorneys and solicitors.

Although catholic barristers, apart from those included in the Articles of Limerick, had been debarred from practising as early as 1691, and even those included in the Articles of Limerick, as early as 1704, catholics continued throughout the eighteenth century to be admitted as students to the inns of court in London, where they might qualify as barristers while disabled from being called to the bar. Such barristers, called 'paper men' in the profession, could build up quite lucrative practices in such activities as conveyancing, in giving opinions on legal matters put to them, and acting as agents in various capacities.

It would be next to impossible to quantify how many Irish catholics availed of the opportunity offered them by the different inns of court in London to qualify as barristers of this sort. Bartholomew Duhigg, the protestant barrister already mentioned, tells us that 'several gentlemen occasionally qualified themselves for conveyancing, or chamber practice, and even became members of the Inns, whereby an instant accession of able and eminent men was added to the legal roll of each kingdom'.[27] It seems likely that several of these, perhaps the majority, not being prepared to put up with the limits imposed on them if they remained catholic, later conformed to the established church. Colum Kenny has arrived at a figure of ninety-two as the number of such converts,[28] but how many continued

26 O'Byrne, E. (ed.), op. cit., passim. 27 Duhigg, B., op. cit., p. 460. 28 Power, T. P., 'Conversions among the legal profession in Ireland in the eighteenth century' in Hogan & Osborough, op. cit., p. 159. As students of the London inns the ninety-two were distributed as follows:– Middle Temple: 68, Gray's Inn: 17, Lincoln's Inn: 4 and Inner Temple: 3. It appears from this that the Middle Temple accounted for around 75 per cent of catholic law students. The reason for its popularity was presumably that it was more sympathetically disposed towards catholics than the other inns.

to remain within the catholic fold can only be a matter for conjecture. While noting Duhigg's claim that they were to be found in both kingdoms, it seems likely that the bulk of those who did not conform remained in London, where, considering the much greater volume of business transacted, far better opportunities would have been available for building up conveyancing and chamber practices of various kinds. It must be of some significance that not a single person claiming to be a conveyancer is to be found in the Catholic Qualification Rolls for Dublin city which commence in 1778, although it may be the case that any catholic engaged in any legal business would have been reluctant to disclose the fact.

It is worthwhile, at this point to take a look at two prominent legal families, the Blakes and the Burkes, with a view to assessing their vicissitudes religion-wise throughout the eighteenth century.

To begin with the Blakes, fourteen of the name were students in the Middle Temple in the eighteenth century.[29] Interestingly, of the fourteen nine are described as 'son and heir', 'eldest son' or 'only son' and all but two of the fathers are described as esquire. These are features which we find repeated throughout the Middle Temple registers, indicating that the barrister profession in Ireland was predominantly the preserve of the landed gentry and that, far from, as might be expected, the profession being regarded as an opening for younger sons, more often it was the eldest son who was sent to study at the inns of court. On the supposition that most of these returned home to manage the estate after qualifying, it appears that a knowledge of the law was regarded, at least by some families, as desirable in the running of an estate and that the landed gentry were not all the brainless nincompoops they are generally perceived to have been. In the case of a catholic landed family, some knowledge of the law was highly desirable for an heir, given the precarious position of such families under the property provisions of the penal laws, and the likelihood is that some eldest sons were put to the law for that precise purpose and with no intention of functioning as 'paper men'.

As for the Blakes, in five instances it appears from an examination of the Convert Rolls that the family was already protestant when the son entered the Middle Temple, viz. Dominick of Fartigare (1739), Francis and Peter (brothers) of Corbally (1721), Oliver of Ardfry (1712) and Patrick of Drum (1777). In four instances conversion to the established church occurred subsequent to entry, viz. Denis of New Grove entered 1732, conformed 1736; Ignatius of Grange entered 1722, conformed 1728; Martin of Killernan, Co. Mayo entered 1751, conformed 1765; and Ulick of Menlo entered 1738, conformed 1748. There remain five instances – Andrew of Castle Grove (1773), Martin of Moyne, Co. Mayo (1759), Patrick of Kiltollagh (1720), Robert of Co. Kilkenny (1774) and Xavier of Oranmore (1721) – where it is not possible to say whether the son in question was a protestant on entry or a catholic entrant who remained a catholic. Andrew of

29 MacGeagh, Henry F. (ed.), *Register of admissions to the Middle Temple*, London 1949, passim. Addresses of Blake and Burke families are in Co. Galway unless otherwise stated.

Castle Grove is the only one of these to appear on the King's Inns list of admissions, but the date of admission is not stated, and he may possibly have been a catholic who was admitted following the 1792 act. The other three do not appear in the King's Inns list and they could have been either protestants who died young or dropped out, or catholic 'paper men'.

In the case of the Burkes, thirteen of that name were students in the Middle Temple in the eighteenth century. In the following instances the family was already protestant when the son was admitted to the Middle Temple: Edmund of Dublin, the noted statesman (1747), Hubert of Gortmorris (1727), John of Tyaquin (1729), Thomas of Dublin (1729), Richard, son of Edmund above (1775), Ulick of Tyaquin (1775), and Robert of Annagh (1758). William of Carrowntrilly (1738) and James of Attyflyn (1774) appear in the King's Inns list and are therefore by definition protestant, but whether they were protestants when admitted to the Middle Temple is not clear. Richard H. of Drumkeen, Co. Limerick (1796) may have been a catholic. We are then left with Patrick of Killimor (1707), Richard of Burke's Field (1747) and Tobias of Milford (1703). None of these appears in the King's Inns list and could have been either protestants who died young or dropped out, or were catholic 'paper men'.

One of the best known of those who carried on a chamber practice was Daniel MacNamara (1720–1800), a member of the MacNamara family of Ardcloney, County Clare. He first came into prominence in the early 1770s as the agent in London of the Catholic Committee and he was to continue in that capacity for many years.[30] In addition to a highly successful career as a conveyancer, he was the London agent in political mattters for several public men in Ireland, including the chief justice, Lord Clonmel. He held court at his villa in Streatham with a great show of hospitality, and the Prince of Wales and members of both houses of parliament were among those who patronized his soirees.[31] The story that Thurlow, the British lord chancellor, confessed that, but for the penal laws, MacNamara, and not he, would have been lord chancellor,[32] might appear at first sight apocryphal, but when one takes into account the esteem in which MacNamara was held, there is every likelihood that it was only too true.

Arthur Murphy, the playwright, was another prominent Irishman of catholic birth who studied at the Middle Temple. Born at the home of his mother's people, the Frenches of Clooneyquin, Co. Roscommon, he was educated by the English Jesuits at St Omer. Although the *Dictionary of National Biography* states that he was refused admission to the Middle Temple because he was an actor, the

30 MacNamara, N.C., *The story of an Irish sept*, London 1896, p. 300. I have failed to find MacNamara's name in the registers of any of the four London inns. It may be of some significance that in the minutes of the Catholic Committee MacNamara is never accorded the title of counsellor, but is referred to as Mr MacNamara or as D. MacNamara Esq. It may be that he was only an attorney or qualified as a lawyer on the continent.   31 Lawless, Valentine, Lord Cloncurry, *Personal recollections*, Dublin 1849, p. 40.   32 Trench, Charles Chenevix, *Grace's card: Irish catholic landlords 1690–1800*, Cork 1997, p. 223.

registers of that body are quite clear that he entered there in January 1757. The great sums he made from his plays as well as a legacy he received enabled him to retire from the bar in 1788. Arthur's elder brother, James, was also a student at the Middle Temple. He emigrated to Jamaica with the intention of practising as a lawyer there, but he died soon after arrival, aged about thirty-four.[33]

A general move towards catholic relief was initiated in 1774 with the intro-duction of a special oath of allegiance for catholics. This was followed by the relief act of 1778 which rescinded the restrictions on catholic ownership of prop-erty. A further relief act in 1782 removed the restrictions on the exercise of the catholic religion and, to an extent, on catholic education. But strangely, at a time when reliefs were being granted in these other spheres, a 1782 act to regulate the admission of barristers represented a backward step as far as catholics were con-cerned.[34] This act provided that none but protestants should be admitted as stu-dents to the Society of King's Inns. It also required intending students to apply for admission to the society before proceeding to apply for admission to one of the inns of court in Britain. The act also extended the period of study by four additional terms, which students had the option of keeping at the King's Inns. The act did not apply to students whose names had been entered in any of the inns of courts in Britain on or before the first day of Hilary term (i.e. January) 1782, and there were remissions for certain graduates of Dublin, Oxford and Cambridge universities.

It could be argued that in barring catholics from the King's Inns, the act was doing no more than restating the status quo. However, the ban was being restated at a time when there was a movement towards catholic reliefs in other fields, and when some relief might have been expected also in the admission of catholics to the legal professions.

Following the catholic relief of 1782, the Catholic Committee continued to maintain pressure for further reliefs, but faced with opposition from all sides in the Irish parliament, they decided towards the end of 1791 on direct recourse to the king and the government in London, with a view to the latter intervening with the Dublin administration on their behalf. Shortly after the opening of the new session of the Irish parliament on 19 January 1792, the Catholic Committee passed a resolution to the effect that their petition to government at that time was limited to the following four objectives:

(a)   admission to the profession and practice of the law;

(b)   capacity to serve in county magistracies;

(c)   a right to be summoned, and to serve on grand and petty juries;

(d)   the right of better-off catholics to vote in county, as distinct from borough, elections.[35]

33 *Dictionary of national biography.*   34 21 and 22 George III c. 32.   35 Edwards R. Dudley,

The claim for admission to the practice of the law was perhaps prompted by a clause in a wide-ranging English catholic relief act of the previous year (31 George III c. 32) which allowed catholic counsellors-at-law, barristers, attorneys, solicitors, clerks and notaries in England and Wales the full practice of their professions subject to their taking the special oath of allegiance and abjuration for catholics set out in the act. What had been granted in England and Wales could scarcely be refused in Ireland, and it was no great surprise, therefore, to find that when Sir Hercules Langrishe introduced a new relief bill in the Irish house of commons in February 1792 one of the concessions proposed was the admission of catholics to the practise of the law. However, none of the other reliefs sought by the Catholic Committee were conceded and indeed the proposal for the granting of the franchise to catholics, even in the restricted form sought, met with an angry response from the house and was rejected by a large majority. Langrishe's bill did contain a couple of minor reliefs, not sought by the Catholic Committee, in regard to the inter-marriage of catholics and protestants and catholic education.

The bill had been prepared by Langrishe with the help of Edmund Burke who, as the son of an attorney, a barrister himself and the father of a barrister, could be said to have had more than a casual interest in the legal profession. In contrast to the house's angry reaction to the franchise proposal, the relief bill had a rather easy, though somewhat lengthy, passage through the house. Langrishe introduced the bill in the commons and circulated the text on 4 February 1792.[36] It had its second reading on 11 February, when Mr Staples enquired whether the bill represented the *ne plus ultra* of catholic demands.[37] Langrishe was able to refer him to a 'declaration of a host of Roman catholics' that, 'grateful for what had already been granted, they would with joy and humility receive whatever the wisdom and liberality of parliament thought proper to bestow'.[38] The bill's most persistent opposer was George Ogle, who initially tried to delay the bill by seeking more time to consult his Wexford constituents. He believed the bill to be a serious threat to protestant ascendancy. Although he protested he was not the religious enemy of any man, neither was he 'the friend of those who would force the Roman Catholics into power and turn the Protestants out'.[39] He considered a protestant bar as necessary as a protestant parliament.[40]

The Honourable Denis Browne supported the bill with a view to removing 'religious discord so long ruinous to the country'.[41] Other speakers spoke in similarly broad general terms. Those who, like Ogle, opposed the bill, concentrated on the threat to protestant ascendancy, and those in favour pointed out the need to conciliate catholics. Specific comments on the admission of catholics to the

(ed.), 'The minute book of the Catholic Committee 1773–92' in *Archivium Hibernicum*, vol. 9, pp 144–8. 36 *Commons Journal Ireland*, vol. 15, part 1 under dates mentioned. 37 *Irish Parliamentary Register*, vol. 12 (1792), p. 62. 38 Ibid., p. 63. The declaration appeared in an address to the lord lieutenant by Lord Kenmare and his fellow seceders from the Catholic Committee. 39 Ibid., p. 118. 40 Ibid., p. 240. 41 Ibid., p. 117.

legal professions were somewhat sparse. The Honourable George Knox asked
with a rhetorical flourish:

> Are they [the legal profession] engaged in a selfish opposition to a meas-
> ure by which so many of them must suffer? No, they support it. Do they
> wish for a monopoly of the profits of the bar? No, they throw open its
> doors, despising every gain but what arises from the honourable conten-
> tion of industry and talents.[42]

But later, although he supported the bill, he hinted at possibilities therein for
proselytising catholic lawyers. He believed that the prejudices of catholics would
be removed by the study and practice of the law, and their antipathies abated by
their introduction to a protestant society. They would find in the bench an object
of ambition placed before their eyes, which was attainable only by conformity.[43]
George Ponsonby gave the bill his 'most hearty consent', adding that:

> In a free country the law holds the first rank. In every great revolution for
> the establishment of liberty, lawyers have taken the lead in the glorious
> work. This was the case in America and France. Therefore, Sir, in giving
> the catholics this profession, you give them an influence short of nothing
> but that of sitting in this house: and, Sir, in giving such an influence, let us
> accompany and secure it by liberal education.[44]

Col. Hutchinson, a barrister himself, favoured the opening of the bar to
catholics because he wished 'to call catholic eloquence to the support of protestant liberty'.[45] Michael Smyth, another barrister, was almost ecstatic in his welcome of catholics to the profession:

> Sir, we will admit, cheerfully admit, our Roman Catholic brethren into
> the profession of the law; we will receive them with open arms; we will
> enable and encourage them to qualify for that important station; we will
> contend and struggle with them in the honest and honourable pursuits of
> fortune and fame.[46]

Grattan made a lengthy speech, couched for the most part in rather general
terms. He attacked the concept of protestant ascendancy and argued the need to
conciliate the catholics by giving them further reliefs, if a strong state, capable of
withstanding the threat of a union with Britain, were to be established. He nevertheless envisaged protestants remaining in control of such a state. He argued
that the mass of protestants, despite their boasted ascendancy, had, under the
current unreformed regime, little power. 'The Protestant ascendancy', he said,

42 Ibid., p. 149.   43 Ibid., p. 149.   44 Ibid., p. 157.   45 Ibid., p. 139.   46 Ibid., p. 136.

'returns for corporate towns about ten or twelve members; the rest are returned ... really by individuals .... We are governed by the ascendancy of the treasury'.[47]

On 18 February George Nugent, member for the borough of Fore in Westmeath, and son and heir of the convert earl of Westmeath, reported progress by the committee examining the bill. On 23 February the bill was reported from the committee with amendments and was agreed to by the house on 24 February.[48] Rounding off the debate on that occasion Langrishe claimed that catholics were being admitted to 'participation in the most honourable, the most lucrative and the most comprehensive profession in the country'.[49] The bill was then carried to the lords, for their concurrence, by Langrishe, accompanied by a great number of the members. On 6 March it was agreed to by the lords with an amendment and on 18 April it was accorded the royal assent.[50]

The resulting act, 32 George III c. 21, referred in section 1 to restrictions in 6 Anne c. 6 (in regard to solicitors) and in 1 George II c. 20 (in regard to barristers and attorneys) and provided that the oaths and declarations therein mentioned be no longer required after 24 June 1792 and substituted therefor the special oath for catholics in the 1774 act. Section 2 removed restrictions in 6 Anne c. 6 on the employment by barristers, attorneys and solicitors of catholic apprentices and clerks, but subject to such apprentices and clerks being required to take the oath in the 1774 act. Section 3 removed the bar on barristers having catholic wives and section 4 repealed the part of the 1698 solicitors act (10 william III c. 13) which obliged solicitors to educate their children as protestants.

Section 5 repealed the clause in the 1734 act requiring solicitors and attorneys to be protestant from the age of fourteen or for two years before being admitted an apprentice. Section 6 repealed the clause in the 1727 act (1 George II c. 20) in regard to lawyers who were converts to the established church. Section 7 removed the prohibition in the 1782 act (21 & 22 George III c. 32) on catholics being admitted to the degree of barrister-at-law in the King's Inns, Dublin and, mindful of the position of certain catholics who had earlier entered one of the English inns of court without first having applied for admission to the King's Inns in Dublin, as required by the 1782 act, section 7 also provided that any person whose name had been entered as a student in any of the inns of court in England previous to 21 January 1792 should be admitted to the King's Inns as of the date of his entry into the English inn of court,[51] but subject to (section 8) such

---

47 Ibid., pp 163–73. Grattan's speech, as reported, extends to eleven pages of the *Parliamentary Register*. In addition to the ten or twelve members mentioned by Grattan as returned for boroughs, two members for each county (i.e. sixty-four members) were returned by popular, protestant franchise. This means that out of a house of commons of 300 members, only a quarter were returned by popular franchise. **48** *Commons Journal Ireland*, vol. 15, part 1 under dates mentioned. **49** *Irish Parliamentary Register*, vol. 12 (1792), p. 246. **50** *Commons Journal Ireland*, vol. 15, part 1 under dates mentioned. **51** This provision was not in the original bill, as circulated, but was introduced by Langrishe as a sort of after-thought at the committee stage. The reason he gave for this amendment was that 'the liberality of the gentlemen of the law in not opposing the entry of Roman Catholics into that profession, was so strong

person taking the oath in the 1774 act before being called to the bar. Section 32 prevented catholics from being promoted to the inner bar.

There were further sections in the act, with which we are not concerned here, removing restrictions in previous acts on catholics intermarrying with protestants, on the keeping of apprentices by catholics in trade and manufacture and on foreign and home education of catholics.

The act was not long in achieving concrete results, for there were, as we have seen, a number of catholics, already qualified as barristers in the various inns of court in London, who could be said to be waiting in the wings to be called to the Irish or English bars.[52] These included the following who were admitted to the Middle Temple on the dates mentioned: Martin Lynch, eldest son of Martin, Esq., Cullin, Co. Mayo (1778), James Laffan, eldest son of Thomas, gent, Kilkenny (1781), Michael Keogh, son of Michael, Esq., Crumlin, Dublin (1784), Robert Bellew, eldest son of Patrick, Esq., Ballindinish, Co. Cork (1787) and Valentine Maher, son of Nicholas, Esq. Thurles, Co. Tipperary (1787), and the following who were admitted to Lincoln's Inn on the dates mentioned: William Cruise, son of Patrick, Rahugh, Co. Westmeath (1773), William Bellew, son of Sir Patrick, Barmeath, Co. Louth (1782) and Matthew Donelan, son of John, Esq. Ballydonelan, Co. Galway (1783). Also included was Christopher Bellew, eldest son of Dominick, Esq., Mount Kelly, Co. Galway, who was admitted to the Inner Temple in 1781.

Of the above, William Cruise and Christopher Bellew were called to the English bar. The majority of the remainder were called to the Irish bar. It will be noted that nearly all of them were sprung from the catholic landed gentry.

There was also a concerted move by many, mainly gentry and middle-class families, to have their sons enrolled in the King's Inns in Dublin prior to their being entered in one of the London inns of court.[53] Among the sons of the gentry were Daniel O'Connell, 'The Liberator', Carhen, Co. Kerry, Denys Scully, Kilfeacle, Co. Tipperary, Dominick Rice, Dingle, Co. Kerry, James Bagot, Castlebagot, Rathcoole, Co. Dublin, Nicholas O'Gorman and his brother Richard, Ennis, Co. Clare, Richard Farrell, Swords, Co. Dublin and Michael Fitzsimons, Glencullen, Co. Dublin. Merchants' sons included Theobald MacKenna, Carrick-on-Suir, Co. Tipperary, Thomas Moore, the future poet, Aungier Street, Dublin, Patrick McSheehy, Killarney and James Bernard Clinch, James's Street, Dublin. The Dublin medical profession was represented by John and Peter Purcell, sons of Dr John of Sackville Street, William Doyle son of Surgeon Doyle, Ush-

an argument in favour of extending the facility of admission to the bar'. The clause proposed by Langrishe was further amended so as to cover any protestants who might be in the same situation as catholics.   52 The list, which does not claim to be definitive, has been compiled by reference to a number of sources viz., P. Beryl Phair, *King's Inns admission papers*, Eileen O'Byrne, *The convert rolls*, Brian MacDermott, *The catholic petition of 1805*, the registers of the four London inns and the Thomas U. Sadlier ms 554–5 in NLI.   53 Compiled by reference to the same sources as at note 52.

er's Island, Edmund Daly son of Dr John Michael, Mary Street and James Brett, son of Dr Charles, Wood Street.

The majority of the foregoing were involved to a greater or lesser degree in the activities of the Catholic Committee in the early years of the nineteenth century. These activities were to culminate in the unsuccessful petition of 1805 to the English parliament for catholic emancipation.[54] A prominent figure in the Catholic Committee at this time was Denys Scully, son of a wealthy landowner from Tipperary. Although the young Daniel O'Connell had been the principal speaker at a catholic anti-Union meeting in Dublin in 1800, he remained in the background, as far as Catholic Committee affairs were concerned, for some years after that and did not emerge as a leader until 1809.

As already mentioned, the Society of King's Inns introduced new rules, effective from January 1794, for the admission of barristers and attorneys to the society.[55] It will be noted that these new rules coincided with two other major developments in the legal professions viz. (a) a great influx into the attorney profession following the 1791 chancery rule requiring all chancery solicitors to be attorneys, and (b) the admission of catholics to the practice of the law. It is pertinent to consider, then, whether the new rules were in any way intended to pre-empt an inflow of catholics to the professions and to make entry difficult for them.

Certainly, if the King's Inns authorities were so minded, some of the new rules could be used to keep catholics out. Under rule 6 of the attorneys' rules would-be apprentices were required to swear an affidavit stating, *inter alia*, the place of abode of their parents and the course of education they had already passed through. Here the course of education was likely to be of a lower level in the case of catholics and this factor could militate against them. Rule 7 (attorneys) provided, on completion of apprenticeship, for the public examination of the would-be attorney in the society's dining-hall before the benchers and the society. Since the persons conducting the examination would be all protestants, it is easy to see how a catholic appearing before such examiners might feel at a disadvantage. In the case of barristers, rule 9 required an aspiring student to state the course of education through which he had passed, and, on his completing the necessary terms in the inn of court, rule 15 gave the benchers the option of admitting, rejecting or postponing for further consideration, the applicant, or of remitting him to a further prosecution of his studies. Again, both these rules could be used arbitrarily to the disadvantage of catholic students.

As to whether they were so used, it has to be said in the case of barristers, judging by the several statements in the house, when the bill was going through,

---

54 MacDermott, Brian, *The catholic petition of 1805*, Dublin 1992, passim.　55 For 1794 rules see Duhigg, B. op. cit., p. 583 et seqq. Subsequent to the 1791 chancery rule the terms 'attorney' and 'solicitor' became almost interchangeable, but the preferred title for many years thereafter was 'attorney'. Hence the absence of any comment by me at this point on the position of solicitors.

that catholics would be welcome at the bar, and by the actual inflow of catholics
to the different inns of court in the years following1792, that, generally, no ob-
structive tactics were engaged in by the society or its members. The situation,
however, may have been quite different in the case of attorneys. In their case, in
addition to the disadvantages mentioned above, there was the initial and very real
problem for a catholic desiring to enter the profession of finding a master attorney who would be prepared to take him on as an apprentice, bearing in mind that
the masters were all protestants. When one takes into account that catholics applying to be freemen of their guilds under the 1793 relief act, were nearly all
refused simply on account of ther religion, it does not seem likely that the attitude of protestant attorneys in Dublin to taking on catholic apprentices was going to be any more favourable. In Dublin, where the bulk of the attorney profession was centred, the entire protestant body at this time was pervaded by what
amounted to a paranoia about the danger posed for protestant ascendancy by the
projected improvements in the situation of catholics. The probability is, therefore, that, although I have not discovered any hard evidence to that effect, for
some years after 1792, catholics found it difficult to gain entry to the attorney
profession.

But it appears that, once these initial disadvantages had been overcome, the
attorney profession proved easier of access for catholics than that of barrister.
The main reason for this was that attorneys and solicitors, in contrast with barristers, came from a lower stratum of society, with a lower standard of education,
a situation which obviously favoured the recruitment of catholics. Hence it was
that, as will be seen below, when the first figures showing numbers of catholics
and protestants in the various professions were published in the 1861 census,
catholics were seen to have made appreciably more headway in the attorney and
solicitor than in the barrister profession.

Under section 9 of the Catholic Relief Act of 1793 the ban on catholic membership of the inner bar was continued, but, while catholics were barred by the
same section from high court judgeships and all higher positions in the legal
hierarchy, they were in future eligible for appointment as county court judges, as
chairmen of quarter sessions and as lesser magistrates. But attempts to put this
eligibility into practice could be thwarted by protestant opposition, as when
William Bellew was offered a county court judgeship in Co. Louth in return for
supporting the Union, and the local protestant gentry combined to prevent the
appointment. Bellew had to be content with a pension instead.[56]

It was not until the relief act of 1829 that catholics were allowed entry to the
inner bar, to high court judgeships and higher legal positions. One of the first
catholics admitted to the inner bar was Richard Lalor Shiel in 1830; he was later
a member of parliament and supporter of O'Connell. Sir Michael O'Loughlin, a
Clareman, was the first catholic to sit on the bench since 1690 when he was ap-

56 MacDermott, B., op. cit., p. 175.

pointed a baron of the Exchequer Court in 1836. He had previously been appointed solicitor-general for Ireland in 1834, and had been elected MP for Dungarvan in 1835 and appointed attorney-general. Appointment as master of the rolls followed in 1837 and he rounded off a hectic five years by being made a baronet in 1838.[57]

Starting from such a low base, catholics had a great deal of ground to make up before they could attain even a moderate representation in the legal professions. The 1861 census is the first to show a breakdown of the numbers of catholics and protestants in the various professions. In Leinster in that year, out of a total of 551 barristers 150, or 27.2 per cent, were catholic, and out of a total of 1,093 attorneys and solicitors 380, or 34.8 per cent, were catholic. For the whole country in that year, out of 734 barristers 208, or 28.3 per cent, were catholic, while out of 1,829 attorneys and solicitors 665, or 36.3 per cent, were catholic.[58] It is of interest that in 1861 75 per cent of barristers and 60 per cent of attorneys and solicitors were located in Leinster.

In the 1881 census a combined figure for barristers and solicitors showed that, for the whole country, out of a total of 2,123 in these professions 837, or 39.4 per cent, were catholic. The comparable figure for the two professions for 1861 was 34.1 per cent. In 1901 the total number of barristers and solicitors in the whole country was 2,216 of which 898, or 40.5 per cent were catholic. In 1911 the total in the two professions in the whole country was 2,246 of which 999, or 44.5 per cent, were catholic.[59] The percentage of catholics in the two professions that year showed very great disparities from province to province – 78.0 per cent in Connacht, 71.5 per cent in Munster, 45.8 per cent in Leinster and 22.6 per cent in Ulster. Just over half of all members were located in Leinster. Following the establishment of the Irish Free State in 1922 it can be assumed that there was a rapid increase there in the proportion of catholics in the legal professions. In Northern Ireland, on the other hand, the assumption must be that there was no great change over the first fifty years. However, in the past twenty years or so there has been a startling upturn there to the extent indeed that today the majority of barristers and solicitors are believed to be catholic.[60]

---

57 *Dictionary of national biography.*   58 *Census of Ireland 1861*, Part IV, p. 689.   59 *Census of Ireland* for 1881 and 1911. The term 'attorney' had disappeared following the enactment of the Supreme Court of Judicature (Ireland) Act of 1877. It will be noted that the total for barristers and attorneys/solicitors (2,563) for 1861 was significantly higher than the total for those occupations in 1881 and 1911. I have not discovered the reason for this.   60 *Sunday Tribune* of 19 October 1997, disclosures in Department of Foreign Affairs memo.

5

Catholic involvement in freemasonry

Freemasonry had its origin in the guilds of free or travelling masons of the middle ages. These guilds derived a special importance from the fact that their members were responsible for the building of the great cathedrals, churches and castles of that time in Europe. Their *raison d'être* is readily explicable, then, in modern parlance, as combinations of craftsmen with the general aim of protecting their conditions of employment and their standard of living. That with the passage of time such guilds for their own protection might have developed certain customs, rituals and signs and have become secret, oath-bound societies is also understandable. What is difficult to comprehend, however, is why at a certain stage these guilds came to be infiltrated by persons who were not masons at all and who proceeded to usurp and make their own the whole fabric of masons' rituals and customs and to adapt them to their own perceived needs. These newcomers came to be known as speculative or accepted masons and essentially they could be said to be merely playing at being masons. Their elaborate masquerade was so successful that lodges of speculative masons became the rule and lodges of real masons the exception.

We are told that the purpose of freemasonry today is, and indeed has been for nearly three hundred years, to promote the spiritual, moral and social development of the community through the influence, example and contributions of its members. A worthy aim indeed, but one which could be attained just as readily without resort to arcane customs and rituals, and without, as someone has rather uncharitably put it, pretending that members are somehow involved in the building trade. The appeal of such an organization to the middle classes stems in large measure from the fact that it provides a *modus operandi* for people to meet with others of their own class, thus fulfilling a function rather like a modern-day golf club. For people taking up residence in a new town or city, membership of such an organization is a means of getting to know people and of easing oneself into a new environment. Overtones of elitism and exclusivity serve to make membership attractive to social climbers and the upwardly mobile generally. To be fair, the same could be said about equivalent catholic organizations.

Recent research indicates that freemasonry in its modern, speculative form originated in Scotland about 1600 and that it spread from there to England and later to Ireland, where the first so far discovered documentary evidence of it is to be found in a satirical speech delivered by a student, John Jones, in Trinity College, Dublin in 1688.[1] Lodges in these islands throughout the seventeenth century appear to have existed independent of each other, with no central body to relate to. This situation was to change in 1717 when the Grand Lodge of England was founded in London as a central body for the affiliation and administration of English lodges. The foundation of the Grand Lodge of Ireland must have followed soon after this, for it can be inferred from a lengthy report of a meeting of over one hundred masons at the Great Hall, Kings' Inns, Dublin on 24 June 1725 to elect a *new* grand master and other dignitaries, that the Irish Grand Lodge had been up and running for at least a year prior to the date mentioned.[2] The report mentions six lodges 'of gentlemen freemasons who are under the jurisdiction of the Grand Master' and, at another point, 'the masters and wardens of the several lodges'.

In the years following the establishment of the Grand Lodge freemasonry made great strides in Dublin. By 1735 there were fifteen lodges in the city as compared with thirty-seven for the entire country, including Dublin.[3] In the following ten years a further ten lodges were established in the city.[4] In most cases lodges held their fortnightly meetings in inns or taverns, although exceptionally meetings were held in private houses. We can get some idea of the area of the city served by the different lodges in the 1730s and 1740s from the venues for such meetings. Thus, lodge no. 2 met at The Hercules in Patrick Street and at The Green Posts in Meath Street; no. 3 at The Bull's Head in Ormond Market near Capel Street; no. 6 at The Recorder's Head in Meath Street and at Mr Bray's of Ash Street nearby; no. 7 at The Cock and The Punch Bowl in Cork Hill and at The White Lion in George's Lane (now South Great George's Street); no. 8 at The Eagle in Cork Hill and The Plume of Feathers in Park Street, the Coombe; no. 54 at Mr Russell's in Church Street; no. 100 at The Black Lion in Park Street, and no. 141 at The Struggler in Cook Street.[5]

As to catholic involvement at this early period, Viscount Netterville was elected grand master in 1732 but he had already forsaken the Roman Catholic for the established church in 1728. However, Netterville's successor as grand master in 1733 and 1734 was the catholic Henry Benedict Barnewall, Viscount Kingsland, while another catholic, James Brenan, a Dublin physician, was appointed grand warden during Kingsland's first year of office.[6] When Kingsland was elected for a second year in 1734 he appointed Brenan deputy grand master, a post the latter

1 Lepper, J.H. & Crossle, Philip, *History of the Grand Lodge of free and accepted masons of Ireland*, vol. 1, Dublin 1925, pp 36–7.   2 *Dublin Weekly Journal*, 26 June 1725. The report can be read in Patrick Fagan, *The second city: portrait of Dublin 1700–1760*, Dublin 1986, pp 253–4. It is of interest that there was one lodge of real masons present at this meeting.   3 Smith, W., *A pocket companion for freemasons*, Dublin 1735, p. 78.   4 Information supplied by Freemasons' Hall, Dublin.   5 Smith, W., op. cit., p. 78.   6 Spratt, Edward, *The new book of constitutions ... of the free and accepted masons*, Dublin 1751, p. 123.

retained until his death in December 1737. It should be mentioned that, while the post of grand master was a somewhat honorary position, nearly always occupied by a titled person, the task of effectively administering the organization fell to the deputy grand master and the other grand officers. Robert Nugent was appointed a grand warden in 1732 when he was still apparently a Roman Catholic. He later converted to the established church and achieved high office in Britain as Earl Nugent. Apart from the foregoing it appears that no catholic has ever held any official position in the Grand Lodge of Ireland. Walter Wade, who was deputy grand master towards the end of the century, converted from catholicism to the established church in 1781 prior to his marriage that year to the quaker, Mary Chambers. Dowell O'Reilly, who was grand secretary in 1782 and a grand warden 1783–5, was 'the first of the family that conformed to the established church', although some of his descendants, including a grandson, Myles O'Reilly MP, were catholic.[7]

Freemasonry also made rapid progress early in the century on the continent of Europe, where it was established in France in 1721, in Holland in 1724, in Portugal in 1735 and Germany in 1737.[8] As a secret, oath-bound society it soon came to the notice of the Vatican and Clement XII in his bull *In eminenti* condemned the movement in 1738.[9] After reflecting on the great evils, both for the tranquillity of states and the safety of souls, which he apprehended would result from these secret societies, Clement 'resolved and decreed that the before-mentioned societies ... should be condemned and proscribed'. He went on:

> Wherefore to each and all of the faithful of Christ we ordain stringently and in virtue of holy obedience, that they shall not under any pretext enter, propagate or support the aforesaid societies known as Freemasons or otherwise named; that they shall not be enrolled in them, affiliated to them or take part in their proceedings; assist them or afford them in any way counsel, aid or favour, publicly or privately, directly or indirectly, by themselves or by others in any way whatever; under pain of excommunication to be incurred by the very act without further declaration from us.

The bull went on to say that absolution from this penalty should not be obtainable through anyone other than the pope himself, except at the hour of death.

---

7 Lepper & Crossle, op. cit., pp 464–72. The date of Dowell O'Reilly's death (1738) given by Lepper & Crossle does not appear to be correct; a report of his daughter Elizabeth's marriage in the *Cork Advertiser* for 10 October 1816 refers to him as the late Dowell O'Reilly of The Heath, Esq. He was probably the Dowell O'Reilly, Dublin city, Esq., whose will was proved in 1809, indicating that he died around that date; see Sir Arthur Vicars, *Index of prerogative wills*. For his defection to the established church see John O'Hart, *Irish pedigrees*, Dublin 1892, p. 746. For Walter Wade see Eileen O'Byrne, *The convert rolls*, Dublin 1981, and E. Charles Nelson & Eileen McCracken, *The brightest jewel: a history of the National Botanic Gardens*, Kilkenny 1987, passim.   8 *The Catholic encyclopedia*, Washington DC.   9 Cahill, Edward, *Freemasonry: its character and purpose*, Dublin 1944, p. 7.

Despite its uncompromising language, the bull was virtually ignored in Ireland in common with the catholic states of Europe. A further condemnation of free-masonry by Pope Benedict XIV in 1751 in the bull *Providas Romanorum* was likewise ignored, and it was not a matter of the faithful not knowing about these papal decrees. Clement XII's bull was so well-known in Dublin that a pamphlet in answer to it was published in that city in 1751 by an apparently protestant writer.[10]

During the second half of the 1740s several new lodges were established in Dublin, nine new ones in 1747 and eight in 1749. A total of seventeen new lodges were established in the city in the period 1750–9. There was then a gradual slow-ing down, with eight new ones in the 1760s, six in the 1770s and only two in the 1780s. From 1783 until 1818 no new lodges were set up in Dublin, apart from a Barristers' Lodge in 1790 and a Medical Lodge in 1794, both of which, it will be argued, appear to have been fronts for the United Irishmen. By the 1790s most lodges, in contrast with earlier in the century, were holding their meetings at addresses other than inns and taverns. It was then the practice, no doubt for reasons of economy and convenience, for several lodges to use the same meeting-place. While in 1794 twenty-four of the twenty-nine active lodges met at what appear to have been private addresses, three met at The Eagle in Eustace Street and two at The King's Arms in Fownes Street. All except one – no. 2 which met at 17 Church Street - had their meeting-places at the date mentioned on the South side of the city, twelve of them in Bride Street or Meath Street or lanes off those streets. It is a measure of the general decline of masonry that, although some 82 lodges had been formed in the city throughout the century, only twenty-nine were active in 1794.[11]

The Vatican does not appear to have made any serious effort to promulgate in Ireland the papal condemnations of freemasonry until 1760. In July of that year Cardinal Corsini, in his capacity as cardinal protector of Ireland, wrote to the four Irish metropolitans to convey the grief and concern of the Congregation of the Holy Office of the Inquisition at hearing that many Irish parish priests and ecclesiastics had become freemasons.[12] That anguish and grief was much increased when the Congregation found that, whilst some of these acknowledged their er-ror and submitted with humility to the pastoral admonition of their respective bishops, there were others who, obstinate in their error, falsely contended in their own defence that freemasonry flourished with impunity, not only in Britain and Ireland, but all over France. Corsini maintained that Clement XII's bull, as confirmed by Benedict XIV, evidently contradicted this contention, for it lay under censure those of every denomination or condition all over the Christian world who disobeyed the papal decree, which, Corsini contended, was deemed

10 Clarke, Bernard, *An answer to the pope's bull with a vindication of the real principles of freema-sonry*, Dublin 1751, passim. See Haliday pamphlets in the Royal Irish Academy, vol. 236. 11 *Sentimental and Masonic Magazine*, April 1794, pp 293–4. 12 Russell Library, Saint Patrick's College, Maynooth, Renehan MS vol. 43, p. 57

canonical by all governments and kingdoms, was accepted as being consistent with the rights of the civil law and should, therefore, be duly observed. It was the desire of the Holy Office, then, that the metropolitans would bring the provisions of Clement XII's bull to the attention of their suffragans, emphasizing the punishments contained therein and the obligation everyone was under punctually to observe them. Corsini concluded with the hope that, with the cooperation of the suffragans, the false opinions in this matter would be entirely removed, and the faithful enabled to fulfill their duty to obey the papal decree through making the situation clear to them.

Corsini's strictures again apparently fell on deaf ears for the freemason movement continued to spread rapidly both in Dublin and the provinces as the 1760s advanced. Ultimately, there were very few towns of any size which did not have their freemason lodges, and larger towns, such as Tralee, Co. Kerry, could have several lodges. Many villages also had their lodges. For example, the villages of Kinnegad, Castlepollard and Finea in Co. Westmeath all had lodges.[13] The fact that catholics as well as protestants were members meant that the lodge served an important function as a meeting place for the two communities. The role of the lodges in fostering good relations between catholics and protestants and indeed in promoting an environment where protestants were prepared to accept the necessity of relief measures for catholics, has never been adequately studied, much less sufficiently recognized, by historians. The fact that lodges were in effect secret, oath-bound societies rendered them easy preys for organizations wishing to use them as fronts for illegal, anti-government activities. Early in the century the Jacobites used the lodges in Britain, Ireland and the continent for such purposes,[14] while towards the end of the century the United Irishmen were up to the same game especially in Ulster[15] but also, as will be argued, in Dublin. There is the probability that from the 1750s onwards lodges were used as meeting-places by catholics to discuss their grievances and to formulate plans of action.

With regard to the extent of the catholic presence in freemasonry in the country as a whole in the eighteenth century, Lepper and Crossle in their history of Irish freemasonry in the eighteenth century make the following claim:[16]

> At the period Lord Donoughmore [Richard Hely-Hutchinson] was elected our Grand Master [1789] the majority of the Freemasons in Ireland were Catholics, and we can point with pride to the inherent love of Freemasonry which existed so strongly amongst the Irish people that when once within the walls of an Irish masonic lodge there were no such things as distinctions of class, of creed, of politics, every Brother, no matter who or what he was, meeting upon the same level ...

13 Crossle, Philip, *Irish masonic records*, Dublin 1973, passim. 14 Murphy, Seán, 'Irish Jacobitism and freemasonry' in *Eighteenth-Century Ireland*, vol. 9 (1994), pp 75–82. 15 Stewart, A.T.Q., *A deeper silence: the hidden roots of the United Irish movement*, London 1993, passim. 16 Lepper & Crossle, op. cit., p. 423.

In considering whether the claim that the majority were catholics is well grounded, it is pertinent to look at the membership situation generally about 1770.[17] At that time, if the army lodges are excluded, out of a total of about 300 lodges, some 40 per cent were in the province of Ulster and so can be assumed to have been predominantly protestant. Dublin city lodges accounted for about a further 20 per cent and it will be argued later that membership in Dublin generally was largely protestant. The rest of the country accounted for the remaining 40 per cent and even if there was a majority catholic representation in these lodges – a proposition which is highly debatable – the protestant majorities in the Ulster and Dublin lodges would appear to be more than sufficient to ensure that the majority of the freemasons in the country as a whole were protestant. The contrary claim made by Lepper and Crossle that the majority of Irish freemasons at this period were catholic does not appear to be sustainable.

As to the particular situation in Dublin city, the extent of the movement there in the eighteenth century can be gauged from the fact that, apart from lodges catering for the military, 82 separate lodges were established in that period in the city, and of these 47 were founded before 1750.[18] The membership records of seventeen of these lodges are no longer extant; the lodge numbers in these cases were afterwards assigned to provincial lodges and the extent to which there were admissions to these lodges in Dublin from the mid-1750s onwards appears to have been small. For the remaining 65 Dublin lodges names of those admitted to membership appear to be complete from 1758 onwards, but the names of about 150 persons (of which forty-six are for 1757), admitted to various lodges before that date, are also available in the Grand Lodge registers. Dublin lodges had two identity numbers – a number in the register for the country as a whole and a number in a separate exclusively Dublin sequence.[19]

The membership registers preserved in the Freemasons' Hall, Molesworth Street, Dublin are divided into six columns setting out particulars of (a) serial number; (b) Christian name and surname; (c) date admitted to membership; (d) date, if made master; (e) date, if made warden and (f) a general remarks column which usually gives the date of certification of membership but occasionally contains remarks such as 'left', 'dead', 'excluded', 'abroad' and, very rarely, 'excluded for high crimes'. Addresses are never given and, except in the cases of some attorneys, physicians and clergymen, occupations are only occasionally given and then usually to distinguish two members of a lodge with the same name. Occasionally members are designated as 'esquire' or 'gent'. Clergymen are designated 'Revd' but we cannot be certain that all clerical members are designated in this way. Assuming those designated 'Revd' represents the full extent of clerical membership, clergy participation in the freemasons in Dublin was very low indeed.[20]

17 Crossle, Philip, op. cit., p. 15.   18 Information supplied by Freemasons' Hall, Dublin.   19 See Grand Lodge membership registers in Freemasons' Hall, Dublin.   20 Only 21 of about 5,300 admitted to membership in the period 1758–99 were designated 'Revd'.

The total number admitted to the Dublin lodges in the 42 years from 1758 to 1799 inclusive was about 5,300. The active membership at any given point in time probably averaged no more than 1,500. In the absence of records it is not possible to offer any comment on membership figures prior to 1758 except that the high figures recorded for the three years 1758–60 may be the apex of a curve extending back to the early 1750s. For the years 1758–99 total numbers admitted to each lodge are set out in the table in Appendix 8, p. 151. This table shows that from the late 1750s to the mid-1760s there was a relatively heavy influx of new members, followed by a significant falling off from 1766 onwards, a trend which was not reversed until the mid-1790s. For example, admissions to membership of 2,161 for the fourteen years 1758–71, compare with 1,369 for the fourteen years 1772–85 and with 1,762 for the fourteen years 1786–99. Apart from one Cork lady who, it is claimed, gained admission in rather dubious circumstances, membership was entirely male. The minimum age for admission to membership was fixed in 1730 at twenty-one but in 1741 this was changed to twenty-five and so remained until 1813 when the minimum age of twenty-one was reverted to.[21]

It is clear that certain lodges catered for particular professions or a particular stratum of society.[22] Clearly, the most exclusive was the Grand Master's lodge, which was founded in 1750 and is not to be confused with the Grand lodge of Ireland, although membership of the Grand Master's lodge automatically qualified one to take part in the proceedings of the Grand lodge. Details of admissions to the Grand Master's lodge are available only from 1771 and these show that members were predominantly non-catholic, upper-class, professional, with not a few titled persons. Lodge no. 198 was also upper class with several esquires, gentlemen, physicians and other professionals and better-heeled merchants. It is not surprising that it catered for a higher degree of mason, the Royal Arch. Likewise Lodge no. 188, with several attorneys among its members, would have been upper class and largely protestant. Lodge no. 203, with all twelve members described as 'gents', was set up in 1754 but only lasted until 1759. Lodge no. 620, known as 'The First Volunteer Lodge of Ireland', was established in 1783 and was held in 'the Corps of Independent Dublin Volunteers'. Like the Volunteer organization generally, it would have been predominantly protestant. Lodge no. 207 was known as the Philanthropic Lodge, but whether it had any connection with the Philanthropic Society, a Jacobin, Painite club which flourished in Dublin in the 1780s and 1790s, has not been discovered. A Medical Lodge established in 1794 and a Barristers' Lodge established in 1790 both appear to have been fronts for the United Irishmen and this aspect will be considered later.

But there was also a proletarian dimension to eighteenth-century Dublin freemasonry, and it was a dimension which became more pronounced as the century advanced. By the 1790s many lodges were holding their meetings in the run-

21 Lepper, J.H. & Crossle, Philip, op. cit., p. 270.   22 The information given here about different lodges is the result of a perusal of the membership registers.

down, overcrowded Liberties area and there was not a single lodge meeting in the wealthy, largely protestant eastern half of the city.[23] A report by Watty Cox on the Dublin masons parading for a charity sermon in 1815 gives a very unflattering insight into the movement at that time.[24] This report is included as Appendix 11 to this chapter (see pp 155–8). Cox mentions the presence at this parade of forty-one army lodges 'from as many cellars in Barrack Street' (now Benburb Street) close to the Royal (until recently Collins) Barracks. Cox had earlier reported that 'at this day [1814] Barrack Street in Dublin is full of Freemason lodges, and a proper estimate may be made of their reputation, when one considers the depravity and wretchedness which exist in that abode of licentiousness and gallantry'.[25]

The multiplicity of army lodges in the city and their insalubrious meeting-places points to a high proportion of non-commissioned officers and privates among the members. Parkinson claims that a camaraderie between the officers, NCOs and men was cultivated within these army lodges where 'the more thoughtful type of soldier found a refuge from the hardships and monotony of service' and where 'officer, NCO and man, meeting on the same level, bred a mutual respect, devoid of servility'.[26] But this is to disregard entirely the great gulf which existed socially between the officers and men in the British Army at that time and down to modern times. Cox, in his report, mentions the ragged condition of the members of some other lodges and maintains that the grand master, the duke of Leinster, absented himself from the parade because he was ashamed to be seen at the head of 'one of the most ridiculous and ragged rabbles ever exposed to public ridicule'.

That there was, despite papal condemnations, a significant catholic dimension to freemasonry in Dublin in the eighteenth century cannot be gainsaid, but how to quantify that dimension is a difficult and daunting task. In a situation where the membership records, with few exceptions, merely tell us the first name and surname of the member, the only pointer to religious persuasion consists in whether the surname, and to a lesser extent the first name, was one which appertained usually to protestants or catholics. It is recognized of course that catholic-sounding names are an unreliable guide to religious affiliation since we are deal-

---

23 See list of lodges in the *Sentimental and Masonic Magazine*, April 1794, pp 293–4. 24 *Irish Magazine and Monthly Asylum for neglected biography*, December 1815, vol. 8, p. 575. Cox had earlier in his magazine (vol. 7 [1814], p. 486) disclosed a deep antipathy to freemasonry, but implied his previous membership, when he stated: 'We know what this craft of masonry is; we have witnessed it in all its whimsies; in short we are intimately acquainted with its mysteries and history, and we are not afraid to pronounce it one of the most silly amusements that ever beguiled the hours which fools, rogues and idiots lay apart to play the part of children.' As regards the army lodges, since the army until the 1790s was predominantly non-Irish and exclusively protestant, these lodges could have little relevance to an examination of the catholic dimension in Dublin freemasonry. They have, therefore, been excluded from any but a cursory mention in this chapter. 25 Ibid., vol. 7 (1814), p. 487. 26 Parkinson, R.E., *History of the Grand Lodge of free and accepted masons of Ireland*, Dublin 1957, vol. 2, p. 290.

ing with a time when, to a far greater extent than in Dublin today, people with catholic-sounding names were in fact protestant. On the other hand, many with protestant-sounding names were in fact catholic – after all Linegar, Lincoln, Carpenter and Troy are the names of four eighteenth century catholic archbishops of Dublin.[27] Nevertheless, it can be advanced as a reasonably acceptable principle that the great majority of people with catholic-sounding names were catholic and the great majority of people with protestant-sounding names were protestant. Thus a heavy concentration of catholic-sounding names in a lodge can be taken as denoting it as catholic-oriented, and on this basis we can identify lodges numbered 54, 64, 137, 173, 241, 263, 319, 324, 348, 353, 375 and 382 as being largely catholic. In considering how much note was taken of the papal decrees of 1738 and 1751, it is of some significance that three of the lodges listed (54, 64, and 137) were founded in the period 1736–46, while the remaining nine were formed in the period 1747–63.

The following are thumb-nail sketches of the foregoing lodges. The dates of establishment of the different lodges is taken from a list supplied by Freemasons' Hall, Dublin. To demonstrate the apparent catholic ethos of these lodges, names of persons admitted in the late 1750s and early 1760s are set out in footnotes.[28]

Lodge no. 54   Founded in 1736, this lodge was meeting at Mr Russell's of Church Street on the north side of the city *c.*1744.[29] It will be seen from Chapter 1 that this area was over 70 per cent catholic by 1766. There was an intake of 22 apparently catholic members in the period 1758–61, four of these being designated 'merchant' (George O'Connor, Daniel Keogh, James Purcell and Henry Dowling) and one as a 'gent' (Peter Masterson).[30] The James Purcell mentioned was probably the same James Purcell who was a signatory, with over three hundred others of the catholic gentry, merchants and citizens of Dublin, of an address to the lord lieutenant in December 1759.[31] The lodge declined in the years 1762–9 with only one new member admitted in that period. There was a reactivation in the 1770s but new members appear to have been mostly protestant. It may be that it was around this time it moved to the South Side; a list for 1794 shows that at that date it was meeting at 15 Ross Lane off Bride Street.[32] During the 1780s and 1790s intake of new members was probably divided equally between protestants and catholics. The lodge ceased to function in 1817.

27 Some surnames are more catholic or more protestant than others and there are some quite common names (e.g. Smith, White, Brown, Jones) where representation might be close to 50/50.   28 Where the meeting place of a lodge is not known, the area of the city catered for by the lodge has been determined by a comparison of members' names with the list of merchants etc. in *Wilson's Dublin Directory* and with Mrs Wall's list of catholic merchants etc.; see note 46 below.   29 Smith, W., op. cit., p. 78.   30 The remaining 17 members were as follows: John Netterville, John Colier, Thomas Perry, Philip McGullycuddy, William Gillway, Pat Howard, Owen Cassety, Daniel Quinn, Thomas Wade, Nicholas Brown, Andrew Herman, William Cross, Peter Hand, James Sweeney, Barnard Reid, Francis Morgan and Pat Cavanagh.   31 *Dublin Gazette* of 15 December 1759.   32 See *Sentimental and Masonic Magazine*, April 1794, pp

Lodge no. 64 This apparently South Side lodge was founded in 1737. There was an intake of 24 mostly catholic members in the three years 1758–60.[33] It remained very active and very mixed religion-wise for the remainder of the century. It was meeting at 43 Meath Street in 1794 and ceased to function in 1825.

Lodge no. 137 Founded in 1743, this lodge was meeting at Mr Bray's of Swan Alley, St Audoen's parish *c.*1744. This was throughout the century a very catholic area (see Chapter 1). There was an intake of 26 mainly catholic members in the years 1758–62, followed by a moderate intake of mostly catholics for the remainder of the sixties.[34] There was a very mixed intake of members for the remainder of the century. It was meeting at 82 Bride Street in 1794 and it closed in 1837.

Lodge no. 173 Founded in 1747, this lodge had an intake of 52 mostly catholic members in the period 1758–62.[35] Annual admissions were moderate after that, apart from 1769 when there were eleven. It appeared to draw its membership from the parishes of St Paul and St Michan on the North Side. There were no new members from 1771 on, and it ceased to function in 1774. The Thomas Lee who joined in 1768 was in all probability the catholic linen-draper of that name from Pill Lane who was a great friend of Charles O'Conor of Belanagare and who married a sister of Archbishop Carpenter.

Lodge no. 241 This lodge was founded in 1753 and catered mainly for a North Side membership. An intake of 20 new members in the years 1758–60 was rather mixed.[36] It was followed by moderate intakes for the following years and ceased in 1777.

293–4 for this and for addresses of other lodges at that time.   33 The names of the 24 were: James Kelly, Michael Clarke, Edward Clarke, Samuel Baston, James Laughlin, Thomas Murray, Pat Earls, Peter Dowling, Thomas Dolan, Alex Mc Crea, James Reid, Daniel Croane, Michael Miler, William Underhill, John Campbell, Jeremiah Bowen, Michael Coffey, Andrew Coffey, Cornelius Lyne, James Kelly, William Finley, William Jenkins, James Ferrall, and Laurence Ball.   34 The names of these 26 were: John King, John McNamara, John McCauley, Arthur Matthews, John Callen, Edward Brennan, Robert Cusick, Stephen Kelly, James Coffey, Thomas Furey, James Graham, John Nicholson, Ralph Parr, Patrick Hamilton, John Power, Oliver Parker, James Harris, John O'Brien, John Brannon, William Lee, Joseph Fullam, Hugh Gallagher, James Tuite, Edward Mullen, Martin Ward and Patrick McGuinness.   35 The names of 28 admitted in the years 1758–60 were: John Carden, Michael Dalton, Tim Murphy, William Dooley, Thomas Connor, Thomas Reilly, Patrick Murray, Robert Ormsby, Miles Keough, Dennis O'Brian, Thomas Daley, William Raper, Hugh Monks, James Scanlon, Henry Kelly, John Stewart, Pat Farrell, William Brown, Owen Keating, Henry Smyth, Edward Fagan, Simon Cavanagh, John Dillon, Thomas Scurlock, Richard Allright, William Ryan, Andrew Mooney, and Thomas Jarrett.   36 The names of these 20 were: Andrew Walsh, John Smart, Denis Dunne, James Scanlon, John Knight, Patrick Connelly, Pat Tygh, John Matthews, George Bonnell, Thomas Axe, Jeremiah Morran, John Daly, John Felton, Herbert Wallbank, Timothy Mullally, Nat Hoyle, William Bourke, Walter Waldren, Patrick Walsh and Michael Geragherty.

Lodge no. 263 Founded in 1755, this lodge had a mixed intake, 40 in the years 1758–62, and it is not clear which side of the city it catered for.[37] It is of interest that 29 members were 'excluded'. It ceased in 1774.

Lodge no. 319 It appears that 33 men with predominantly catholic names came together in 1759 to form this lodge.[38] There was an addition of a further twelve mainly catholic members in 1760. There was a falling-off between 1761 and 1770, the number of admissions each year averaging only three. It drew its membership mostly from the parishes of St Catherine and St Audoen and ceased in 1786.

Lodge no. 324 Founded in 1759, membership was drawn mostly from the parishes of St Paul and St Michan. In its early years it appears to have had a large number of catholic members but from the 1770s onwards it was a very active lodge with mostly protestant members.[39] In 1794 it was meeting at 9 Eustace Street on the south side. It ceased in 1818.

Lodge no. 348 This lodge was founded in 1760 and catered for a South Side membership. It has all the appearances of having been set up by catholics who however ceased to be attracted after 1766.[40] There were no new members in the period 1772-96. It was revived in 1797 but ceased in 1830.

37 The names of these 40 were: William Nowlan, John French, James Jacob, John Carroll, Charles Taylor, John Eccles, John Toole, John Pilkinton, Francis Graghan, William O'Brien, Daniel Galway, Patrick McGee, Tobias Murphy, John Bowes, Daniel Casey, John Casey, John Jennings, Michael McCormick, James Keating, Thomas Reagan, Andrew Kelly, John Bassnett, Joseph Renard, Patrick Dundon, John Maloney, Pat Keane, Thomas McDonagh, William Leeson, Philip Boyle, John Kelly, Denis Boyle, William Hopkins, Thomas Pilkington, James Oxborough, William McCoome, Thomas Ennis, Michael Fitzgerald, Cornelius Manning, Cornelius Donavan and William Keating.   38 The names of these 33 were: Richard McDaniel, John Gaffney, Pat Lawless, John Leacock, Richard Coffey, William Clinch, Darby McDaniel, Francis Ivory, Pat Dempsey, Pat Cooney, William Kennedy, Pat Boyle, Abraham Taylor, Francis Dungan, John Sullavan, Robert Pearson, William Mahon, Samuel McCartney, David Cunningham, Daniel Magurk, Peter Geoughagan, Thomas Keane, George Carter, Edmund Byrne, Pat Smyth, Michael McCormick, Jacob Cavanagh, Pat Coffey, Joseph Archbold, Rodger Keene, Randle McDaniel, Farrel Reilly and Thomas Head.   39 The names of 40 admitted in the years 1759–62 were: James Hanna, John Pascal, Edward Fox, John Forster, Joseph Cox, George Bradburn. Thomas Hodgen, Pat Kenedy, William Byrne, Pat Donnelly, John Farrell, Joseph Plemeth, John Byrne, Richard Graham, William Fetherston, Brian Green, Edward Byrne, Daniel Noone, Hugh Woods, Thomas Rozzell, Thomas Brotherton, Laurence Hanna, John Kelly, Darby Dunavan, Pat Walsh, Andrew Byrne, Peter Brodie, Pat Smyth, Richard Smyth, James Delaney, Phelix McGauran, Thomas Davis, William Hopkins, Chris Clinch, Patrick Trenor, John Willey, Maurice Donnelly, William Collins, Patrick Duff and Thomas Doyle.   40 The names of 31 admitted in the years 1760–1 were: James Walsh, John O'Brien, Andrew Keating, James Flood, William Harris, James Murphy, John Ratchford, William O'Connor, William Keating, William Whelan, Stephen Lynch, Thomas Barnett, William Clancy, John Keine, Tim O'Connor, Michael Fitzgerald, John Barker, William Coffey, Edward O'Neill, John Griffin, Stephen Doyle, George Irwin, Daniel Flood, James Cavanagh, Peregrine Smyth, Nicholas Doran, James Cooke, John Harris, Thomas Ryan, Thomas Lamb and John Cross.

Lodge no. 353 A South Side lodge founded in 1760, it had an intake of 51 largely catholic members in its first four years,[41] but catholic interest seems to have declined after that, the average intake being around three for the following 36 years to 1799. It was meeting at 2 Hoey's Court on the south side in 1794. It ceased in 1818.

Lodge no. 375 This South Side lodge was founded in 1761 with an initial intake of 17 mostly catholic members.[42] There was a moderate intake in the following years until 1771 when there was an intake of ten. There were no new members after 1774 although the lodge did not officially cease until 1801.

Lodge no. 382 A South Side lodge founded in 1762, it gives the impression of being rather mixed religion-wise.[43] It ceased to operate in 1787.

It is evident, then, that there was a large influx of catholics into these lodges in the late 1750s and early 1760s. In some cases it appears that groups of catholics came together to form lodges. A quite significant falling-off in catholic membership can be detected from about 1770. In order to quantify the extent of this falling-off, the period 1758–99 has been divided into three fourteen-year periods – 1758–71, 1772–85 and 1786–99. Details extracted of admissions of persons with the seventy-three most frequently occurring catholic surnames for these three periods show that there were 506 such surnames in the first period, 243 in the second period (i.e., a reduction of 52.2 per cent) and 345 in the third (a reduction of 32.0 per cent).[44] We have already noted that the reduction generally in admissions as between the second and the first period was 40.4 per cent and between the third period and the first was 26.2 per cent.

It appears from this that while there was a reduction in admissions generally in the 1770s and 1780s, the decrease in the admissions of catholics was far more pronounced than the general decrease, and more pronounced still than admissions of protestants. After all, it must be of some significance that while seventeen persons named Byrne were admitted to lodges in the period 1758–71, only three of that name were admitted in the period 1772–85 and that twenty-nine

41 The names of 25 admitted in the years 1760–1 were: John Mohan, Randel Gillam, Nicholas Byrne, Pat Teelan, William Alexander, Pat White, James Robinson, Nicholas Fagan, Hugh Crawford, Nicholas Byrne Sen., Simon Pearson, Pat Tearnan, Richard Smyth, Chris Adamson, John Fitzpatrick, Terence McGuier, James Connely, Nicholas Coyle, Peter Cahill, Alex Bussby, Maurice Collins, Matthew Reilly, John Joseph, Pat Gallagher and Gregar McGuire. 42 The names of the 17 admitted in 1761 were: Hugh Carr, Murtagh O'Connor, Michael Byrne, Garrett Reilly, Andrew Carr, John Bourk, John Carey, John Whitford, Terence McLaughlin, John Coffey, Thomas Lyness, John Carr, John Orr, Farrell Malone, Owen McGinness, Terence McCabe and David Jones. 43 The names of the 16 founding members were: Walter Nugent, John Boothman, Henry Sharp, Richard Malloy, Nicholas Cunningham, Nat Whitestone, Daniel Larkin, James Micheau, George Tracey, Pat Slaughaurty, Barry Murphy, John Carty, Richard Murray, Richard Smyth, Richard Kane and Mat Molloy. 44 See Appendix 9, pp 152–3.

persons named Kelly admitted in the period 1758–71 compare with only ten for 1772–85. It will be noted from the information already given that some lodges with a high catholic intake in the 1750s and 1760s ceased to function or went into a decline in the 1770s or 1780s, viz. lodges nos. 173, 241, 263, 319, 348 and 375. This falling-off in catholic admissions was probably not unconnected with the death of the liberal archbishop Patrick Fitzsimons in 1769 and the succession the following year of the ultramontane John Carpenter. While there is nothing in Carpenter's surviving 'Epistolae' to indicate that he proceeded during his term as archbishop to enforce the papal ban on catholic membership of the freemasons,[45] it has to be said that this is the sort of action he would have taken covertly and without committing anything to writing, in view of the danger of antagonizing the protestant establishment through the condemnation of a movement to which so many protestants belonged.

As to the degree of participation by catholics in the Dublin lodges, a test can be applied to a list of 1,250 catholic merchants, manufacturers, tradesmen and traders, compiled by Mrs Maureen Wall from the Catholic Qualification Rolls for the period 1778–82.[46] These are the kind of people one would expect to have been members of the freemason lodges. A comparison of the names on Mrs Wall's list with an alphabetical index I prepared of some 5,300 admissions to the Dublin lodges in the period 1758–99, shows that only 326 (or 26 per cent) of the names on Mrs Wall's list are to be found on the freemason list, and it can be concluded from this that at least 74 per cent of the people on Mrs Wall's list were *not* freemasons. Furthermore, in the case of the 326 mentioned, there would be a significant number where, while the names on the two lists were the same, the persons concerned were not the same – in other words, the Patrick Barrett, for example, who appears on Mrs Wall's list may not be the same Patrick Barrett who appears on the freemason list. After making a reasonable allowance for this factor, it seems safe to conclude that something less than 20 per cent of the persons on Wall's list were in fact freemasons. While, at first sight, this might appear a rather low participation rate, it has to be considered quite high when it is taken into account that at the time in question only about 5 per cent of the adult male population of Dublin were freemasons. In any event, while the exercise quantifies the extent to which Dublin catholic merchants etc. were freemasons, it is of no great help in determining what proportion of Dublin freemasons were catholic.

To arrive at a more positive assessment of the degree of catholic participation in Dublin freemasonry in the eighteenth century, a count has been made of all catholic-sounding surnames among admissions to lodges in the period 1758–69, and this gives a figure of 810. Now, while it is true that a certain proportion of

45 Curran M.J. (ed.), 'Archbishop Carpenter's Epistolae' in *Reportorium Novum* vol. 1, nos. 1 & 2, passim.   46 Wall, Maureen, 'The Catholic merchants, manufacturers and traders of Dublin 1778–1782' in *Reportorium Novum* vol. 2, no. 2, 299–323.

these were in fact protestants, it is also true that a proportion of those in the register of members with protestant-sounding names were in fact catholics. If we assume that these two factors more or less cancel each other out, we are left with a figure of 800 as an approximation of the number of catholics admitted to lodges in the period 1758–69, and, relating this to the total number admitted in that period (1,900), the indications are that about 40 per cent of those admitted in the period 1758–69 were catholics.[47] Since this was the high point of catholic membership of the freemasons in Dublin in the eighteenth century, it can be concluded for that century generally that, although catholic membership was sizeable, it never amounted to a majority in Dublin. This high catholic involvement was never accorded any acknowledgment in the form of appointments to higher posts in the Grand Lodge of Ireland, apart from the appointments in the 1730s already mentioned.

With the succession of another liberal, John Troy, as archbishop in 1786, a softening in the Irish church's attitude to freemasonry was considered desirable. Thus, in November 1788, probably at the instigation of Troy, the four metropolitans in a letter to the pope, which was concerned also with a relaxation of fasting at certain times, sought a revocation as far as Ireland was concerned of the major excommunication of catholic freemasons contained in Clement XII's bull.[48] The letter pointed out that even the British royal princes themselves, almost all the nobility, civil administrators, military officers, members of parliament and innumerable others had been enrolled in freemason lodges condemned by the pope. It emphasized the huge difficulty, or rather impossibility, in those circumstances of declaring a major excommunication against those catholics who were attached to such lodges, without great peril to the catholic religion and no trivial danger to bishops and priests pronouncing the excommunication. Since for these reasons the papal bulls could not be complied with and were therefore useless as far as the kingdom of Ireland was concerned, the archbishops presumed to supplicate his Holiness that he would deign to revoke in respect of that kingdom the censure of major excommunication against catholic members of the freemasons. They requested that for the future it should be open to Irish bishops, already appointed and to be appointed, to deal with catholics already enrolled in freemason

47 Whether these two factors do in fact largely cancel each other out is of course crucial to the conclusion arrived at. That both factors were significant cannot be doubted. An examination of Mrs Wall's list of catholic merchants etc. (see note 46) shows that about 20 per cent had protestant-sounding names. On the other side of the equation we have only to peruse the Convert Rolls to get a sense of the extent to which people with catholic surnames had become protestant.   48 Moran Patrick, *Spicilegium Ossoriense*, Dublin 1874–84, vol. 3, pp 418–21. The original is in Latin. It is probable that some of Troy's relations were freemasons. A Henry Troy was a member of lodge no. 207 while a Michael Troy was a member of lodge no. 241. There is no evidence that the archbishop's father, James Troy, was a member but he could have joined prior to the late 1750s when the extant registers commence.

lodges or to be enrolled, in the manner which is seen by the bishops themselves to be more appropriate towards winning their souls for the Lord.

While Fr Valentine Bodkin, Roman agent for some of the Irish bishops, in a letter dated 24 June 1789 to Archbishop Butler of Cashel, stated that the metropolitans' letter 'was not well received in Rome',[49] it was not until June 1791 that Rome saw fit to issue an official reply to the metropolitans. In this reply Cardinal Antonelli dubbed freemasonry as a Trojan Horse employed to injure the security of both the church and state.[50] It was profound wisdom, he maintained, that had prompted Clement XII and Benedict XIV to excommunicate all catholics who dared to join that society. In a period even more dangerous to religion, he went on, Rome had no intention of abandoning the foresight and good sense of past pontiffs and he regretted that many Irish catholics should have succumbed to freemasonry.

By that stage (1791) the question of whether the excommunication of catholic freemasons should be enforced had been overtaken by events in the form of the French Revolution. Rightly or wrongly, French freemasonry was regarded as having in some degree contributed to that catastrophic event and certainly some of the most prominent *philosophes* – Rousseau, Voltaire, Helvetius – whose ideas had fired the revolution, were freemasons. In the changed circumstances of 1791, then, the metropolitans can hardly have been in any humour to challenge further the diktat of Rome. I have not discovered when exactly Troy proceeded to enforce the ban. The year 1797 has been mentioned in a recent work as the date on which the papal bulls against freemasonry were promulgated in Ireland, but the author did not cite his authority for this.[51] Granted, Troy's pastoral letter of February 1797 condemned the taking of all unnecessary oaths and, while this was aimed primarily at the United Irishmen and the Defenders, it could be taken as applying also to freemasons. But in view of the turbulence of the times it seems highly unlikely that Troy proceeded to enforce the ban on freemasons in the period 1797–1800. The state of unrest was such that Troy did not dare to undertake visitations of his diocese during those years and it would have been nothing short of foolhardy to antagonize the establishment at that time by condemning freemasonry and excommunicating catholic members.

Indeed, the evidence of the membership registers is that an increased number of catholics were admitted to the Dublin lodges during the late 1790s, apart from 1798, when the number admitted was small due to the unrest caused by the rising. The increase in the years immediately prior to 1798 was probably not unconnected with the lodges in some cases being used as fronts for the United Irish-

49 Tierney, Mark (ed.), 'The papers of James Butler II' in *Collectanea Hibernica* no. 20, p. 95.
50 McNally, V.J., *Reform, revolution and reaction: Archbishop John Thomas Troy and the Catholic Church in Ireland 1787–1817*, Lanham, Md. 1995, p. 47.   51 Trench, Charles C., *Grace's card: Irish catholic landlords 1690–1800*, Cork 1997, p. 34. For further information on Troy's pastoral letter of February 1797 see *Reportorium Novum*, vol. 1, p. 499 et seqq.

men. This reason cannot, however, be advanced for the large number of admissions in 1799. The intake of 229 new members that year was the largest annual intake in the 42-year period 1758–99 and it must be seen in some sense as a reaction to the rebellion the previous year. It must also be seen as evidence that Troy had not by that time formally condemned the freemasons, since many of those admitted to the lodges in 1799 were apparently catholics. In the relative peace of the new century and in a climate of growing catholic self-confidence and resurgence it can be assumed that Troy found time to enforce the ban. In the neighbouring diocese of Meath Bishop Plunkett was also active against the freemasons. His report of a visitation to the parish of Killeigh/Kilbride (near Oldcastle, Co. Meath) in 1806 states that 'the discipline of the church with regard to freemasonry [was] enforced against a few members of that society' and two years later in the same parish he reported that freemasons had been excluded from the Sacraments.[52]

FREEMASONS AND THE UNITED IRISHMEN

The Dublin Society of United Irishmen was formed in November 1791 and initially operated as a constitutional organization with republican proclivities. Following the enactment of the Convention Act in 1793, it was in May 1794 dispersed by order of the government and its assets were seized. Thereafter it operated as a secret society, carrying on its activities in some instances by taking over established radical clubs or by infiltrating freemason lodges and using them as fronts for subversive activities. The government was not unaware that the lodges were being infiltrated. The chief secretary, Thomas Pelham, is on record in 1797 as requesting the grand master, Lord Donoughmore, to check those who sought to turn the order into 'a political engine'.[53]

The two most obvious examples of United Irishmen infiltration in Dublin were the Medical Lodge and the Barristers' Lodge.[54] The Medical Lodge was set up in February 1794 with just three members, the master being William McNevin, the catholic physician and United Irishman, and the two other members, surgeons James Tandy Wilkinson and Robert Hamilton, being wardens. Wilkinson

---

52 Cogan, Anthony, *The diocese of Meath ancient and modern*, Dublin 1870, reprinted Dublin 1992, vol. 3, pp 354 & 373.   53 Smyth, J., 'Freemasonry and the United Irishmen' in D. Dickson, D. Keogh & K. Whelan (eds), *The United Irishmen: republicanism, radicalism and rebellion*, Dublin 1993, p. 152.   54 For Medical and Barristers' Lodges see register of members in Freemasons' Hall and the *Sentimental and Masonic Magazine* for April 1794, pp 293–4. The full list of members of the Medical Lodge in order of admission was as follows: William James McNevin MD, James Tandy Wilkinson, Robert Hamilton, Gerard Macklin, John Creighton, Abraham Bolton, William Lawless, Richard Kiernan MD, Thomas Smith, John Connor, Thomas Tuke, Edward Geoghegan, Huson Bigger, Joseph Stringer, James Rivers, Robert M. Peelo and William Gannon. I have not positively identified William Gannon; he was possibly William Gannan the peruke-maker, on Mrs Wall's list.

is known to have been a United Irishman and it must be presumed that Hamilton was one also. In 1794 this lodge was held in The Eagle in Eustace Street. There was an intake of nine new members in July 1795, including Richard Kiernan, the catholic physician and United Irishman and two other known United Irishmen, William Lawless and Thomas Smith, both surgeons. There were further intakes of two members in 1796 and three in 1797, making a total of seventeen members in all. While I have positively identified only six of these as United Irishmen, the likelihood must be that they were all United Irishmen. Of the seventeen at least five were catholic, that is, physicians McNevin and Kiernan and surgeons Edward Geoghegan, William Lawless and James Rivers. The probability is that the lodge was intended as a medical corps for the United Irishmen in the event of hostilities. The fact that at least fourteen of the seventeen members were surgeons supports this view. In the aftermath of the rebellion the Medical Lodge was 'erased' by order of Grand Lodge in July 1799.

What happened in the case of the Barristers' Lodge was somewhat different. This lodge was formed in February 1790 but had only five members, all lawyers, when Bagenal Harvey, the Wexford United Irishman, William Henn and Charles McCarthy, all lawyers, joined on 6 June 1793. The fact that within months Harvey was master of this lodge and Henn and McCarthy wardens may mean that the lodge was moribund when these three joined. There were only two more admissions, both lawyers, to the lodge, William Horan in July 1793 and Robert Crowe Bryanton in May 1794. The lodge met on Saturdays during law terms. The fact that the lodge was 'erased' in July 1799 at the same time as the Medical Lodge, would seem to identify it as a United Irishman cell.

The registers in Freemasons' Hall show that there were several other lodges where, from a position where annual intakes had been nil or a mere trickle, there were relatively large intakes of new members in the years preceding the rising, suggesting that they also were being used as fronts for United Irishmen activities. Indeed, there was overall a very significant increase in the number of new members in the four years 1794–7, when the total was 729 as compared with 458 for the preceding four years. The following lodges must be viewed as cases in point in this regard: no. 7 (intake of fourteen in 1795 and seven in 1797), no. 100 (intake of twenty in 1796 and twenty-one in 1797), no. 118 (intake of sixteen in 1795), no. 137 (intake of sixteen in 1796), no. 141 (intake of nineteen in 1796 and seventeen in 1797), no. 153 (intake of fifteen in 1796), no 202 (intake of twenty-five in 1797), no. 324 (intake of twenty-seven in 1795, thirteen in 1796 and seventeen in 1797), no. 348 (intake of thirteen in 1794) and no 584 (intake of twelve in 1794 and eleven in 1796).

A comparison of the names in Dr McDowell's list of United Irishmen[55] dur-

---

55 McDowell, R.B., 'The personnel of the Dublin Society of United Irishmen' in *Irish Historical Studies* vol. 2, pp 12–53. Since Dr McDowell's list is concerned only with the United Irishmen's constitutional period, it is quite incomplete as a list of the UIM's total membership.

ing their constitutional period with the list of freemasons shows that the same names occur on both lists in a significant number of instances in the case of the foregoing lodges, but the usual caveat has to be entered that, while the *names* are the same, the *persons* in some cases may have been different. Without getting too deeply involved in this subject, since we would be thereby straying from the primary subject of this chapter, a few more fascinating possibilities should be mentioned. Was William McKenzie, the attorney and United Irishman, the same William McKenzie who was admitted to lodge no. 7 in 1793, becoming a warden the following year, and in 1794 to lodges nos. 137 and 584? There must be a strong suspicion that it was the same person and that he was using the lodges mentioned as recruiting grounds for the United Irishmen. Likewise, can we detect the hand of Dr McNevin and John Gorman Kennedy behind the influx in 1797 of twenty-five members to lodge no. 202, which McNevin and Kennedy had joined a few years earlier? In the case of lodge no. 190 Dr Theobald McKenna, the United Irishman, and James Tandy (probably the famous Napper or his son) joined this lodge on 3 November 1791 with nine others, and may have been not unconnected with the admission of twelve new members in 1796. One cannot regard as other than highly suspect the admission of two known United Irishmen, Edward Hudson and Walter Cox, to lodge no. 324 with twenty-five others in 1795, with further intakes of thirteen in 1796 and seventeen in 1797. Can a United Irishmen cell be detected within the prestigious lodge no. 198 itself with the presence there of such notable United Irishmen as Oliver Bond, merchant, John Talbot Ashenhurst, public notary, John Grogan, Esq. of Co. Wexford and Walter Wade, the physician and botanist? The involvement of Dublin freemason lodges with the United Irishmen is a subject which deserves a more thorough examination than can be afforded it here. In the meantime, it is a sobering reflection that the lists of Dublin freemasons for this period preserved in Freemasons' Hall may in many cases be lists of United Irishmen.

FREEMASONS AND THE 1798 REBELLION

The Grand Lodge as early as March 1793, no doubt reacting to sectarian tensions manifesting themselves particularly in the northern counties, reminded the respective lodges that

> it is utterly inconsistent with the fundamental principles, the ancient charges and the uniform practices of Freemasons, to permit any discussions or publications on religious or political subjects among them, because these, of all others, are known to arouse the worst passions in men,

Information about membership in the UIM's subsequent illegal period is necessarily sketchy. Some members, e.g. Dr William Drennan, broke with the association once it became illegal.

and excite among the kindest brethren the most rancorous and lasting animosities. True masonry prefers no sect and acknowledges no party.[56]

With the outbreak of the rebellion on 23 May 1798, Grand Lodge decided to suspend meetings and did not meet again until 1 November 1798. Although many Freemasons were or had been United Irishmen, it is understandable that, in view of the ensuing debacle, Grand Lodge was anxious to distance the organization from any connection with the rising. Accordingly, at the meeting on 1 November 1798 it was ordered that the several lodges in the city be directed to enquire into the conduct of their members during the late rebellion and report thereon at the next meeting of Grand Lodge. Following complaints that two members (Southwell McClune and James McNulty) had been concerned in the rebellion and had thereby acted contrary to the principles of masonry, it was ordered that they be summoned to attend the next meeting.[57] However, there is nothing subsequently in the minutes to show that either of these orders was followed up.

At the meeting of Grand Lodge on 6 December 1798 it was resolved unanimously that 'any discussion of political, religious or controversial subjects was utterly subversive of and abhorrent from [*sic*] the fundamental principles of masonry, by whatever authority attempted to be introduced'.[58] This resolution was apparently the culmination of differences (see below) between the deputy grand master, Walter Wade, who appears to have been a United Irishman during the organization's constitutional period, and the other members of Grand Lodge. That body took a further step towards orthodoxy at its meeting on 4 February 1799 when it resolved unanimously that the true principles of masonry inculcate an affectionate loyalty to the king and a dutiful subordination to the state.[59] Nevertheless, Grand Lodge appears to have had no desire to conduct a witch-hunt against members who had been implicated in the rising, as long as they did not seek to continue to use their lodge to air their political views. Rather, the aim of Grand Lodge was to mend fences and they were lucky at this time to have in Lord Donoughmore a grand master with the requisite tact and understanding to heal threatening divisions and to prevent rifts.

DANIEL O'CONNELL AND THE FREEMASONS

The most famous catholic member of the Irish Freemasons was undoubtedly Daniel O'Connell. With twenty-five others O'Connell joined Dublin lodge no. 189 on 2 April 1799.[60] This was a South Side lodge which had been founded in

56 *Sentimental and Masonic Magazine*, March 1793.   57 See Grand Lodge minutes under relevant dates.   58 Ibid.   59 Ibid.   60 See membership registers in Freemasons' Hall, Dublin. The number of this lodge is given incorrectly as 198 by Lepper and Crossle in work cited above and the error has been repeated by other writers.

1758 and met at 82 Bride Street in the 1790s. Apart from an intake of twelve new members in 1760, it had not been notably successful in attracting new members, the average annual intake for the period 1761–82 being only four. The situation got even worse after that, with an average intake of less than two per year in the sixteen-year period 1783-98. A perusal of the names of the members indicates that it was religion-wise a mixed lodge. The acquisition by such a lodge of twenty-six new members on the same day in April 1799 invites speculation as to the underlying motive. It must be asked whether it was a calculated move by this group to take over the lodge. It may well be that there were some existing members of the lodge who from the inside aided and abetted a take-over bid. One suspects that the Stephen Rice who became a member of the lodge in 1774 belonged to the legal family of that name with which O'Connell was on friendly terms, although it was probably not the Stephen Henry Rice who partnered O'Connell and Revd John Blennerhassett in the formation of lodge no. 886 in Tralee in 1800, a project which proved abortive because the requisite fee was not paid.[61] It is also possible that the Edward Byrne who joined lodge no. 189 in 1769 was one and the same as Edward Byrne, the wealthy merchant who played a prominent part in the Catholic Committee in the 1780s and early 1790s.

The take-over bid, if such it was, was highly successful to the extent indeed that within the year O'Connell had been elected master of the lodge. This entitled him to attend meetings of the Grand Lodge of Ireland and in fact he proceeded without delay to take a prominent part in the business of that body. Was all this manoeuvring simply intended to launch O'Connell into prominence in the freemasons with a view to enhancing his legal career – in April 1799 he was only twenty-four years old and a young barrister not too encumbered with briefs – or had the influx into lodge no. 189 a wider political agenda? It has to be remembered that O'Connell was at this time preparing to launch himself also on a political career. Nine months later, on 13 January 1800, he was to be the main speaker at a catholic meeting in the Corn Exchange, Dublin at which a resolution was passed deploring the impending Act of Union. Was lodge no 189 being used in this intervening period as a means of getting around the Convention Act of 1793 through serving as a front for meetings of catholics at which discussions could take place and plans could be prepared? It is quite on the cards that it was.

61 The Stephen Rice who became a freemason in 1774 may have been the person who appears in the King's Inns Admission Papers as Stephen Edward Rice, who was admitted to the Middle Temple in 1776 and was a son of Thomas Rice of Dublin. The Stephen Henry Rice mentioned above was probably the person who appears in the Admission Papers as Stephen Rice, son of Dr Henry Rice of the Island of Dominica, educated at Trinity College Dublin and admitted to the Middle Temple in 1787. He afterwards had a legal practice in Tralee, Co. Kerry. O'Connell recorded in his Journal for 5 January 1797: 'I dined yesterday with the three Rices in Eustace Street. Stephen Rice seems to me to possess more information than any man in whose company I have ever been. How different, how decisively different is his knowledge to mine! He made me creep into my ignorance.'

The names of the persons admitted to lodge no. 189 with O'Connell were: William Byrne, Charles Colgan, Tobias Colgan, Michael Roach, Thomas Ging, George Payne, Thomas Douglas, John Masterson, Sylvester Fox, James McLoughlin, William Clarke, John Havey, Pat Shuttleton, John Seavers, John Bray, Frederick Byrne, Joseph Morris, Thomas Lynch, Benjamin Teeling, John Thomson, William Morgan, James O'Neill, Christopher O'Brien, Morris Lenaghan and Thomas Hautenville.

William Clarke, Christopher O'Brien, James O'Neill and John Thompson, listed here, may possibly have been the attorneys of those names practising in the courts at the time in question. But it seems more likely that William Clarke was the man of that name who had been one of the representatives of St Paul's parish on the Catholic Committee and who was apparently a brewer in North King Street.[62] Likewise Christopher O'Brien may alternatively have been the merchant of that name in Moore Street, James O'Neill the salesmaster of that name in Smithfield and John Thompson the draper of that name in Bridge Street. In the case of the remainder, since neither the addresses nor the occupations are given in the Grand Lodge registers, it is not possible to identify positively the persons listed, but the great majority of the names can be seen to correspond with names in *Wilson's Dublin Directory* list of merchants etc. or in Mrs Wall's list, already mentioned. It can thus be deduced that they came mostly from the South Side of the city and followed a diversity of occupations such as merchant, grocer, draper, brewer, tanner, publican, apothecary, watchmaker, hatter, salesmaster, coppersmith, saddler, wool merchant.[63]

It says a lot about the remarkable charisma of the young O'Connell that, shortly after he began to appear at meetings of Grand Lodge, he was in June 1800 appointed chairman of a sub-committee charged with the important task of approaching Lord Donoughmore about the latter's continuance in office as grand

62 Edwards, R. Dudley (ed.), 'Minute book of the Catholic Committee' in *Archivium Hibernicum* vol. 9 (1942), p. 117.   63 For what it is worth, the persons in Wilson's or Wall's lists corresponding to other names above are: William Byrne, grocer, Francis Street; Charles Colgan, grocer, Church Street; Thomas Ging, tanner, Mill Street; George Payne, coppersmith, Back Lane; John Masterson, merchant, Lattin's Court, Greek street; Sylvester Fox, merchant, Usher's Quay; James McLaughlin, publican, Canal Harbour or apothecary, Temple Bar; John Havey, merchant, Thomas Street; John Seavers, saddler, Ormond Quay; Frederick Byrne, draper, Werburgh, Street; Joseph Morris, hatter, Castle Street; Thomas Lynch, grocer, Church Street; John Thompson, draper, Bridge Street or wool merchant, Mark's Alley, Francis Street; and William Morgan, watch-maker Ormond Quay. John Bray may have been related to Robert Bray, mercer, Francis Street who was a United Irishman, and Benjamin Teeling may have been related to John Teeling, distiller, Marybone Lane, also a United Irishman. Michael Roach may have been the Michael Roche who signed the Catholic Petition of 1805 and was reportedly worth £100,000 (see Brian MacDermott, *The catholic petition of 1805*, p. 157). Thomas Hautenville was presumably the person of that name who was admitted a freeman of Dublin in 1793 as a free brother of the Tailors' Guild – see National Library ms ILB 94133 D2. We are then left with Tobias Colgan, Thomas Douglas, Morris Lenaghan and Pat Shuttleton for whom no identification can be suggested.

master. Normally it should have been the duty of the deputy grand master, Walter Wade, to communicate with Donoughmore on this point but Wade had made himself obnoxious to the other members of Grand Lodge, perhaps because of his United Irishman sympathies, and it appears he was not prepared to adhere to Grand Lodge's prohibition on discussion of political, religious and controversial subjects.[64] The Grand Lodge professed to be embarrassed by Wade's dereliction of duty and was concerned about the serious consequences they apprehended from his continuance any longer in office. As the letter sent to Donoughmore by O'Connell as chairman of the sub-committee does not appear to have been published before, it is included as Appendix 10, pp 154–5. Lord Donoughmore was inclined initially to come down on the side of Wade but further embarrassment for Grand Lodge was avoided by Wade's voluntary withdrawal and Donoughmore's agreeing to continue as grand master for a further year.[65]

O'Connell also figures in the minutes of the meeting of Grand Lodge on 24 June 1800 when he was appointed to a committee 'to distribute the collection of the day to such subjects as they deem worthy'. The minutes of the meetings of Grand Lodge for the period 1802 to mid-1806 are missing, with the result that O'Connell's involvement at Grand Lodge level during those years cannot be ascertained. It can be said, however, that he never became a member of the Grand Master's Lodge, unlike his friend, Stephen Henry Rice, who became a member of that lodge in 1801.

How far O'Connell's involvement with freemasonry may have helped his legal career is arguable, although being enabled to rub shoulders with the likes of Lord Donoughmore cannot have done his career prospects any harm. One piece of legal business came his way certainly through such involvement when he was employed as counsel for Grand Lodge in their proceedings against Alexander Seton from 1806 to 1816. Seton had been deputy grand secretary but had been dismissed from that position for 'organizing a system of resistance to the grand officers and Grand Lodge'. Seton was ordered to deliver up books and other Grand Lodge documents in his possession. However, he was not prepared to go quietly and in June 1806 he organized an invasion of Grand Lodge, mostly by brethren from the north of Ireland who proceeded to re-elect Seton as deputy

---

64 McDowell, R.B. (ed.), op. cit. Walter Wade, described in McDowell's list as a chemist and apothecary, appears to have been Walter Wade, the physician and botanist. Wade was originally an apothecary like his father. I note that Lepper & Crossle, op. cit., pp 311–12, claim that Wade's dispute with the Grand Lodge arose from a difference over whether it was in order for the Grand Master's Lodge to continue to nominate the grand master and other officers as had been the custom. The Grand Lodge of Ireland decided in December 1799 that, notwithstanding this custom, they alone were competent to elect the grand master and the other grand officers, a decision with which Wade is reported to have disagreed. I believe that a close reading of the minutes of the Grand Lodge and of O'Connell's letter to Lord Donoughmore point to a more serious rift originating from the Grand Lodge's decision to clamp down on discussion at lodge meetings of political, religious and controversial subjects. **65** See Grand Lodge minutes under relevant dates.

grand secretary. He was finally expelled in April 1807 but the lodge's lawsuit against him was still active in 1816.[66] The following comment in 1806 by Seton, apparently about O'Connell, is interesting in view of O'Connell's subsequent reputation at the bar:

> Since writing the above I have received a note from a gentleman to say that he is under the opinion of counsel prepared to proceed at law. Not knowing who his counsel may be, I can only say that if he is not a better mason than he seems in my opinion to be a lawyer, he never will shine as an ornament to the order.[67]

Incidentally, Seton was a member of the sub-committee, already mentioned, of which O'Connell was chairman and so they would have been personally known to each other.

Whatever about advancing his legal career, O'Connell must have found his involvement in the freemasons a distinct advantage politically when in the agitation for full emancipation for catholics he sought the support of Lord Donoughmore, who was favourably disposed to the catholic cause to the extent that in June 1810 he had sponsored an unsuccessful petition for catholic emancipation in the house of lords. Donoughmore continued in the following years to lend his support to O'Connell in the latter's fight for emancipation. In a letter dated 9 September 1821 to Donoughmore, O'Connell acknowledged his indebtedness:

> For myself personally, I am under obligations to your Lordship and your family which no time can weaken nor can any opportunity ever occur to enable me sufficiently to testify my sense of the favours which I have received.[68]

It is somewhat ironical, considering the lambasting meted out to freemasonry by catholic apologists such as Frs Coyle and Cahill in the early decades of the twentieth century, that the freemason grip may have played some part in catholic emancipation.

It should be remembered that for much of the time he was involved in freemasonry, O'Connell was passing through a phase when he was a catholic only in name, although he was at the same time a very active supporter of catholic causes. His preferred religion, if it could be called such, was deism, which, while it acknowledges the existence of God, does not lend support to any of the revealed religions. It can be said then that, during this period, not only was O'Connell not

66 Lepper & Crossle, op. cit., passim and Grand Lodge minutes under relevant dates. **67** Grand Lodge minutes of 5 March 1806. 68 O'Connell, Maurice R. (ed.), *The correspondence of Daniel O'Connell*, 8 vols, Dublin 1972–80, vol. 2, p. 332.

a practising catholic, but that he was not a christian of any other denomination either. O'Connell was still apparently a member of the freemasons in May 1816, when Grand Lodge ordered their agent to take the best means of putting an end to the Seton lawsuit and to act under the direction of Brother Counsellor O'Connell.[69] In a speech in 1814 the counsellor had eloquently defended freemasonry, the basis of which he described as 'philanthropy unconfined by sect, nation, colour or religion'.[70]

By this time he had forsaken his earlier involvement with deism and had become apparently an exemplary catholic. Indeed, in a letter to his wife dated 15 August 1816 (the feast of the Assumption) he confided, following a bout of illness incurred while he was on circuit, that he 'was well enough this morning to go to my duty [to go to Confession and receive Communion] and attend three Masses'.[71] He formally renounced his past membership of the freemasons in a letter to *The Pilot* dated 19 April 1837, when he acknowledged that he had been a freemason and a master of a lodge, but claimed that this was at a very early period of his life and either before an ecclesiastical censure had been published in the Catholic Church in Ireland prohibiting the taking of the masonic oath, or at least before he was aware of that censure. He went on:

> I now wish to state that having become acquainted with it, I submitted to its influence, and very many years ago unequivocally renounced freemasonry. I offered the late archbishop Dr Troy to make that renunciation public but he deemed it unnecessary ... Freemasonry in Ireland may be said to have (apart from its oaths) no evil tendency, save as far as it may counteract in some degree the exertions of those most laudable and useful institutions ... the temperance societies. But the great, the most important objection is this, the profane taking in vain the awful name of the Deity – in the wanton and multiplied taking of oaths – of oaths administered on the book of God either in mockery or derision.[72]

CONCLUSIONS

1   The great majority of freemasons in Dublin in the eighteenth century were people in trade, such as merchants, shopkeepers and publicans, together with artisans and small manufacturers, but there was a proletarian dimension to the movement which became more pronounced as the century advanced. Really respectable people, such as physicians and the clergy, shunned the Craft, although there were a few lodges catering for the professional and upper classes.

69 Lepper & Crossle, op. cit., p. 377.   70 Parkinson, R.E., op. cit., p. 106.   71 O'Connell, Maurice R., op. cit., vol. 2, p. 111.   72 Parkinson, R.E., op. cit., vol. 2, pp 106–7.

2   It was claimed for the lodges that they were the only places where catholics could mix with protestants on an equal basis and that this was calculated to improve relations between the two persuasions. Although this may have been true for the rest of the country, the tendency in Dublin for catholics to congregate in certain lodges must have greatly reduced opportunities for inter-community co-operation and understanding.

3   It is remarkable that in the 1750s and 1760s, when catholics in Dublin were trooping into the lodges, the Catholic Committee, established in 1756, found it very difficult to attract members. It may be that the Committee, with its emphasis on the gentry and the professional classes, scared away the people in trade who were the backbone of the freemasons.

4   Although catholic participation in freemasonry in Dublin in the eighteenth century was sizeable, they were never in the majority. Catholic membership appears to have been at its peak in the 1750s and 1760s but to have shrunk during Carpenter's term as archbishop (1770–86). The next archbishop, Troy, was initially inclined to be indulgent to freemasons and in 1788 sought, with the three other metropolitans, a relaxation of the papal ban. This was turned down by Rome in 1791 and with the coming of the new century the ban was enforced in Dublin and elsewhere.

5   Considering that fortnightly meetings, particularly in the first half of the century, were held mostly in inns and taverns, it is not surprising that eighteenth-century freemasonry, in contrast to the prim, highly respectable body of modern times, had something of a reputation for roistering and conviviality. As early as 1750 it was being said that participation in the craft made men idle, fond of drink and company and consequently negligent of their families.[73] Daniel O'Connell, after he had ceased to be a member, accused freemasonry of 'counteracting in some degree the exertions of the temperance societies'.[74] O'Connell himself recalled in the winter of 1801 'supping at the Freemasons' Hotel, at the corner of Golden Lane, with a jovial party', following which he helped to put out a fire on the way home.[75] It is probable that the popularity of the lodges in the eighteenth century had less to do with their philanthropic aims than with their attraction as centres of joviality and good fellowship.

6   The secretive nature of the lodges was largely responsible for their being used as fronts for the activities of illegal and subversive bodies. Organizations or movements which resorted to such subterfuge were the Jacobites in the first half of the century, and in the second half the United Irishmen, the Defenders and catholics generally wishing to meet but anxious to avoid the attentions of the authorities. There is convincing evidence that some Dublin lodges were fronts for the United Irishmen. Furthermore, several organizations established in the late eighteenth century, i.e. the Orange Order, the United Irishmen and the De-

73 Clarke, Bernard, op. cit., p. 47.   74 Parkinson, R.E., op. cit, p. 107.   75 Houston, Arthur, *Daniel O'Connell: his early life*, London 1906, p. 247.

fenders, while discarding the more arcane customs of freemasonry, based their organizations in greater or lesser degree on the freemason model. In particular, the Orange Order and the other Orange institutions, are in many respects carbon copies of the freemason model. As regards the United Irishmen, Dr William Drennan, when he first mooted the setting up of a Dublin Society of United Irishmen, is on record as having in mind something on the lines of the freemason lodges.[76]

7   It is probable that Daniel O'Connell used lodge no. 189 as a launching pad both for his legal and political careers. Furthermore, he must have found his involvement in the freemasons a distinct advantage when enlisting the support of Lord Donoughmore, a former grand master, in the cause of catholic emancipation.

APPENDIX 8

Numbers admitted to Dublin Lodges in the years 1758–99

Year admitted	No.	Year admitted	No.	Year admitted	No.
1758	158	1772	177	1786	113
1759	204	1773	123	1787	84
1760	217	1774	131	1788	88
1761	160	1775	133	1789	117
1762	178	1776	82	1790	91
1763	151	1777	107	1791	120
1764	181	1778	78	1792	127
1765	166	1779	80	1793	120
1766	114	1780	63	1794	115
1767	112	1781	93	1795	143
1768	129	1782	66	1796	206
1769	132	1783	51	1797	165
1770	127	1784	78	1798	44
1771	132	1785	107	1799	229

Note These figures of admissions do not take account of cases where a person was a member of two or more lodges.

76 Chart, D.A. (ed.), *The Drennan letters*, Belfast 1931, p. 54.

APPENDIX 9

Numbers admitted to lodges for different catholic surnames

Name	1758–71	1772–85	1786–99	Total
Burke/Bourke	6	5	9	20
Boyle	8	1	1	10
Brady	1	2	4	7
Brennan	7	2	–	9
Butler	1	4	8	13
Byrne	17	3	11	31
Carr	4	4	–	8
Carroll	6	3	7	16
Casey	2	1	7	10
Cavanagh	6	1	3	10
Clarke	14	8	10	32
Coffey	10	2	1	13
Collins	4	5	4	13
Connell	3	2	3	8
Connor	15	13	10	38
Connolly	10	3	4	17
Cullen	6	4	2	12
Dalton	3	4	2	9
Daly	13	–	7	20
Delaney	4	3	4	11
Dempsey	4	3	4	11
Dillon	3	2	5	10
Donovan	6	1	1	8
Doyle	7	3	8	18
Dunne	11	6	7	24
Dwyer	4	2	2	8
Egan	3	1	4	8
Fagan	3	2	4	9
Farrell/Ferrall	13	6	6	25
Fitzgerald	9	3	6	18
Fitzsimons	3	1	4	8
Flanagan	4	2	2	8
Flinn	2	4	3	9
Flood	6	3	1	10
Ford	1	3	5	9
Gallagher	5	3	1	9
Geoghegan	6	1	3	10
Harte	3	2	3	8
Healy	7	6	–	13

Appendix 9 (contd)

Name	1758–71	1772–85	1786–99	Total
Higgins	6	6	3	15
Hogan	4	1	4	9
Hughes	7	6	5	18
Kane/Keane	12	1	5	18
Kearns	3	2	3	8
Keating	15	3	4	22
Kelly	29	10	13	52
Kennedy	5	4	8	17
Lawlor	3	2	4	9
Lynch	4	4	3	11
McCarthy/Carty	6	–	3	9
McCormack	5	1	4	10
McDermott	2	3	9	14
McDaniel	10	4	2	16
McGuire	5	3	9	17
McLaughlin	7	5	2	14
Magee	5	–	3	8
Malone	4	4	3	11
Martin	3	4	4	11
Matthews	4	3	5	12
Moore	6	3	10	19
Murphy	16	9	7	32
Murray	10	4	7	21
Nolan	4	1	8	13
O'Brien	13	3	9	25
O'Neill	7	3	5	15
Quinn	5	1	2	8
Reilly	19	11	8	38
Reynolds	8	3	4	15
Ryan	8	2	2	12
Sheridan	4	2	3	9
Sullivan	3	4	1	8
Walsh	14	5	14	33
Ward	10	2	3	15
TOTALS	506	243	345	1,094

Note The different surnames above can be assumed to include the usual variations, in particular the prefixing of O or Mac/Mc, where appropriate, although the use of O and Mac/Mc was largely shunned by catholics in the eighteenth century.

Letter from Daniel O'Connell to Lord Donoughmore

My Lord,

We have the honour of laying before your Lordship a resolution of the Grand Lodge of Ireland which was unanimously agreed to at a numerous meeting on Thursday the 5th June and of requesting that your Lordship will have the goodness to inform them through us whether you will do the Craft the high honour of continuing in office another year, or whether your Lordship will be pleased to put a successor in nomination.

We beg leave to inform your Lordship that the Grand Lodge of Ireland sincerely regret that, through the failure of the constituted mode of collecting your Lordship's sentiments on such occasions, they should have been compelled to the necessity of opening this communication.

We feel, however, the highest satisfaction that it has afforded us individually an opportunity of joining in the expression of the general sentiments of personal esteem and affection and of gratitude which the Brethren entertain for your Lordship's parental care and government of the Order during the eleven years you have so worthily filled the station of Grand Master; and should any insinuation to the contrary have reached your Lordship's ear, we entreat you to dismiss it as being wholly without foundation. It is with the utmost regret that, in discharging the duty imposed upon us by the Grand Lodge, we find ourselves under the painful necessity of communicating to your Lordship their unalterable disapprobation of an individual so highly honoured as to be your Lordship's deputy. It would be as superfluous as it would be distressing to enter into minute details on this subject, but we feel ourselves bound to inform your Lordship that it is the unequivocal conviction of the Grand Lodge that the general tenor of the conduct of the individual alluded to, most manifestly tends to involve the Craft in difficulties and disorders which, if not prevented, must lead to destruction. Should your Lordship then do the Order the high honour of continuing another year in office, the Grand Lodge do not pretend to dispute your Lordship's right to the appointment of a deputy, but they anxiously entreat your Lordship not to raise once more to that exalted situation a man in whose former misbehaviour they only find an earnest of future misconduct.

We are, therefore, compelled to assure your Lordship that the Order has been kept in continual uneasiness by your deputy's unceasing recurrence to past transactions which your Lordship as well as the Grand Lodge by their act of amnesty, and which on their part has been rigidly adhered to, wished to consign to oblivion. And that this letter is itself an evidence of the total dereliction of his duty in not holding with your Lordship the communication which the approaching election demands. Add to this, my Lord, that he has completely abandoned the Throne on the last two nights of meeting at a season when his attendance was most necessary; and his absence the Grand Lodge are well warranted in considering as a continuation of a system adopted by him for the purpose of embarrassing the Order. And hence your Lordship will clearly see that his remaining longer in office is inconsistent not only with the dignity but even with the safety of Masonry.

We have further to inform your Lordship that a Grand Lodge of emergency is appointed for Thursday the 19th instant to elect officers previous to St John's Day. We, therefore, request your Lordship will be pleased to enable us to report to them on that occasion your Lordship's determination.

And we have the honour to be, with sentiments of the highest consideration and respect of your Lordship, the most devoted and humble servants

Danl O'Connell
WM [Worshipful Master]

Signed in behalf of and by order of the
committee appointed to carry the within
resolution into effect

Note The copy of the foregoing letter preserved in the Grand Lodge minutes is undated but the indications are that the original was dated mid-June 1800.

APPENDIX 11

Freemason charity sermon November 1815[77]

The neighbourhood of Dame-street and George's-street was much amused at a ridiculous parade of a set of persons calling themselves Free-Masons, collected together by public advertisement. It was on the Sabbath of the 26th of November. The avowed object was to attend a Charity Sermon in St Patrick's church [cathedral], to be performed by one of the brethren, named [Revd. J.A.] Coghlan.

We have frequently noticed [reported] the description of persons who composed the different cellar lodges of Barrack-street,[78] where every cavern is a lodge

---

77 It can be presumed that this report, like nearly all of the *Irish Magazine & Monthly Asylum for neglected biography*, was written by Walter Cox. While Cox sometimes wrote with little regard for the truth, the present piece has at least the appearance of being substantially true. The son of a blacksmith, Cox was born in Westmeath in 1770. Migrating to Dublin, he worked there as a gunsmith and later as a journalist. There can be little doubt that he was the Walter Cox who was admitted to lodge 324 with twenty-six others in 1795. He was a United Irishman who, according to Madden, turned informer in 1798. The *Irish Magazine*, which he founded in 1807, continued until 1815. Renowned for his scurrility, he was such a thorn in the side of the establishment that they were glad to offer him a pension in 1815 on condition that he left the country. This he did but returned in 1835, two years before his death.   **78** Barrack Street, now Benburb Street, near Royal (until recently Collins) Barracks, was the location of several military lodges.

room, but never did our imagination strain itself so far as to draw such a picture of Dublin Freemasonry as itself exhibited on this holy occasion.

The Duke of Leinster, who is Grand Master, promised to head the procession; and having placed himself, in cog, at one of Grierson's windows,[79] from it he recognized the miscellany of Brothers, but had not courage sufficient to encounter the sneers of the populace, by a public acknowledgment of being the head of one of the most ridiculous and ragged rabbles ever exposed to public ridicule. His Grace sent an excuse, and a promise of fifty pounds to the charity.

A military band, at a signal given, struck up 'God save the King', which was a notice to the Brethren in the adjacent whiskey shops, that the procession was commencing, and in a few minutes, more than a hundred, in a state of intoxication, rolled from their respective tippling stations, into the Exchange.

At half past one they moved, preceded by all the Grand Officers but the Duke, and one Gentleman, who was prevented from attending by Brother Sirr,[80] who had rather inadvertently committed the Senior Grand Warden to Newgate, on the preceding Monday, for forging stamps.

After the Grand Lodge, a Liberty Lodge, which holds its mystic meetings in Crosstick-Alley,[81] paraded, and indeed they furnished a very candid representation of the decay of everything in that extensive district, but loyalty, which, thanks to a large barrack and some charity bread, weekly distributed, keeps the spirit of the constitution in pretty good order ...

They were succeeded by another lodge much better dressed, having better access to the shelves of a shoemaker, or to the pendant drapery which hangs ready-made in Plunkett-street, where the linen of the unfortunate, who have been compelled to resign worldly affairs at Kilmainham, offer themselves to other customers, until time prepare them for the paper manufacture.[82] These well-dressed Brothers were all Policemen, preceded by Brother Farrell, as Master, Bullbrooks and Saw Shin, Wardens.

Next were the loose Brethren of no. 21, as the fast ones were under the keys of Brothers Ormsby and Bournes,[83] or recruiting [recuperating ?] themselves over their noggins of Kale [broth], in the Dominions of Ben II, King of the Beggars. Beresford's Black, Master, Brothers Gribbin and Biblemouth, Wardens.

The next, were the Golden-lane Lodges, whose respective strength, being much reduced, by claims made on their members, which required their attendance in the several depositories, caused by disputes with their bread merchants,

79 The duke of Leinster was elected grand master in June 1813. Grierson's were king's printers with premises in Parliament Street.   80 Brother Sirr was Major Henry Charles Sirr, the head of the Dublin police and a prime target for Cox's scurrility since the inception of his magazine. 81 Crosstick Alley joined Meath Street with Ashe Street in the Liberties.   82 Plunkett Street was just off Patrick Street. 'Those who have been compelled to resign worldly affairs at Kilmainham' were those who had been hanged at Kilmainham Jail.   83 Lodge no. 21 in the Dublin nomenclature was lodge no. 324 (Cox's old lodge) in the national nomenclature. There is a play here on the words 'fast' (locked up) and 'loose' (at large). F.G. Bournes was the gaoler (i.e. governor) of Newgate and presumably Ormsby was also on the staff of that prison.

or by the mistakes of jurymen,[84] the aggregate of the outs was not sufficient to compose more than one respectable body, so, uniting their respective standards, they marched as one lodge to the place of Charity.

More than four hundred Brothers, not classified, followed, and were they not sanctioned by the respectability of Luke Dignam[85] and Nosey Mehain, they would have been mistaken for a crowd of Beggarmen who had put on their worst garments, to show they were not making anything of the bad times than public misfortune allow to other people, who depend on the casual benevolence that yielding to fear or charity, relieve those who love working as, it is said, the Devil loves Holy water.

The most remarkable was the Santry Lodge, and to the credit of the Santry Bank, its Governor Lord Santry, the Clerks and Runners made as elegant a turnout as any we remember. My Lord was dressed with a superb blue ribbon, to which a gold Cross, a pistol and whistle hung. He was mounted on his Dunboyne hunter, covered with housings embroidered richly with the Eye, Ladder and Cock, emblems of sight, elevation and vigilance, as useful on Santry road as in Masonry. His Lordship's Wardens were Nosey McKeown and Val Dulcimer. The Deacons, armed with white rods, pistollated, or crowned with pistols, were Jumping Moloney and Stop Chaise Magee.[86]

The military lodges, forty-one in number, from as many cellars in Barrack-street, such an assemblage of mutilated Brethren we did not expect to see out of the Hospital of Incurables.[87] Among three hundred there were not thirty who had on anything like a nose, more than sixty were on sycamore legs, and not less than a hundred, though deficient in several members, were rendered still more incapable of any progressive movement, by an occasional application of whiskey. The tippling souls had the precaution to take out their wives, and as living crutches, they succeeded in keeping matters as upright as things would permit. This part of the fraternity were as loyal as the air of Barrack-street can inculcate; as the first duty of a soldier and a subject, they damned the Irish and sang God Save the King, until they arrived before the pulpit, which would not be very easy to accomplish had not Major Sirr very prudently allowed the Police Horse to act as a body guard, as his honour perceived some indications of an offensive movement on the part of the populace, which might have interrupted the cause of Charity, by breaking the remnant bones of the benevolent Brethren. The public may form

---

84 Possibly refers to those committed to jail for debts. 85 Luke Dignam was presumably the tavern-keeper of that name in Trinity Street. 86 Santry Road on the northern outskirts of the city was renowned for footpads. According to vol. 7, p. 287 of the *Irish Magazine* Nosey McKeon kept a gaming-house in Dame Street and Stop Chaise Magee was 'a fashionable robber'. The title Baron Barry of Santry became extinct in 1751. As to who was masquerading as Lord Santry in 1815, it was presumably a member of the Domville family who had acquired the Santry estate some time after 1751. 87 The mutilated state of the members of the military lodges was of course the legacy of years of war.

a very accurate estimate of the liberal contributions which the purses and charity of these fellows were capable of affording.

Mr McNulty, the Brewer, and Mr Hayes, the Distiller, for the first time in their lives went to church,[88] to the edification of the brotherhood; and some entertain hopes on their parts that their respective liquids will hereafter meet a liberal preference with every brother who has a mouth and a ten penny.

---

88 That is, to a protestant church. The usage was that protestants went to church while catholics went to chapel. McNulty and Hayes were apparently catholics.

6

Catholic merchants, traders and manufacturers

In any treatment of the subject of this chapter some consideration should first be given to the position of catholics *vis-à-vis* the Dublin guilds. The guild system in the city can be traced back to the Norman Invasion itself, when in 1171 Henry II granted to 'his men of Bristol' the right to set up guilds. Although the merchants' guild, established in the early thirteenth century, in its earlier form represented more than fifty different occupations, there was a tendency with the passage of time for separate guilds to be established for the different trades and occupations so that by the end of the seventeenth century there were twenty-three guilds in existence catering for merchants, tailors, butchers, tanners, goldsmiths, barber-surgeons, skinners, saddlers, bakers, glovers, carpenters and other building trades, cooks, gardeners, smiths, shoemakers, weavers, tallow-chandlers, coopers, hatters, cutlers-painters-printers-stationers, furriers, brewers and joiners. Only one new guild was established in the eighteenth century, the apothecaries who had previously been included with the barber-surgeons.[1]

There was a link between the guilds and the government of the city in that the common council of the corporation was formed from representatives of the various guilds – thirty-one from the merchants and two, three or four each from the others, depending on size or importance. Being a freeman of a guild and consequently, though not invariably, a freeman of the city, carried with it the added privilege of a vote in parliamentary elections for the two Dublin city seats. The system as outlined could be said to be an early manifestation of corporatism, but, lamentably, it was one from which the voices of the journeymen and workers were entirely absent.

The protestantization of the country in the sixteenth century was felt also in the guilds where the oath required of freemen was such as no catholic could take. Even in Charles II's supposedly more liberal reign, stringent regulations against catholics continued in operation in Dublin and were even added to. Under an order dated 20 September 1672 by the lord lieutenant and council, the master and wardens of the Dublin guilds were among those required, *inter alia*, to take the oath of supremacy.[2] Meanwhile in 1662 the guild merchant resolved that no

---

1 Webb, John J., *The guilds of Dublin*, Dublin 1929, reissued London 1970, passim.   2 *Irish*

brother should henceforth take an apprentice who was a catholic and in 1679 the same guild deprived catholics of the privilege of being a quarter-brother.[3] The latter was a person who paid a fee every quarter to the guild concerned, the return from which must have been minimal for he was not allowed to take any part in the administration of the guild. However, the rules of the guild were not the law of the land and the restrictions mentioned did not prevent catholics from functioning as merchants without reference to the guild. In any event, the rules do not appear to have been enforced with much vigour. The fact that in 1724 a number of catholic merchants signed the guild's protest against Wood's Half-pence (see below), is a tacit acknowledgement of their existence at that time.

The position of catholics changed fundamentally and briefly with the coming of James II to the throne in 1685, when catholics took control of the guilds and of the corporation and a catholic became lord mayor of Dublin. With the defeat of James catholics returned to the same parlous situation as before, but it appears that in most guilds they were accepted as quarter-brothers. By 1707 so many papists had 'repaired to the city' and followed so many trades therein that the common council resolved that it was the duty of all masters and wardens of guilds, and of magistrates to oblige all persons (except weavers in the linen trade) who were permitted to follow their trades 'as quarterers or otherwise', not to keep more than two apprentices at a time and that for no less a term than seven years.[4] This resolution was given legislative effect by section 37 of the popery act of 1709 (8 Anne c. 3).

Catholics, however, did not consider it any great boon to be allowed to carry on their trade or business subject to the quarterage payments mentioned, particularly as they got nothing in return for such payments. One of the earliest objections to the quarterage system is to be found in Fr Cornelius Nary's pamphlet *The case of the Roman catholics of Ireland* (1724) where he points out that 'neither are any of the tradesmen or shopkeepers of this religion suffered to work in their respective trades, or sell their goods in any of the cities of Ireland, except they pay exorbitant taxes which they call Quarterages to the respective masters of their corporations'.[5]

Meanwhile the catholic tradesmen of Cork city were becoming more restive and vocal and by 1731 they were threatening to prove in court the illegality of claims for quarterage payments. Matters, however, did not come properly to a head until 1759 when, following the committal to prison by the mayor of Cork of

statutes, vol. 3, p. 207. Similar orders were made at the same time in respect of the other Irish cities and corporate towns. These orders must be seen as qualifying considerably Cornelius Nary's claim in *The case of the Roman catholics of Ireland* (p. 115) that in the reign of Charles II 'Roman Catholic merchants, dealers and tradesmen were aldermen and burgesses in cities, and freemen in towns and corporations over all the kingdom'.   3 Webb, J.J., op. cit., p. 148.   4 Gilbert, John T. (ed.), *Calendar of the ancient records of Dublin* (CARD), vol. VI, pp 379–80.   5 Nary, Cornelius, *The case of the Roman catholics of Ireland* included in Hugh Reily's *Genuine history of Ireland*, 1762 edition, p. 118.

certain catholic traders for non-payment of quarterages, a case was brought on behalf of the traders in the court of king's bench, where judgment was given against the mayor. There was then the extraordinary upturn where a catholic trader 'publicly arrested the mayor and behaved with great disrespect'.[6]

Following this reversal the guilds tried a different tack by promoting legislation in the Irish parliament with the object of legalizing quarterage payments. Such legislation required the approval of the English privy council and when the bill was first sent to the council in 1768, it was thrown out by the 'benevolent intervention' of the lord lieutenant, Lord Townshend, who again effectively scuppered a similar bill in 1772 by simply not transmitting it to London. An important factor in the defeat of these bills was the lobbying carried on in Dublin and London by the Catholic Committee which had been formed in 1756.[7]

The lord lieutenant's treatment of the quarterage bills was the prelude to a number of measures for catholic relief – a special oath for catholics in 1774, and relief acts in 1778 and 1782. In 1792 an act concerned mainly with the admission of catholics to the legal professions included a clause (section 16) repealing the provision in the 1709 popery act limiting the number of apprentices a catholic, engaged in trade or manufacture, might take.

By section 7 of the major relief act of 1793 it was enacted, *inter alia*, that 'it shall and may be lawful for Papists ... to be a member of any lay-body corporate' without taking the oaths and subscribing the declaration against transubstantiation up to then required, 'any law, statute or bylaw of any corporation to the contrary notwithstanding'. Catholics availing of this provision were, however, required to take a special oath set out in the act together with the special oath for catholics in the 1774 act.[8] But despite the very clear intention of the section that catholics would be enabled to be freemen of guilds and, furthermore, to be freemen of the city and entitled to a vote in parliamentary elections for the two Dublin seats, only a handful succeeded in being admitted freemen of guilds and none at all freemen of the city, although the latter point was contested in the court of king's bench.[9]

However, with the exception of the goldsmiths, the guilds by then had ceased to have any control over the trades for which they were originally established and their sole *raison d'être* was the continuance of protestant domination of Dublin corporation and the exclusion of Dublin catholics from the parliamentary franchise.[10] The refusal to admit catholics to the guilds did not, therefore, prevent them from achieving success in their chosen trade or craft.

6 Wall, Maureen, *Catholic Ireland in the eighteenth century*, Dublin 1989, pp 65–6. 7 Ibid., pp 68–9. There were further unsuccessful quarterage bills in 1773, 1775 and 1778. 8 33 George III c. 21. 9 *Municipal Corporations of Ireland: First report of the commissioners – Report on city of Dublin*, 1836, p. 279. 10 The position of catholics in Co. Dublin, which included the suburbs of the city, was quite different. There, as in the case of the other counties, from 1793 to 1829 catholic freeholders of forty shillings valuation and upwards were eligible to vote in elections for the two county seats in accordance with section 1 of the 1793 relief act.

We can now turn to a consideration of the extent of catholic participation throughout the century in the different sectors of trade, commerce and manufacture and in different crafts and occupations. With regard to trade there were several pronouncements, mainly by protestant commentators from the early years of the century onwards, on the size, nationally, of catholic involvement. We have already noted above the complaint of Dublin Corporation in 1707 that great numbers of papists had 'of late repaired to this city to follow several trades therein'.

In 1717 Archbishop King, in a letter lamenting the departure of large numbers of protestants to the West Indies, pointed out that papists, being made incapable to purchase lands, 'have turned themselves to trade and [have] already ingrossed almost all the trade of the Kingdom'.[11] King returned to the subject in April 1728 when he enumerated the advantages which the catholic merchant had over the protestant:

> As to the trade of the Kingdom, they [catholics] have got the best of it into their hands and have several advantages of the Protestants. A Popish merchant is better received in Popish countries with which we trade, than protestants; and the generality of farmers and graziers in Ireland being Papists, they choose to put their goods into the hands of those of their own religion; and, lastly, the country assists them in running their goods [smuggling] both out and inward.[12]

Meanwhile in 1724 Fr Cornelius Nary, pointing out in his *The case of the Roman catholics of Ireland* reasons why it would be impolitic for the government to proceed with passing into law a stringent popery bill then before parliament, claimed that 'Roman Catholic merchants and dealers carry on more than half the trade of the Kingdom, and pay more Custom and Duty for imported goods, than all the Protestants in it'.[13] If the bill should pass, he went on, all these merchants and dealers would be necessitated to leave the country, to the great diminution of the revenue, and 'God knows in how many years this could be retrieved, if ever'.

In 1749 the anonymous author of the pamphlet *The ax laid to the root* complained that popish merchants 'had jockeyed out the Protestant merchants, who were treated with less favour in Popish countries'.[14] Later in the century, in February 1774, Clotworthy Rowley, in a debate in the Irish house of commons, claimed that catholics in Ireland possessed three-quarters of the trade.[15]

11 King, Sir Charles, *A great archbishop of Dublin*, London 1906, p. 208 – Archbishop King's letter of 6 February 1717 to the archbishop of Canterbury.   12 Ibid., letter dated 27 April 1728 from King to Edward Southwell. The latter had been chief secretary in Ireland in 1710 and secretary of state, London, in 1720.   13 Nary, C., op. cit., pp 130–1.   14 Fagan, Patrick, *Divided loyalties: the question of the oath for Irish catholics in the eighteenth century*, Dublin 1997, p. 79.   15 Brady, John, *Catholics and catholicism in the eighteenth century press*, Maynooth 1965, pp 156–7. Rowley put forward the interesting theory that 'the greatest part of the trade of any country is carried on by those who are not of the established religion of that country: in Turkey by Jews and Christians; in India by the Gentoos; in France by the Huguenots; in Amsterdam

It is evident that in all these cases the commentator had in mind, not Dublin, but the country as a whole, and that in nearly all cases it suited his line of argument to exaggerate the extent to which trade was in catholic hands. The first pronouncement by Dublin Corporation was factual and restrained enough and hardly exaggerated the position. The comments by Archbishop King, the first made to the archbishop of Canterbury and the second to Edward Southwell, were made in the context of King's alarmist claims about the deterioration of the protestant interest in Ireland. It also obviously suited Cornelius Nary's book to exaggerate the catholic presence in trade. The claim of the author of *The ax laid to the root* was probably factual; it was made in the context of a proposal to allow catholic merchants to purchase lands and so give them a stake in the country and a real, though selfish, interest in being loyal to the government, but with a consequent diminution in the amount of trade in their hands. Clotworthy Rowley's claim was made in the course of a debate on a bill (defeated) to permit catholics to take lots of ground on building leases for an unlimited term of years.

In recent times the claims of the foregoing commentators regarding the size of catholic representation in trade in the country as a whole have been challenged by various writers, including Cullen, Connolly[16] and Dickson, the latter being of the view that 'even by 1775 less than a third of Dublin's wholesale merchants were catholics'.[17]

We are here concerned specifically with the situation in Dublin and, not alone with catholic representation in trade, but in the other fields mentioned in the title of this chapter. As to the reasons for catholic success in trade, a few more can be added to those mentioned by Archbishop King.

Firstly, it has to be said that engaging in trade or manufacture at all would be considered *infra dig.* by any family, catholic or protestant, with pretensions to nobility or gentility. Even catholic families down on their luck following the forfeiture of their estates, could have qualms about going into trade as an alternative means of earning a living. Thus, when John O'Brien sought to be appointed bishop of Cloyne in 1747, an attestation of his nobility, made to the Pretender on his behalf by certain catholic gentry from Co. Cork, pointed out that O'Brien's parents had 'always preserved the sentiments and good principles of their loyal ancestors, from whom they have never degenerated by following any vile or mechanical profession, but have always lived in a decent and credible manner in a farming way ...'.[18] However, this is a point which should not be laboured to any great extent, even in the case of protestants, for the reality was that the majority of protestants did not belong to the landed gentry, but were to be found in the

by those of all religions; in England by the Dissenters and here [Ireland] by the Roman Catholics who possess three-quarters of the trade.'   16 Cullen, Louis M., *Anglo-Irish trade 1660–1800*, Manchester 1968, p. 23 and Connolly, S.J., *Religion, law and power: the making of protestant Ireland 1660–1760*, Oxford 1992, p. 148.   17 Dickson, David, *New foundations: Ireland 1660–1800*, Dublin 1987, p. 121.   18 Fagan, Patrick (ed.), *Ireland in the Stuart papers*, Dublin 1995, vol. 2, p. 69.

cities and larger towns carrying on the usual trading, commercial and manufacturing businesses.[19]

Secondly, as we have seen in chapter 1, the quadrupling of Dublin's population between 1700 and 1800 was accomplished almost entirely by migration from the provinces, for the most part from the Leinster counties, all staunchly catholic. This migration of catholics has to be seen as the primary reason for the change in Dublin's status as a mainly protestant city at the beginning of the century to its being a mainly catholic city at the close. It was to be expected that many of these migrants would make good in the big city — it is a phenomenon which constantly repeats itself — and in the fullness of time set up as merchants, grocers, publicans, drapers etc. and as craftsmen of various types. It was also to be expected that the increased catholic population would rally to the support of catholic businesses, for catholics were notorious for patronizing their co-religionists to the exclusion of protestant businesses.

THE MERCHANTS

Having adverted to the reasons for a significant catholic presence in trade, commerce and manufacture, we can now proceed to try to evaluate, however roughly and unsatisfactorily, sector by sector, the extent of such presence in Dublin city, starting with the merchants. It should be noted that the term 'merchant' was often used in the eighteenth century as an umbrella to cover a whole range of persons engaged in all kinds of trade and even manufacture. In the list in *Wilson's Dublin Directory* of 'merchants, traders and others', commencing in 1762, persons calling themselves merchants accounted for only about 20 to 25 per cent of the total. In the list of 307 catholic 'gentry, merchants and citizens of Dublin' who signed the address to the lord lieutenant in December 1759, merchants accounted for only about one-third.[20] The term 'merchant', it is suggested, had connotations of respectability which led to its being used as a cloak for the less respectable. We are here concerned with the narrower concept, with the dictionary definition of merchant as 'a wholesale trader, especially with foreign countries'.

When in 1724 the Dublin merchants issued a statement proposing what amounted to a boycott of Woods' Halfpence, it was signed by 298 merchants who were free of the guild and, therefore, by definition protestant, and by seventy-four who were not free of the guild.[21] Some of these latter would have been catholic but probably not many of them for it is known that catholics, intent on keeping a low profile and literally minding their own business, generally did not intervene in the Woods' Halfpence dispute. Some seven of the names on the list, however,

19 Fagan, P., op. cit in note 14, p. 21.   20 *Dublin Gazette* of 1 December 1759.   21 Ibid. of 18–22 August 1724.

can be identified from other sources as catholic viz. Thomas Woulfe, Miles Reily, Thomas Luttrell, Pat Creagh, George Usher, Edmund Goold and Thomas Hall.[22] Assuming that no more than twenty of the seventy-four were catholic, protestant merchants, between free and not free, would have totalled about 350. For there to be any substance, in the case of Dublin, in the claims made by Nary and King about this time, as to the size of catholic involvement in trade, there would need to have been close on 400 catholic merchants in Dublin. This in turn would mean that the total number of merchants in the city would be close to 750. But the first list published by Wilson in 1762 contained only about 470 merchants and this was twenty-eight years after 1724 and in respect of a greatly expanded city. Even after allowing for some significant deficiency in Wilson's 1762 list, it seems clear that in 1724 the number of catholic merchants in Dublin must have been considerably less that the number of protestant ones and that claims that 'they had ingrossed almost all the trade' (King) or 'carried on more than half the trade of the Kingdom' (Nary) were wide of the mark where Dublin was concerned. I am assuming in all this – and it seems a reasonable assumption – that on average the volume of business carried on by a catholic merchant was no greater, and probably significantly less, than that carried on by a protestant merchant.

Turning to the mid-century, in the list of freemen for 1749 already mentioned, out of 2,272 freemen from all twenty-four guilds, 487, or 21 per cent, belonged to the merchants' guild. To get some idea of catholic participation, the figure of 487 protestant merchants can be compared with the number of merchants, including catholic and protestant, in Wilson's list for 1762, which, as we have noted above, was about 470. Again, after allowing for some deficiency in Wilson's list, it seems clear from these lists that catholic merchants at the time in question can have been only a minority.

The 307 catholics who signed the address to the lord lieutenant in December 1759 provide a sort of profile of catholic participation in various trades and crafts at that time. The names of the signatories have been arranged alphabetically and are set out in appendix 12, pp 184–6. The occupations of the signatories did not appear in the original press announcement, but they have now been deduced for some 277 of them from various sources and are included in the appendix.[23] We cannot, of course, guarantee that all of these identifications are correct but over

---

22 Woulfe and Reily are mentioned in a house of lords investigation in 1733 (see chapter 2), Luttrell, Creagh and Usher in a postulation of Stephen MacEgan as archbishop of Dublin in 1729, Goold in the 1759 address to the lord lieutenant and Hall may be the 'honest Catholic [wine] merchant' mentioned by Swift – see Harold Williams (ed.), *The correspondence of Jonathan Swift*, Oxford 1965, vol. 4, p. 469.   23 Some 200 have been identified from the list of merchants etc. in *Wilson's Dublin Directory* for 1762. Others have been identified from Mrs Maureen Wall's CQR list mentioned in note 26 below, subscribers to contemporary catholic-oriented books, Sir Arthur Vicars' *Index of prerogative wills, Diocese of Dublin index to the act or grant books and original wills* and contemporary newspapers.

90 per cent of them probably are. There can be no doubt that the name John Corry disguises John Curry, the physician and Charles O'Conor's main associate in the campaign for relief from the penal laws, for it is known from O'Conor's correspondence that Curry signed this address.[24] The James Troy, who figures in the list, was in all probability the father of Archbishop Troy.

The address arose from catholic anxiety to show loyalty to the government following the outbreak of the Seven Years' War and the threat of a French invasion of Britain or Ireland. However, the subscribers are by no means a complete list of the catholic gentry, merchants and citizens of Dublin at that time, since the address was opposed by many catholics, including the archbishop, Lincoln. Of those identified some eighty-four were merchants of various kinds, thirty-four grocers, eighteen brewers, seventeen linen drapers, eight tanners, seven each woollen-drapers, chandlers, apothecaries and weavers, five each clothiers and salesmasters, four each distillers, booksellers, gents, physicians and butchers, three each haberdashers, shoemakers, surgeons, glovers and pinmakers, followed by an assortment of occupations with one or two each. In a few cases one has to choose between two or more competing occupations. For example, John Kelly could be the physician or the brewer or the wine merchant of that name. Similarly, Thomas Brown could have been a carpenter, feather merchant or handkerchief printer. Many of those not identified may have belonged to the mysterious, eighteenth century category called 'gent'.

A greater degree of transparency with regard to the number of catholic merchants manifests itself with the advent of the Catholic Qualification Rolls (CQR). These rolls, as already noted, had their origin in the provision in the 1778 and 1782 relief acts requiring catholics, who wished to avail of the reliefs in those acts, to take the special oath already set out in a 1774 act. Rolls, which came to be known as the Catholic Qualification Rolls, were required to be maintained in the Rolls Office containing the names of persons who had taken the oath and these were transferred to the Public Record Office in 1867. The rolls themselves were destroyed in the fire in the Public Record Office in 1922 and, as far as Dublin is concerned, all that remains is an index covering the periods 1778–90 and 1793–6. As well as the date on which the oath was taken, this index, ideally, contains the name, address and occupation of the person concerned.[25]

Some years ago Mrs Maureen Wall extracted from this index for the period 1778–82 information on occupations in respect of 1,250 merchants, manufacturers and traders from Dublin city. Although the information extracted is spread over five years, in fact 85 per cent of those listed took the oath in the period

24 Ward, R.E., Wrynn, J.F. & Ward, C.C. (eds), *Letters of Charles O'Conor of Belanagare*, Washington DC 1988, p. 80.   25 See Fagan, P., op. cit. in note 14 pp 179–85 for further information. As far as Dublin is concerned, the index stops short at 1796, although there were manifestly a larger number of enrolments after that date.

October–December 1778.[26] The information on Wall's list would be all the more valuable if the number in a particular occupation could be compared with the number for that occupation in Wilson's list, on the assumption that the latter represented the total number in that occupation in the city. However, a number of limitations to such an exercise, on further consideration, emerged. Firstly, of the 1,250 persons in Wall's list, only 369, or 30 per cent, appear in Wilson's list for 1780. This surprisingly small percentage can be explained to some extent by the fact that Wall's list covers a wider spread of occupations than Wilson's – occupations not covered by Wilson account for about 150 persons of the 1,250 on Wall's list – but the absence of catholics from Wilson's list was probably due in the main to an innate fear of exposing themselves, even after the relief measures in the 1778 act, although there would be some small operators who considered themselves unworthy of inclusion.

Secondly, while ideally the information in Wall should be compared with that in Wilson for the year 1779 or 1780, it so happens that the only year for which Wilson's list is compartmentalized to show the numbers in each trade or occupation, is 1768, and while the total numbers in Wilson's list remained constant at around 2,700 for the years in question, there must have been differences in the numbers in each trade or occupation. Thirdly, there were a number of catholics in the various trades and occupations who did not bother to take the oath, or who did so before or after the period covered by Wall. However, for the purposes of this exercise, these could be said to offset more or less the number of protestants in those trades or occupations who do not appear in Wilson. Subject to these limitations we can proceed to compare the number for each occupation in Wall with the comparable number in Wilson, the latter increased to take account of the number in Wall who are absent from Wilson. In the following pages, as we proceed to perform a like exercise for different trades and occupations, this latter will be referred to *as the number in Wilson as adjusted.*

In the case of the merchants, Mrs Wall's list disclosed 178 Dublin merchants of all kinds who had taken the oath. However, some ninety-five of the merchants on Wall's list are not to be found in Wilson's, and the number, 483, in the latter's list requires to be increased to that extent, resulting in a revised total of 578. A comparison of the 178 merchants in Wall with this revised total leads to the conclusion that only about 30 per cent of Dublin merchants were catholic in 1780. What percentage of the total volume of trade this represented is another and, it appears, a quite unquantifiable matter. Certainly, some of the catholic merchants, such as Denis T. O'Brien, the Dermotts, Thomas Braughall and Edward Byrne, carried on very substantial businesses. According to William Drennan, Byrne was in 1801 'the first merchant' in the city.[27]

---

26 Wall, Maureen, 'The Catholic merchants, manufacturers and traders of Dublin 1778–1782' in *Reportorium Novum*, vol. 2, no. 2, pp 298–323. There was a requirement in the 1778 relief act to take the oath before 31 December 1778. When the courts opened in October there was, then, a scramble to take the oath before the end of the year.   27 Chart, D.A. (ed.), *The Drennan letters,*

THE COMMITTEE OF MERCHANTS

By 1760 many members of the merchant guild had become disenamoured of the guild as a vehicle for promoting the trading and commercial interests of merchants. Accordingly, in 1761 a group of merchants of the city decided to form themselves into 'a voluntary society composed indiscriminately of all merchants who were willing to join in defraying the necessary expense of such an institution, the mere objects of which were the defence of trade against all illegal impositions and the solicitation of such laws as might be beneficial to it'. The reason given for the setting up of this breakaway body was the 'long experience of the utter inattention of corporate bodies to the interest of trade ... the generality of them entirely taken up in contests for little distinctions of pre-eminence among themselves and eagerly engaged in the pursuit of honours or emoluments of magistracy'.[28] The society elected a committee of twenty-one wholesale merchants, generally known as the Committee of Merchants, to carry into effect its purposes, one of the more practical of which turned out to be the organization of lotteries for the benefit of the Dublin hospitals.

The minutes of the committee are available only from June 1767. At that time there were four catholic merchants, Anthony and Owen Dermott, Michael Cosgrave and John Connor, who regularly attended meetings, but there were presumably catholic members from the outset in 1761 since the society from which the committee was elected was composed, as stated above, *indiscriminately* from all merchants.[29] Catholic representation later increased to five.

On Lord Townshend's appointment as lord lieutenant in August 1767 the committee were quick to present a humble address to him indicating how happy they should think themselves if under his government 'we shall be able to point out any regulations relative to commerce that may prove worthy of your approbation and countenance'. In October of the same year they presented a petition to parliament for the erection of an exchange on Cork Hill. However, this spurred Dublin Corporation to present a rival petition for the same purpose, which in

Belfast, 1931, p. 311, William Drennan to Mrs McTier, Dublin 17 April 1801. **28** Royal Irish Academy mss 12.D.29 & 3.C.25, titled incorrectly as 'Merchant Guild minute books'. In fact they are the minute books of the breakaway Committee of Merchants. The mss are duplicates of each other, except that 12.D.29 commences on 17 June 1767 and ends on 30 April 1782 while 3.C.25 commences on 10 February 1768 and ends on 10 February 1783. In the absence of pagination the various events recorded below will be found in the mss under the dates mentioned. The information here about the committee's origin is contained in *The case of the merchants of the city of Dublin* dated 21 January 1768. **29** The members of the Committee of Merchants are listed in *Wilson's Dublin Directory* for the years 1776 to 1783, when the committee was dissolved. The same five catholics were on the committee throughout these years viz. Anthony and Owen Dermott, Michael Cosgrave, Thomas Braughall and Denis T. O'Brien. Alexander McDonnell, Lurgan Street, who appears on the committee for the first time in 1780, was an alderman and therefore a protestant and should not be confused with the catholic Alexander McDonnell, Francis Street.

turn prompted the committee to remark that there never would have been an exchange if the city had to wait for the corporation to make the first move about it. Nevertheless, when the proposal was proceeded with, the committee agreed in January 1768 that the planning, building and administration of the exchange should be in the hands of a named committee, all of whom appear to have been protestants, and that all future additions to this committee should be wholesale freemen (and therefore protestants) from the guild of merchants. Catholic merchants were afforded some recognition in the appointment of Anthony Dermott as one of the three trustees for the funds of the exchange.[30]

From April 1769 onwards the committee carried on a protracted campaign against the building of a new custom house (at its present location), involving petitions to parliament, to the lord lieutenant, to the king and to the English privy council when the heads of a bill in the matter had been submitted to the latter. They argued that the new custom house would be too far removed from the new exchange and from the main manufacturing area on the south-west of the city, but their principal fear was that a custom house on the site proposed would strengthen the case for a new bridge on the Liffey east of Essex Bridge, a development they were strongly opposed to since it would upset the status quo. They also opposed a proposal for building new courts of justice in College Green, although the site was only about five minutes walk from the old Four Courts near Christ Church.

In March 1778 the committee made representations in regard to the (Dublin) Circular Road bill. In January 1780 they expressed concern about regulations regarding the importation of sugar from the Colonies and in July 1780 they were having problems with regard to drawback on hops. The catholic members, in particular Anthony Dermott, played a prominent part in the committee. Dermott occasionally took the chair at meetings. In January 1770 he produced to the committee heads of a bill, prepared at the request of Sir Lucius O'Brien MP, for carrying into execution a scheme for inland navigation from Dublin to the Shannon. In February 1772 he was a member of a subcommittee of eight appointed to wait on key members of parliament in regard to a bankruptcy bill.

The declaration of the legislative independence of the Irish parliament in 1782 led to a much greater degree of activity in that parliament and a great increase in commercial regulations, heightening the need for a proper chamber of commerce for the city. Plans for such a chamber were announced in 1783. Membership would be open to any merchant or trader resident within the city 'or its dependencies' on payment of one guinea. The operation of the chamber would be in the hands of a council whose business it would be to confer when necessary with persons in high stations, to have a watchful attention to the proceedings of

---

30 Cullen, L.M., *Princes & pirates: the Dublin Chamber of Commerce 1783–1983*, Dublin 1983, p. 36. Dermott and other catholic merchants were also prominent in setting up fire and general insurance companies in the 1770s.

parliament respecting trade in both kingdoms, to inspect into methods of transacting business in Dublin and to contrive and recommend improvements therein.

Clearly, such a chamber would render the Committee of Merchants redundant. At their last recorded meeting on 10 February 1783 the committee were profuse in their welcome for the proposed chamber and thought themselves happy in resigning their appointment 'when on the liberal plan now proposed, a council of the Chamber of Commerce shall be elected'. There were only six persons present at this meeting, two of them, Denis T. O'Brien and Michael Cosgrave, being catholics.

THE CHAMBER OF COMMERCE

Initially the chamber was a great success. There were 293 subscribers of a guinea and in March 1783 a forty-one member council was elected.[31] Some ten of the forty-one were catholics and this means that proportionately catholic representation on the council of the chamber was much the same as on the Committee of Merchants. Travers Hartley, a dissenter, was elected first president but one of the two vice-president posts went to a catholic in the person of Anthony Dermott. When he died the following year his place was taken by another catholic, Denis T. O'Brien.

For the first couple of years the council was kept very busy with aspects of foreign trade, in particular trade with Portugal, on the subject of which the president and two vice-presidents presented an address to the lord lieutenant. On 10 October 1783, at a largely attended meeting, the council passed a resolution advocating protection of home industry by the imposition of import duties on a range of imported manufactured goods.[32] During 1785 proceedings were dominated by Pitt's Commercial Propositions, amounting to a commercial union between Britain and Ireland, which the chamber opposed and the Irish parliament eventually turned down.[33]

However, the early enthusiasm of members was not maintained and expectations were not realized. Due mainly to friction between radical and conservative members, the chamber began to decline in 1787 and effectively ceased in March 1788, although there was a further meeting in February 1791.[34] The chamber was not re-established until 1805.

The Committee of Merchants, then, during its twenty-two year history af-

---

31 *Wilson's Dublin Directory* for 1784, p. 104 where the names of the forty-one member council are listed. The ten catholic members were: Anthony Dermott (now McDermott), Valentine O'Connor, Batchelor's Walk, Denis T. O'Brien, Michael Cosgrave, Edward Byrne, Mullinahack, Hugh Hamil, North Anne Street, Patrick Dease, Usher's Quay, Francis Cahill, Fisher's Lane, Francis McDermott, Arran Quay and John Comerford, Merchants Quay. All these appear in the index to the CQR and can therefore be deemed to be catholics. 32 Cullen, L.M., op. cit in note 30, p. 49. 33 Ibid., p. 51. 34 Ibid., pp 52–4.

forded catholic merchants an opportunity to play a public part in the commercial life of Dublin and to make an input into measures proposed in parliament or elsewhere affecting business or trade. Of the twenty-one members of the committee, it was usual, at least in its later years, for five to be catholic, a representation which was close to what they were entitled to on the basis of their proportion of the trade of the city. Catholic involvement in the Dublin Chamber of Trade established in 1783 was somewhat less marked, but the chamber had an effective life of only a few years before it closed temporarily in 1791.

DUBLIN CATHOLIC MERCHANTS AND THE CATHOLIC COMMITTEE

We have seen in chapter 2 that the leading lights in organizing funds to finance a lobby in London against two bills sent over in 1733 by the Irish parliament for approval by the English privy council, were two Dublin merchants, Thomas Woulfe and Miles Reily. As the century advanced the Dublin merchants – and here the term is used in the all-embracing sense already mentioned – became increasingly vocal and active in the campaign to gain some amelioration of the penal laws. The Catholic Committee was founded in Dublin in 1756 with considerable merchant support, the first secretary being Anthony Dermott.[35] Merchant influence is apparent in the deliberations of the committee in its early years inasmuch as the successful campaign against the payment of quarterage and against the quarterage bills proposed by the Irish parliament was accomplished mainly by the efforts of the merchants, not only from Dublin but from Cork and other cities as well.

The merchants were indeed a bit too active for some people's tastes. Archbishop Lincoln opposed their address to the lord lieutenant in 1759 ostensibly on the grounds that they were 'no people in the eye of the law'.[36] Catholics' best ploy, according to some clerics, was to continue to keep a low profile and so avoid being taken note of by the authorities. Archbishop Skerritt of Tuam put it this way in a letter to Charles O'Conor in 1778:

> The secular gentlemen of that city [Dublin] assume an authority, which I think they have no right to do, that is, to put everything their wise heads suggest in the name of the whole Kingdom. I was always of the opinion that the less we meddled and the more insignificant we appeared in the eye of the Government, the better, but they by their addresses and representations make the Government think us to be of some consequence, therefore to be guarded against.[37]

35 Ward, Wrynn & Ward (eds), op. cit., p. 9.   36 Ibid., p. 79. The remark was probably a reaction to the pronouncement from the bench in the Saule case – see note 38 following.   37 Ward, R.E. & Ward, C.C. (eds), *Letters of Charles O'Conor of Belanagare*, Ann Arbor, Michigan 1980, addendum to letter no. 68 of 21 February 1760.

The Catholic Committee got a second wind in the early 1770s and once again the Dublin merchants were prominent in its deliberations during the epoch-making period of the relief acts. Disagreements in the committee led to the gentry and clergy members leaving it and to the emergence in 1790 of a vibrant and active organization under the leadership of John Keogh, a wealthy silk mercer. In accordance with the Convention Act of 1793 the committee was compelled to cease its activities, but by then it had, with the very comprehensive relief act of 1793, achieved much of its original aims.

LIFESTYLE OF CATHOLIC MERCHANTS

The lifestyle of the catholic merchants in the first half of the century could be said to be generally understated and unpretentious. Some shunned any public display of wealth, lest such display might excite the envy of protestant neighbours, with the possibility of their ruin through being the object of a discovery suit under the property provisions of the penal laws. As late as the 1750s the Saule case was an example to all of how catholics might expect to be treated if they dared to step out of line.[38]

As the second half of the century progressed, with a growing feeling of acceptance by the administration if not by the majority in both houses of parliament, catholic merchants, traders and manufacturers became much more self-assured and ostentatious. Nevertheless, increased opulence did not bring with it any prospect of membership of the house of commons, or even of Dublin corporation, or (until 1792) of the legal profession. It also rankled with wealthy catholic merchants that, although they could play some part in commercial affairs through the Committee of Merchants and the Chamber of Commerce, and in

---

38 Mitchel, John, *The history of Ireland from the treaty of Limerick to the present time*, London c.1867, vol. 1, p. 80. Saule, a wine merchant, had angered the establishment by providing a refuge for a young catholic girl who was being pressurized into conforming to the established church. The ensuing court case was notable for the pronouncement from the bench that 'the law did not presume a Papist to exist in the kingdom, nor could they so much as breathe there without the connivance of government'. It is noteworthy that this took place in 1758 when the religious provisions of the penal code had been in abeyance for some years and in the same year as a government-sponsored bill, which would have given official recognition to the catholic clergy, had just failed at the last hurdle. It was a year or so before Dublin catholics had presented an address of loyalty to the lord lieutenant and their representative, Anthony Dermott, had been assured by the speaker of the commons that they could not fail to obtain his Majesty's protection so long as they conducted themselves with duty and affection. The judge's statement was a reminder to catholics, who might be inclined to be losing the run of themselves, as to where exactly they stood when it came to the crunch. There was to be a parallel instance over a hundred years later, in 1865, when the Irish regular orders were reminded from the bench that they had been rendered illegal by the 1829 relief act and that accordingly bequests to members of the orders were invalid.

the setting up of fire and general insurance companies, they found themselves debarred from the governance of prestigious bodies like the Bank of Ireland, the Royal Exchange and the Ballast Office.[39]

Increased wealth and self-assurance prompted social ambitions. Some married their daughters into the landed gentry as when Anthony Dermott's daughter, Mary, married Christopher Fitzsimon Esq. of Glencullen, Co. Dublin and brought him a dowry of £4,500.[40] Two daughters of the merchant, Randal MacDonnell, also married into the landed gentry.[41] Edward Byrne's son, another Edward, married a young lady named Roe who was doubly connected with the nobility through being a step-daughter of Lord Clonmel and a niece of Viscount Landaff.[42] Some sought to become landed gentry themselves by acquiring large tracts of land albeit, prior to the 1778 relief act, on the thirty-one year leases applicable to catholics. John Keogh, mentioned above, who retired from his merchant business in 1787, had by then acquired extensive landed interests in Sligo, Leitrim and Roscommon.[43] Thomas Reynolds had a country house at Rathfarnham in addition to his business premises in Ash Street and was in a position to give his daughters considerable dowries when they married in 1754 and 1762.[44] Archbishop Troy's brother, Walter, a mere grocer from Smithfield, acquired land at Porterstown, Co. Dublin and early in the next century we find he had graduated to esquire when his daughter, Margaret, married Dr Thomas Lee, a nephew of another archbishop, Carpenter.[45]

THE GROCERS

After the merchants, the most numerous occupation category, according to the list in *Wilson's Dublin Directory* for 1768, was the grocers, of whom there were 188. The grocers were never catered for by a guild although the larger and more pretentious ones were inclined to describe themselves as merchants and some of them may even have been members of the merchants' guild. With no guild claiming to represent the grocery trade, catholics might be expected to make a good showing. There were about thirty-four grocers among the signatories of the address to the lord lieutenant in 1759 but this is hardly any indication at all of their true strength, since only the more substantial ones would have had the temerity to sign that address. Some 160 grocers in Mrs Wall's list compare with 312 in Wilson's list as adjusted, indicating that about half of Dublin's grocers were catholic in the later decades of the century.[46]

39 See Theobald MacKenna, a catholic activist, on this point quoted in Thomas Bartlett, *The fall and rise of the Irish nation*, Dublin 1992, p. 130.   40 Wall, M., op. cit in note 6, p. 82.   41 Ibid., p. 182.   42 Farrar, Henry, *Irish marriages 1771–1812*, London 1897, p. 68.   43 Wall, M., op. cit. in note 6, p. 81.   44 Ibid., p. 183.   45 Finn's *Leinster Journal* of 19 July 1809.   46 Wall, M., op. cit. in note 26, p. 301.

THE WEAVERS

The weavers' guild was traditionally associated with the earl of Meath's liberty and their hall in the Coombe survived into modern times. They were a very ancient guild which claimed to have been granted their original charter by Henry II in the twelfth century.[47] Members of the guild would have been predominantly master weavers, employing journeymen and apprentices, and today they would be known as small manufacturers. It was a business subject to often intense competition from foreign imports and to the vagaries of fashion, resulting in high unemployment among the journeymen weavers.

The list of freemen of the Dublin guilds for 1749 included 259 weavers, of whom 180 belonged to the established church, sixty-one were dissenters (many of them, no doubt, huguenots) and eighteen quakers.[48] At 30 per cent the weavers had thus a higher proportion of dissenters and quakers than any other guild except the tanners. As for catholic weavers, only seven have been identified among the signatories to the address to the lord lieutenant in 1759. They fare much better on Mrs Wall's list where there are forty-one, including twelve silk weavers and two linen weavers. These forty-one compare with 173 in Wilson's list as adjusted, indicating that just a quarter of Dublin master weavers were catholic.

THE TAILORS

An ancient and fairly numerous guild, with four seats on the common council of Dublin Corporation, the tailors took precedence after the merchants. Their hall in Back Lane is the only guild-hall still in use. They provided 141 of the freemen on the 1749 list, 114 of these belonging to the established church and twenty-seven dissenters.[49] These would be master tailors, employing journeymen and apprentices.

Although the guild of tailors, late in the eighteenth century and into the nineteenth century, have been portrayed, as will be seen below, as a bigoted, anticatholic body, the available minutes of the guild for the years 1726–50 present a somewhat different picture.[50] Here we find that there appear to have been good relations between the guild and the quarter-brothers who would have been predominantly catholic. The quarter-brothers had, four times a year, their own special dinner to which the guild made a contribution. For example, at Easter 1736

---

47 Webb, J.J., op. cit., p. 57.   48 Royal Irish Academy Haliday pamphlet no. 214. The copy of this pamphlet in the academy was annotated in manuscript in 1759 to show the religious persuasion of those listed. The discrepancy in this and other cases between the number of freemen and the number in Wilson's list is due mainly to the former being lists of individuals while the latter is a list of shops and premises.   49 Ibid. under tailors' guild.   50 Gilbert Library, Dublin ms 80, documents of guild of tailors of Dublin under dates mentioned.

the sum of £2 11s. 7d. was allowed for a goose for the quarter-brother day, while in 1746 £2 1s. 1d. was spent on their mid-summer day, 'having invited several of the quarter-brothers according to the usual custom'.

It is probable that the quarterage dispute soured relations between the guild and the quarter-brothers for the guild relied on quarterage payments for a high proportion of its income. In 1727, for instance, total receipts were £414, of which £128 (31 per cent) came from quarterage payments. At a going rate of 5s. 5d. (5s. English) per quarter, the number of quarter-brothers at that time can be estimated at about 120 as compared with 141 free brothers in the guild in 1749.

Some evidence of a catholic presence among Dublin tailors is apparent as early as 1704 when twelve of the sixty-eight sureties for Dublin priests who registered under the 1704 registration of priests act, were tailors.[51] These must have been master tailors of some substance for recognizances were fixed at £50, a considerable sum at that time and equivalent to about £10,000 today. Catholic representation, at least among the master tailors, may have declined as the century advanced, for only two tailors have been identified among the signatories to the address to the lord lieutenant in 1759. Some twenty years later, Mrs Wall's list shows only nineteen tailors and when this is compared with 117 in Wilson's list as adjusted, it appears that only one-sixth of Dublin master tailors were catholic in 1780.[52]

Like nearly all the guilds, before the century was out, the tailors guild had ceased to exercise any influence in the tailoring trade and it continued in existence solely for political reasons concerned with the maintenance of protestant ascendancy in Dublin Corporation and the exclusion of catholics from the vote in parliamentary elections as far as Dublin city was concerned. In the matter of religious bigotry, the tailors' guild must have been in a league all of its own, if we are to accept as genuine this outburst attributed to a tailor member of the common council of the corporation:

> These Papists may get their emancipation, they may sit in Parliament, they may preside upon the Bench, a Papist may become Lord Chancellor or Privy Councillor; bur never, never shall one of them set foot in the ancient and loyal Guild of Tailors.[53]

The commissioners on municipal corporations reported in 1835 that a strong sectarian feeling pervaded in this as in all the other guilds and that only one catholic had been admitted a freeman of it since the 1793 act. The commissioners went on to say that the trade was numerous in the city of Dublin but that the majority were not members of, or connected with, the guild and did not derive the slightest advantage from its existence.[54]

51 *List of popish priests*, Dublin 1705. Only seven of the sureties were merchants. 52 Wall, M., op. cit. in note 26, p. 301. 53 Mitchel, J., op. cit., vol. 2, p. 149. 54 *Municipal Corporations of Ireland, First Report 1836: Report on city of Dublin*, p. 275.

THE BUTCHERS

The butchers had an unsavoury reputation for violence in eighteenth century Dublin. The Ormond-Liberty faction fights, which disgraced the capital for most of the century, were largely fomented by butchers, although hardly by the master butchers who formed the butchers' guild, but rather by their journeymen, apprentices and butcher's boys. A piece of verse celebrating the riding of the city's franchises in 1767 was none too complimentary:

> Next march the butchers, men inured to toil,
> their brawny limbs, like champions, shine with oil,
> murder and slaughter, knocking in the head,
> are their delight, the trade to which they're bred.[55]

It seems strange that such a heavy, laborious and, at that time, dirty trade should largely be the preserve of members of the established church, but such was apparently the position. Antagonism towards catholics following the trade is evident as early as 1697 when the quarter-brothers of the guild petitioned parliament in regard to their being prevented by the master of the guild from following their trade.[56] In the 1749 list of freemen 108 were butchers, of which 105 were from the established church and only three dissenters.

Protestant dominance was no doubt maintained through the way the trade was organized in Dublin, with the vast majority of butchers operating from stalls in the various markets in the city – the Ormond Market on the North Side, and on the South Side the Castle Market (still in existence), Clarendon Market, Newhall Market, New Market and St Patrick's Market. Indeed, out of sixty-four butchers in Wilson's 1768 list, only six were located outside a market. It was a situation which persisted well into the second half of the nineteenth century, when butchers came to be known generally as victuallers. It made sense from a public health point of view to group together, at a few locations, trades, like the butchers, which were likely to cause a nuisance. The administration of these markets appears to have been in the hands of a subcommittee of the corporation, who had in their gift the allocation of stalls and who could be depended on to give short shrift to catholic butchers, although some few of the latter succeeded in obtaining stalls in the Ormond Market.[57]

It was not, therefore, a trade in which catholics flourished. Only four butchers can be identified among the signatories of the 1759 address, and there were only seven butchers in Mrs Wall's list as compared with sixty-nine in Wilson's as adjusted. It is significant that five of the seven catholic butchers operated from

55 Webb, J. J., op. cit., p. 257.   56 Wall, M., op. cit. in note 6, p. 175.   57 See CARD, IX, p. 9 and CARD, X, pp 73–6 for setting of stalls in Newhall Market by a committee of Dublin Corporation and CARD, IX, p. x where the city recorder was directed to defend the city's rights in Ormond Market in a dispute with Lord Buttevant.

addresses outside the markets. The remaining two were located in the Ormond Market. The protestant dominance indicated by these figures must have suffered a severe reversal in the nineteenth century, for the 1871 census shows that in Dublin city there were, presumably including masters and assistants, 603 butchers and meat salesmen, 580 of whom were catholic.[58]

CUTLERS, PAINTERS, PAPER STAINERS, PRINTERS AND STATIONERS

This rather diverse group made up the guild of St Luke, the evangelist, with three seats on the common council and their hall, known as the Stationers' Hall, in Cork Hill. One of the rules of the guild provided that any brother who should take an apprentice should within three months bring him before the master and wardens 'to the intent that they see he be of good conversation and of the protestant religion'.[59] This rule effectively precluded the entry of catholics to the guild except as quarter-brothers.

In addition to the records of the guild, available in the National Library of Ireland, information on the strength of the guild is available from a number of sources. When in 1724, like many other guilds, they published a declaration that members would not accept or use Wood's halfpence, it was signed by sixty-nine free brothers and only twelve quarter brothers.[60] In the 1749 list of freemen of Dublin, seventy-one were free brothers of this guild; nine of these were dissenters and the rest members of the established church.

An examination of the records of the guild in the National Library yields some interesting information on the manner in which catholics were treated in this guild from early in the century. In 1716 the guild resolved that 'no Papist quarter-brother be allowed [to trade] for less than ten shillings a quarter'. The quarterage for protestant quarter brothers was then two shillings. However, the ten shillings charge does not appear to have been adhered to for long, for in 1725 we find Luke Dowling, presumably the catholic bookseller in High Street, complaining that his quarterage of eight shillings was too great for the trade he followed; on a vote it was reduced to four shillings.[61]

In 1728 a catholic, James Hoey, who was Faulkner's partner in *Faulkner's Dublin Journal*, was admitted a quarter brother at three shillings a quarter, but this was increased to four shillings in 1729 'on account of his following a considerable trade'.[62] It can be inferred from these two cases that the extent of the trade carried on was, in the case of catholics, the criterion for fixing the amount of quarterages.

As time went on it appears to have evolved as the policy of the guild to en-

58 *Census of Ireland* 1871, Dublin city, p. 135. 59 Webb, J.J., op. cit., p. 247. 60 *Dublin Gazette* of 18–22 August 1724. 61 National Library of Ireland ms 12,124, vol. 1 under dates mentioned. 62 Ibid. under dates mentioned.

courage non-members, irrespective of religion, to join as quarter-brothers, for in November 1742 a James Griffith was appointed to collect the quarterages, at a commission of three shillings in the pound, and 'to compel hawkers and intruders to come in as quarter brothers of this hall'.[63] This recruitment drive must have been a success for the minutes for 1756 include lists of seventy-nine free brothers and ninety-six quarter brothers. There would have been protestants, as well as catholics, among the quarter brothers, but how many of each is not stated. Religion is stated in the case of the first dozen names on the list (those beginning with A or B) but only four of these are stated to be catholics.[64] This ratio of catholics appears to be far too small, and it may be that the source is not trustworthy.

Turning to Mrs Wall's list, it includes a total of twenty-six persons with occupations catered for by this guild viz. five paper stainers, eight booksellers, seven printers, one stationer and five painters. This compares with seventy-nine in Wilson's list as adjusted, but it is best not to draw any firm conclusions from this since the number in both lists diverge so much from the number in the guild minutes for 1756.

BARBERS AND PERUKE-MAKERS

As already noted in chapter 3 the surgeons and apothecaries originally formed part of the same guild as the barbers and peruke-makers, but the bulk of the surgeons, and indeed the best of them, defected early in the century to form their own society, later to develop as the Royal College of Surgeons, while the apothecaries were incorporated as a separate guild in 1747. The barbers guild lost two of its four seats on the common council to the apothecaries guild on the inception of the latter. The guild's anti-catholic bias is evident from the form of oath administered to freemen on admission under which they undertook, *inter alia*, not to take on any apprentice but of the protestant religion.[65]

As also noted in chapter 3 detailed information on catholic involvement in the guild is available in the guild records for the 1690s and the early 1700s. For 1694, for example, there are lists of sixty-seven free (protestant) brothers, twenty-nine catholic quarter brothers and forty-five 'foreigners' – the latter being, as already noted, predominantly persons, mostly catholics it is suspected, from the provinces. In 1701, in addition to around ninety foreigners, seventeen catholic quarter-brothers were listed, while the number of free brothers had increased to seventy-five.[66] The problem about the lists of catholic quarter brothers in these cases is that they do not indicate the occupations of the persons listed. While some seven of the twenty-nine catholics on the 1694 list have been identified as

---

63 Ibid., vol. 2 under dates mentioned.   64 Ibid. under date mentioned. One was said to be 'a Papist in a good way' , another 'a Papist and a pirate', presumably because he was engaged in pirating editions of books.   65 Webb, J.J., op. cit., p. 247.   66 TCD ms 144/7.

surgeons (see chapter 3), only three can be said with any confidence to have been apothecaries. It, therefore, appears that around eighteen of the twenty-nine on the 1694 list were barbers/peruke-makers. This dominance of the latter was also true of the guild proper, for one of the reasons cited by the surgeons for wanting to leave the guild was that they were continually outnumbered and outvoted by the barbers/peruke-makers.

The high 'foreigner' presence in the trade can be seen as part of a general influx into the city from the provinces in the late seventeenth and early eighteenth centuries, already noted. By 1710 the number of 'foreigners' listed, with names and addresses, had increased to 113, although some few of these had previously appeared as catholic quarter brothers.[67] The majority of these 'foreigners', coming as they did from overwhelmingly catholic areas, can be assumed to have been catholic barber/peruke-makers, and the preponderance of catholic-sounding names among them reinforces such an assumption.

Naturally, the guild sought to control and limit this intrusion of 'foreigners'. In April 1708 it ordered that no person should henceforth be admitted upon quarterage or intrusion otherwise than by petition to the master, wardens and assistants in their common hall. In February 1712 the guild made an order requiring the master and wardens to compel 'foreigners' and intruders to comply with the rules and rights of the guild, while in October of the same year it ordered twelve barber/peruke-makers to pay quarterage of five shillings per quarter. In October 1716 several 'foreigners' and quarter-brothers were reprimanded for failing or refusing to appear in the guild-hall on quarter-days, though they had been duly served with summonses to attend. For each future non-appearance they were ordered to pay a fine of one shilling in addition to their usual quarterage.[68]

There is in the guild records a book of quarter brother bonds for the period 1705–36, the vast majority of those listed being barber/peruke-makers and, it can be assumed, catholics. It is of interest that in some cases a reduced rate of quarterage was provided for in the case of journeymen – for example, where the rate for a quarter-brother was 2s. 8½d. (2s. 6d. English), the rate for a journeyman was fixed at 1s. 6d., and where the rate for a quarter-brother was 10s. 6d. the journeyman rate was 2s. 6d.[69]

In April 1751 a resolution against working on Sunday was signed by twenty-seven free brothers and by thirty-one quarter brothers, the higher number of the latter being probably due to a majority of catholics in their midst. In May 1753 the guild, like most others at this time, passed a lengthy resolution against combinations of journeymen and in 1757 some fifty free brothers and quarter brothers in a press advertisement supported James Gaynor, a quarter brother and probably a catholic, in an ongoing dispute with his journeymen.[70] Charles Lucas's

67 Ibid. under dates mentioned.   68 TCD ms 1447/8/1 under dates mentioned.   69 TCD ms 1447/9.   70 TCD ms 1447/8/1 under dates mentioned.

influence in the guild – he was at one time master – is demonstrated by their support for him in his bid to reform Dublin Corporation, by a resolution supporting the Octennial Bill and by an address to the two Dublin members of parliament in 1769 requesting them to promote a bill legalizing quarterage payments.[71] This latter address is an indication that the guild proper remained strongly anti-catholic in outlook. As further evidence in that regard, it can be mentioned that in April 1771 Thomas Hanley, barber, Mary Street was complimented with the freedom of the guild in consideration of his having reformed from the errors of popery and married the widow of a late free brother, while in April 1772 a like compliment was paid to Francis Conway, barber, College Green in consideration of his having been a good quarter-brother for many years past and having lately reformed from the errors of popery.[72] By that stage, of course, with quarterages rendered illegal by the courts, catholic barber/peruke-makers could, with impunity, thumb their noses at the guild.

Barbers/peruke-makers did not occupy a high position in the social pecking order and this may account for their poor showing in, for example, the address to the lord lieutenant in 1759 and in Wilson's and Wall's lists. None have been identified in the address to the lord lieutenant and only twenty-nine figure in Wilson's list for 1768. Eight peruke-makers and five wig-makers, but no barbers, appear on Mrs Wall's list.[73] It is difficult, then, to attempt any assessment of catholic strength in the trade in the eighteenth century.

TANNERS AND CURRIERS

Tanners were in the business of converting raw hide into leather by soaking in a liquid containing tannic acid. They might, therefore, be more conveniently described as leather manufacturers. One of the staple trades of the city, their guild claimed to have been established by charter in 1289. In 1659 an old edict, requiring leather offered for sale to be assayed and sealed, was renewed, as also a requirement that leather should be sold only in the Corn Market on fixed days.[74] In the eighteenth century tanners tended to be located in the James's Street and Cork Street areas.

With two seats on the common council, the guild cannot have been very numerous at least in so far as free brothers were concerned. In the 1749 list already mentioned, the guild was credited with forty-four freemen, twenty-four of whom were established church, eighteen dissenters and two quakers. Dissenters and quakers thus made up 45 per cent of the free brothers, a higher proportion than in any other guild.

71 Ibid. under dates mentioned.   72 Webb, J.J., op. cit., p. 249.   73 Wall, M., op. cit. in note 26, p. 301. One 'hairdresser' was enrolled in 1786 outside the period covered by Wall and one of Wall's wigmakers is described as a 'ladies hairdresser' in Wilson's list for 1780.   74 Webb, J.J., op. cit., p. 192.

In the trade as a whole, however, that is, free brothers, quarter brothers and tanners who simply ignored the guild, catholics were in a slight majority, at least in the second half of the century, for according to Mrs Wall's list, thirty-four tanners took the catholic oath in the period 1778–82. This compares with sixty-four in Wilson's list as adjusted.

The curriers were an analogous trade, although a separate guild. Their job was to dress and colour tanned leather. In the 1749 list they are credited with only twelve freemen (three dissenters and nine established church). Nine curriers on Wall's list compares with twenty-one on Wilson's as adjusted.

BREWERS AND MALSTERS

Incorporated as a craft guild by William III in the 1690s, these trades were late comers to the guild system.[75] The importance of the brewing and malting industries was recognized by their four seats on the common council, although the number of free brothers in the guild (only eleven, all established church, in 1749) would have entitled them only to the lowest representation. Clearly, this was a trade where the number of free brothers was only the tip of the iceberg and where the vast majority of those involved were carrying on without reference to the guild. For instance, some eighteen (catholic) brewers have been identified among the signatories of the 1759 address to the lord lieutenant.

The Registry of Deeds shows that malthouses were numerous in the city but, strangely, malsters figure very little in either Wilson's or Wall's lists. It may be that some of those described as brewers or distillers were malsters as well, since the malting of grain was an intermediate stage in both the brewing and distilling industries. References to catholic malsters are scant: we read of one Geoghegan, a malster from Loughboy (Bow Lane), whose daughter was abducted in August 1737 when going to Mass.[76]

According to Mrs Wall's list, twenty-nine catholic brewers took the oath in the period 1778–82. This compares with fifty-one in Wilson's list as adjusted, and indicates a catholic share of near 60 per cent.

THE TALLOW CHANDLERS

Chandlers were principally involved in the manufacture and sale of candles and soap, produced from tallow provided mainly by the butchers. An ancient guild, they claimed to have been incorporated by Edward III in the fourteenth century.[77] Although a fairly large guild, they held only two seats on the common council. In 1749 there were eighty-six freemen in the guild, nineteen of whom

75 Ibid., p. 183.   76 *Weekly Newsletter*, August 1737.   77 Webb, J.J., op. cit., p. 57.

were quakers and nine dissenters. Thirty-four catholic chandlers from Dublin took the oath in the period 1778–82 according to Mrs Wall's list. This compares with 106 in Wilson's list as adjusted, and implies a catholic share of less than one-third.

THE SHOEMAKERS

Claiming incorporation by Henry VI in 1427, this was a numerous guild with four seats on the common council.[78] They are credited with seventy-seven free brothers, including nine dissenters, in 1749. These would be generally small manufacturers engaged in the production of boots, shoes etc. The twenty-five shoemakers on Mrs Wall's list compare with eighty-seven on Wilson's as adjusted, indicating a catholic share of less than 30 per cent.

OTHER TRADES AND OCCUPATIONS

We can divide these into trades and occupations with a moderate-to-good catholic participation and those with a low catholic participation. Among those with moderate-to-good catholic participation were: Distiller[79] (15 Wall: 22 Wilson as adjusted), carpenter (40:81), skinner (30:69), woollen draper (40:90), linen draper (34:87), coach-maker (15:42), hosier (12:36), mercer (8:25), ironmonger (8:28) and tobacconist (12:39).

Among trades and occupations with a low catholic participation were: brazier (6 Wall: 38 Wilson as adjusted), breeches maker (2:17), cooper (12:52), goldsmith (3:36), haberdasher (5:45), hatter (7:29), jeweller (4:39), saddler (3:23), staymaker (2:31) and watchmaker (7:38).

An important trade entirely absent, for whatever reason, from Wilson's list were the publicans. Mrs Wall's list, on the other hand, includes thirty-four publicans, five ale drapers and twenty-two inn-keepers, and these must have formed a significant part of what today is known as the licensed trade in the city. Following on from the dominant position of catholics in the brewing and distilling industries, it was to be expected that catholics would also be in the majority where the sale of drink was concerned.

---

78 Ibid., p. 63.   79 One of the distillers, Denis Nowlan, listed by Wall, was located in Leixlip, Co. Kildare. I have, therefore, reduced Wall's figure for distillers from sixteen to fifteen.

CONCLUSIONS

1   While the guild system operated to exclude catholics from any part in the functioning of Dublin Corporation and from a vote in parliamentary elections for the two Dublin city seats – a situation which obtained until the Municipal Reform Act of 1840 – it did not generally operate to exclude catholics from participating in the various trades and occupations catered for by the guilds. Most guilds operated a system under which catholics were required to become what were known as quarter-brothers, involving the payment of quarterly fees. Since there were no tangible benefits to be gained from these quarterages, as they were called, catholics sought to have them declared illegal and eventually in 1759 succeeded in obtaining a ruling to that effect in the court of king's bench. In the second half of the century the role of the guilds *vis-à-vis* the crafts or trades for which they were originally intended to cater, waned perceptibly until by the end of the century they existed, with few exceptions, solely for the political purposes mentioned. Furthermore, it became commonplace to admit to guilds persons, for example, attorneys, who had vocationally no connection with them, but who wished to avail of the advantages to be derived from membership. In the case of the merchants the task of representing and safeguarding their interests was, from the early 1760s onwards, effectively ceded by the guild to the newly-formed Committee of Merchants, a twenty-one man body on which catholic as well as protestant merchants were represented. A Chamber of Commerce, in which catholic merchants were represented, took over from the committee in 1783, and, while at first it was a great success, it closed in 1791.

2   There was a great deal of exaggeration throughout the century, by persons with a particular point to make, as to the proportion of trade in the hands of catholics. In the case of Dublin the true position was that *c*.1780 only about 30 per cent of merchants were catholic and in terms of the volume of trade in catholic hands, the percentage may have been somewhat less than this. It may be significant as a barometer of the catholic share of Dublin trade that 25 per cent of members of the Committee of Merchants and of the council of the Dublin Chamber of Commerce were catholic. Even in the grocery trade, where guilds never had any function, and where other circumstances operated to the benefit of catholics, the proportion of trade in catholic hands *c*.1780 was not much above 50 per cent.

3   The catholic merchants, traders and manufacturers of Dublin were active in the Catholic Committee from its formation in 1756 onwards. Throughout the century they can be seen as a conservative force, with little sympathy in the first half of the century for Jacobite aspirations and no great involvement in radical movements, such as the United Irishmen, towards the end of the century. Their hope and expectation was that, by demonstrating their loyalty to the government, measures of catholic relief might be won. In this connection their interest was more in the removal of penal provisions in regard to property, restrictions on

catholics engaging in trade or manufacture and the admission of catholics to the legal profession, rather than in the removal of religious and educational provisions, which had largely become dead letters anyway. They were foremost in availing of the new concessions won in the relief acts of 1778 and 1782, as witness the number who took the special oath for catholics from 1778 onwards.

4   From the early 1760s Dublin catholic merchants were playing a part in the commercial affairs of the country through participation in the Committee of Merchants and, later, in the Dublin Chamber of Commerce. The most influential catholic figure among the merchants from the 1750s to the 1780s was undoubtedly Anthony Dermott who sometimes chaired meetings of the Committee of Merchants and was elected one of the two vice-presidents of the Chamber of Commerce Council on its formation in 1783. Through personal friendships with protestants he was in a position to play the role of bridge-builder between protestant and catholic and so smooth the way to an acceptance of the need for relief measures for catholics.

5   An effort has been made above to estimate, however roughly, the catholic presence in various other trades and occupations, but, in view of the several imponderables involved, it is best to regard the figures arrived at as no more than indications of trends. It will be seen that catholic representation in the various trades and crafts varied from highs of near 70 per cent for distillers, 60 per cent for brewers and about 50 per cent for grocers, tanners and carpenters to lows of 6 per cent for staymakers, 8 per cent for goldsmiths, 10 per cent for jewellers and 11 per cent for haberdashers.

APPENDIX 12

The humble address of the Roman Catholic gentry, merchants and citizens of Dublin presented to the lord lieutenant and published in *Dublin Gazette* of 15 December 1759, was signed by 307 persons, now put in alphabetical order below.

  N.B. The occupations of the various persons did not appear in the original list. They have been deduced from the sources mentioned in note 23 and may not be correct in some cases.

Andoe, John, distiller
Andrews, Maurice, woollen
   draper
Andrews Pat, woollen draper
Archer, Pat, merchant
Arnald, Richard, distiller
Aylmer, James, salesmaster
Barrett, Ja., saddler,
Barry, John, grocer
Begg, John, merchant
Begg, Francis, haberdasher

Bennett, Thomas, linen draper
Bonfield, Michael, merchant
Bourk, Edmond, grocer
Bourk, Theobald, grocer
Bowes, Philip, bookseller
Bracken, Denis, merchant
Braughall, Edward, merchant
Brenan, John, grocer
Brenan, Thomas, shoemaker
Brett, Christopher, grocer
Brett, Daniel, merchant

Brown, Lau., merchant
Brown, Michael, -
Brown, Pat, linen draper
Brown, Thomas, carpenter
   or feather merchant or
   handkerchief printer
Browne, Joseph, wine merchant
Bryan, Walter, merchant
Butler, Thomas, grocer
Butterly, Matthew, tallow
   chandler

Byrn, Peter, hosier
Byrne, Laurence, grocer
Byrne, Greg, wine merchant
Byrne, Thomas, merchant
Byrne, Phaelix, merchant
Byrne, Charles, linen draper
Byrne Ja. & Ed., merchant
Byrne, Ma. & Ed., grocer
Byrne, Michael, goldsmith
Byrne, Thomas, gent.
Callaghan, James, grocer
Callan, Pat, grocer
Callan, John, flax dresser
Callan, Barth, brewer
Cane, William, guild surgeon
Carroll, Simon, -
Clancy, Thomas, merchant
Clark, John, tallow chandler
Clinch, Michael, brewer
Clinch, William, brewer
Clinch, James, gent
Clinton, Clem, ropemaker
Comerford, John, merchant,
ComerfordPat , tobacconist
Concannon, Lukc, grocer
Connell, William, tailor
Connor, James, merchant
Connor, Peter, Spanish
    leather dresser
Connor, John, merchant
Connor, John, merchant
Copinger, Richard, grocer
Corballis, John, timber
    merchant
Corcoran, Peter, grocer
Corry [Curry], John,
    physician
Cosgrave, James, merchant
Cosgrave, Ed, -
Cosgrave, Michael, mer-
    chant
Costigan, Denis, -
Cox, Thomas, grocer
Crosbie, John, brewer
Crump, John, merchant
Cullen, Pat, merchant
Cullen, Edward, merchant
Curtis, Pat, tanner
Dalton, Richard, hardware
    merchant
Dease, Mat, apothecary
Dease, Michael, wine merchant
Dease, William, -

Dease, Gar, -
Dease, Pat, merchant
Delaney, Dan, clothier
Delaney, William, wine
    cooper
Dempsey, John, merchant
Dermot, Anthony, merchant
Dermot, Owen, merchant
Dermot, Thomas, carpenter
Dickson, John, tanner
Dignam, Ma, -
Dillon, Edward, apothecary
Dillon, John, tallow chandler
Dillon, John, wool merchant
Dillon, James, surgeon
Dillon, Robert, serge m'facturer
Dolan, Pat, -
Doran, Patrick, grocer
Dowdall, Lau, grocer
Dowdall, Matthew, physician
Dowling, John, butcher or
    timber merchant
Doyle, Richard, wine
    merchant
Doyle, Anthony, merchant
Drew, George, merchant
Duff, Pat, linen draper
Duff, John, linen draper
Duffy, Bryan, victualler
Duffy, Bryan, -
Dugan, Michael, broker and
    book collector
Edwards, Thomas, merchant
Egan, William, glover
Egan, Thomas, merchant
Egan, James, vintner
Eustace, Gerard, mercer,
Fagan, Bry., -
Fagan, Patrick, -
Ferrall, John, linen draper
Fitzgerald, John, wine
    merchant
Fitzmaurice, Ja. Ni., -
Fitzsimons, John, baker or
    weaver
Fletcher, James, linen draper
Flood, Thomas, skinner &
    tanner
Fogarty, John, -
Folie, John, merchant
Ford, Pat, grocer
Ford, William, -
Forster, George, tallow chandler

Frayne, George, glover
Frayne, Pat, grocer
Gavin, Martin, haberdasher
Gennet, James, tanner
Geoghegan, Garret, sugar baker
Gold, David, builder
Goold, Edmond, merchant
Grace, John, salesmaster
Grace, William, merchant
Grainger, John, merchant
Grehan, T., brewer
Griffin, Mich, linen draper
Hamil, Hugh, merchant
Hamilton, Laughlin, silk weaver
Harford, Andrew, merchant
    or baker
Hervey, Garret, woollen
    draper
Hickey, Thomas, merchant
Hoey, James, bookseller
Hogan, Ed, shoemaker
Hogarty, Matthew, -
Hourigan, Nich, -
Hussey, James, esquire or grocer
Jennett, John, brewer
Jennett, Christopher, tanner
Joyce, Christopher, dry
    cooper
Kavanagh, Darby, vintner
Kavanagh, Denis, grocer
Kavanagh, John, merchant
Kaven [Kevan?], Val, -
Keating, William, gent
Kelly, Edward, clothier
Kelly, Emmanuel, gent
Kelly, James, linen draper
Kelly, John, physician or
    brewer or wine merchant
Kelly, Mark, merchant
Kelly, Thomas, merchant
Kelly, Thomas, butcher
Kennedy, Thomas, linen
Keogh, John, silk weaver
Keogh, Michael, surgeon
    draper
Kiernan, Francis, merchant
Killin, Lau, -
Lacy, James, hosier
Lawless, Luke, brewer
Lawless, Michael, brewer
Lawless, Nicholas, weaver
Lawless, Pat, brewer
Lawless, Richard, currier

Lawless, Robert, brewer
Leneghan, Peter, merchant
Leonard, Nicholas, weaver
Long, Pat, grocer
Lord, Pat, bookseller
Lynch, Christopher, pin
 maker
Lynch, Christopher,
Lynch, James, pin maker
Lynch, John, grocer
 breeches maker
M'Cabe, Francis, merchant
M'Cabe, Henry, timber
 merchant
M'Dermot, Barney, merchant
M'Donald, Lau, -
M'Guire, P., merchant
M'Guire, Thomas, grocer
McLoughlin, Joseph, grocer
M'Mahon, Pat, grocer
McMahon, Richard, grocer
Madden, James, merchant
Magan, James, apothecary
Magan, Pat, -
Magan, Richard, apothecary
Mahon, Thomas, silk weaver
Mahon, Thomas, merchant
Mahon, Tim, haberdasher
Malone, William, linen
 weaver
Malone, William, merchant
Malpas, John, esquire
Mangan, Nicholas, coach
 maker
Martin, Michael, -
Maryman, John, brewer
Masterson, John, wine
 merchant
Mathews, Sylv, chandler &
 yarn merchant
Mooney, Pat, dry cooper
Mooney, Terence, woollen
 draper
Moore Sen., Pat, grocer
Moore, Edward, grocer or
 brewer
Moore, John, glover
Mulloy, John, starch
 m'facturer
Murphy, George, tobacconist
Murphy, James, grocer
Murphy, Laurence, tanner
Murphy, Michael, grocer
Murphy, Richard, laceman

Murtogh, Dan, dyer
Netterville, E., MD, physician
Netterville, William,   mer-
 chant
Nevin, Daniel, victualler
Nevin, John, merchant
Newman, Thomas, -
Nihil, Lau, -
Nixon, John, Esq. clothier
Norris, Robert, merchant
Nugent, John, linen draper
O'Brien, Den.Tho., merchant
O'Brien, James, mercer
O'Brien, Michael, woollen
 draper
O'Brien, Pat, merchant
O'Brien, Thomas, linen
 draper
O'Donnell, John, upholsterer
O'Neill, Felix, silk throwster
Pearce, James, pump borer
Phealan, Andrew, distiller
Phelan, William, distiller
Plunket, Michael, hair
 merchant
Plunket, Pat, brewer
Plunket, Walter, linen draper
Plunket, William, clothier
Plunkett, Ben, wine
 merchant
Purcell, James, woollen draper
Purfield, Lau., tanner,
Quin, Christopher, wine
 merchant
Reid, Ja, shoemaker
Reily, Caesar, merchant
Reily, Charles, -
Reily, Chas., surgeon
Reily, Chris, salesmaster
Reily, Edward, silk merchant
Reily, Francis, -
Reily, Hugh, grocer
Reily, Hugh, wine merchant
Reily, Hugh, apothecary
Reily, James, salesmaster
Reily, James, salesmaster
Reily, Matt, brewer
Reily, Michael, esquire
Reily, Michael, ironmonger
Reily, Michael, scrivener
  & printer
Reily, Michael, merchant
Reily, Michael, Jun.,
 merchant

Reily, Miles, merchant
Reily, Ms [?] T., -
Reily, Pat, grocer or saddler
Reily, Philip, pin maker
Reily, Richard, wheelwright
Reily, Terence, apothecary
Reynolds, Christopher,
 tallow chandler
Reynolds, James, merchant
Reynolds, Michael, clothier
Reynolds, Patrick, baker
Reynolds, Thomas, weaver
Ross, Pat, -
Russell, Pat, linen draper
Ryan, Thomas, merchant
Savage, John, weaver or
Shannon, Pat, skinner
Shaw, Richard, linen draper
 upholsterer
Sherlock, Eustace, merchant
Sherlock, Pat, -
Sherlock, Tho., wine cooper
Sinnott, James, grocer
Spencer, Alexander,
 merchant
St John, James, -
Stackpoole, John, linen
 draper
Stone, John, merchant
Strong, Barth, tallow
 chandler
Sullivan, Daniel, wine
 merchant
Sweetman, Michael, brewer
Sweetman, Pat, brewer
Sweetman, William, brewer
Talbot, William, merchant
Tiernan, Barnaby, merchant
Tisdall, Thomas, grocer
Troy, Ja., grocer
Wade, Redmond, apothecary
Waldrom, John, linen draper
Wale, Hanley, physician
Wale, John, -
Walsh, Nicholas, merchant
 or linen draper
Weldon, Chris, merchant
Weldon, Everard, woollen
 draper
Weldon, James, -
Weldon, Pat, merchant
Weldon, Peter, -
White, David, tailor
White, Pat, tanner

Bibliography

Anon., *A serious proposal for the entire destruction of popery in Ireland*, Dublin, 1732
——, *Letters of a French visitor*, Dublin 1734
——, *Scheme of proportions which the protestants of Ireland probably bear to papists*, Dublin 1732
——, *The ax laid to the root*, Dublin 1749
Bartlett, Thomas, *The fall and rise of the Irish nation*, Dublin 1990
Bartlett Thomas & Hayton D.W. (eds), *Penal era and golden age: essays in Irish history 1690–1800*, Belfast 1979
Beaufort, Daniel, *Memoir of a map of Ireland*, Dublin 1792
Belcher, T.W. (ed.), *Records of the King's and Queen's College of Physicians in Ireland*, Dublin 1866
[Bindon, David], *An abstract of the numbers of protestant and popish families*, Dublin 1736
Blacker, Beaver H., *Brief sketches of the parishes of Donnybrook and Booterstown*, Dublin 1860
Boulter, Hugh, *Letters*, 2 vols, Dublin 1770
Brady, John , *Catholics and catholicism in the eighteenth century press*, Maynooth 1965
Burke's *Peerage*, 105th edition
Burns, Robert E., *Irish parliamentary politics in the eighteenth century*, 2 vols, Washington DC, 1989 & 1990
Bush, Gervaise, *Essay towards ascertaining the population of Ireland*, Dublin 1789
Cahill, Edward, *Freemasonry: its character and purpose*, Dublin 1944
Cameron, R.C., *History of the Royal College of Surgeons in Ireland*, Dublin 1886
Campbell, Thomas, *A survey of the south of Ireland*, London 1777
Carleton, William, *Autobiography*, London 1896, reprinted Belfast 1996
Census of Ireland for 1821, 1841, 1861, 1871, 1881, 1891, 1901 and 1911
Chart, D.A. (ed.), *The Drennan letters*, Belfast 1931
Clarke, Bernard, *An answer to the pope's bull with a vindication of the real principles of freemasonry*, Dublin 1751
Cogan, Anthony, *The diocese of Meath ancient and modern*, 3 vols, Dublin 1870; reprinted Dublin 1992

Commons Journal Ireland

Connell, K.H., *The population of Ireland 1750–1845*, Oxford 1950

Connolly, S.J., *Religion, law and power: the making of protestant Ireland 1660–1760*, Oxford 1992

Cork Advertiser

Crossle, Philip, *Irish masonic records*, Dublin 1973

Cullen, L.M., *Anglo-Irish trade 1660–1800*, Manchester 1968

——, *Princes & pirates: the Dublin Chamber of Commerce 1783–1983*, Dublin 1983

——, 'Catholics under the Penal Laws' in *Eighteenth-Century Ireland*, vol. 1, pp 23–36

Curran, M.J. (ed.), 'Archbishop Carpenter's Epistolae' in *Reportorium Novum*, vol. 1, no. 1, pp 154–82 & no. 2, pp 381–405

Daultry, S., Dickson, D. & Ó Gráda, C., 'Eighteenth century Irish population: new perspectives from old sources' in *Journal of economic history*, vol. 41, no. 3, pp 601–28

Delany, V.T.H., *The administration of justice in Ireland*, Dublin 1975

Dickson, David, *New foundations: Ireland 1660–1800*, Dublin 1987

——, 'The demographic implications of Dublin's growth 1650–1850' in Lawton, R. & Lee, R. (eds), *Urban population development in western Europe from the late eighteenth century to the early twentieth century*, Liverpool 1989, pp 178–89

Dickson, D., Keogh, D. & Whelan, K. (eds), *The United Irishmen: republicanism, radicalism and rebellion*, Dublin 1993

Dictionary of national biography, London 1895

Diocese of Dublin index to the act or grant books and original wills – Appendix to *26th report of the deputy keeper of the public records of Ireland*, Dublin 1895

Dobbs, Arthur, *Essay on trade and improvement in Ireland*, Dublin 1731

Donnelly, Nicholas, *Short histories of Dublin parishes*, Dublin 1907–12

Dublin Gazette

Dublin Journal

Dublin Postman

Dublin Weekly Journal

Duhigg, Bartholomew, *History of the King's Inns*, Dublin 1806

Edwards, R. Dudley (ed.), 'The minute book of the Catholic Committee 1773–1792' in *Archivium Hibernicum*, vol. 9, pp 1–172

Eustace, P.B. (ed.), *Registry of Deeds, Dublin: abstract of wills*, 2 vols, Dublin 1956

Evans, Ernest, 'The Charitable Infirmary' in *Irish Builder*, vol. 39, pp 6–8

Fagan, Patrick, *The second city: portrait of Dublin 1700–1760*, Dublin 1986

——, *Dublin's turbulent priest: Cornelius Nary 1658–1738*, Dublin 1991

——, *An Irish bishop in penal times: the chequered career of Sylvester Lloyd OFM 1680–1747*, Dublin 1993

——, (ed.), *Ireland in the Stuart papers*, Dublin 1995

——, *Divided loyalties: the question of the oath for Irish catholics in the eighteenth century*, Dublin 1997

Ferrar, John, *History of Limerick*, Limerick 1787

Finn's Leinster Journal

Foster, Joseph (ed.), *Register of admissions to Gray's Inn*, London 1887

——, *The records of the Honourable Society of Lincoln's Inns*, London 1896

Giblin, Cathaldus (ed.), 'Catalogue of material of Irish interest in the collection Nunziatura di Fiandra, Vatican Archives' in *Collectanea Hibernica*, nos 4–16

Gilbert, John T. (ed.), *Calendar of the ancient records of Dublin*, 19 volumes, Dublin 1891–1944

——, *A history of the city of Dublin*, 3 vols; reprinted Shannon 1972

Gilborne, John, *The medical review, a poem*, Dublin 1775

Hayes, Richard, *Biographical dictionary of Irishmen in France*, Dublin 1949

Hogan, Daire & Osborough, W.N. (eds), *Brehons, serjeants and attorneys*, Dublin 1990

Hogan, Dáire, *The legal profession in Ireland 1789–1922*, Dublin 1986

Houston, Arthur, *Daniel O'Connell: his early life*, London 1906

Irish Builder

Irish House of Lords report from the committee appointed to inspect the original papers seized ..., Dublin 1734

Irish Magazine and Monthly Asylum for neglected biography

Irish Parliamentary Register, vol. 12

James, F.G., 'The Irish lobby in the early eighteenth century' in *English Historical Review*, vol. 81, pp 543–57

Jebb, Frederick, *Physiological enquiry into the process of labour*, Dublin 1773

Kenny, Colum, *King's Inns and the kingdom of Ireland*, Dublin 1992

——, 'The exclusion of catholics from the legal profession in Ireland 1537–1829' in *Irish Historical Studies*, vol. 25, pp 337–57

Keogh, Daire, *'The French disease': the Catholic Church and radicalism in Ireland 1790–1800*, Dublin 1993

King, Charles, *A great archbishop of Dublin*, London 1906

Lawless, Valentine, Lord Cloncurry, *Personal recollections*, Dublin 1849

Lepper, J. H. & Crossle, Philip, *History of the grand lodge of the Free and Accepted Masons of Ireland*, vol. 1, Dublin 1925

A list of the names of popish priests, Dublin 1705

Lloyd, Edward, *A description of the city of Dublin*, London 1732

Lords Journal Ireland

Lucas, Charles, *Pharmacomastix or the use and abuse of apothecaries explained*, Dublin 1741

MacAnally, Henry, *The Irish militia 1793–1816*, Dublin 1949

Mac Cóil, Liam, *The book of Blackrock*, Blackrock 1977

MacDermot, Brian (ed.), *The Irish catholic petition of 1805*, Dublin 1992

McDowell, R.B., 'The personnel of the Dublin Society of United Irishmen' in *Irish Historical Studies*, vol. 2, pp 12–53

MacGeagh, Henry F. (ed.), *Register of admissions to the Middle Temple*, London 1949

Mac Giolla Choille, Breandán, 'Test book 1775–6' in *59th report of the deputy keeper of the public records of Ireland 1962*, pp 50–84

MacLysaght, Edward, *Irish life in the seventeenth century*, Dublin 1969

McNally, V. J., *Reform, revolution and reaction: Archbishop John Thomas Troy and the Catholic Church in Ireland 1787–1817*, Lanham, Md., 1995

McNamara, N.C., *The story of an Irish sept*, London 1896

Malcomson, A.P.W., *Eighteenth century Irish official papers in Great Britain*, Belfast 1990

Mitchel, John, *The history of Ireland from the Treaty of Limerick to the present time*, London c. 1867

Moody, T.W., Martin, F.X. & Byrne, F.J. (eds), *A new history of Ireland*, 9 vols., Oxford, various dates

Moran, Patrick, *The Roman catholics of Ireland under the penal laws of the eighteenth century*, London 1900

—— (ed.), *Spicilegium Ossoriense*, 3 vols, Dublin 1874–84

Municipal corporations of Ireland: First report of the commissioners, 1836

Murphy, Seán, 'Irish Jacobitism and freemasonry' in *Eighteenth-Century Ireland*, vol. 9, pp 75–82

Nary, Cornelius, *The case of the Roman catholics of Ireland* included in Hugh Reily, *Genuine history of Ireland*, 1762 edition

Nelson, E. Charles & McCracken, Eileen, *The brightest jewel: a history of the National Botanic Gardens*, Kilkenny, 1987

Newenham, Thomas, *A statistical and historical enquiry into the progress and magnitude of the population of Ireland*, London 1805

——, *A view of Ireland*, London 1809

O'Brien, Eoin, 'The Charitable Infirmary in Jervis Street, the first voluntary hospital in Great Britain or Ireland' in Eoin O'Brien (ed.), *The Charitable Infirmary Jervis Street 1718–1987*, Dublin 1988

O'Byrne, Eileen (ed.), *The convert rolls*, Dublin 1981

O'Connell, Maurice R. (ed.), *The correspondence of Daniel O'Connell*, 8 vols, Dublin 1972–80

O'Hart, John, *Irish pedigrees*, Dublin 1892

Parkinson, R.E., *The history of the grand lodge of the Free and Accepted Masons of Ireland*, vol. 2, Dublin 1957

Pender, Séamus, *A census of Ireland c.1659*, Dublin 1939

Phair, P. Beryl et al. (eds), *King's Inns admission papers*, Dublin 1982

Power, Thomas & Whelan, Kevin (eds), *Emergence and endurance: catholics in Ireland in the eighteenth century*, Dublin 1990

[Prior, Thomas], *A list of absentees of Ireland*, Dublin 1729

Report of the commission on religious public instruction in Ireland 1834

Royal Commission on historical manuscripts, Report no. 11

Rutty, John, *Chronological history of the weather and seasons and of the prevailing diseases in Dublin*, London 1770

Scully, Denys, *Statement of the penal laws*, Dublin 1812

Sentimental and Masonic Magazine

Shortt, Thomas, *New observations on city, town and country bills of mortality*, London 1750

Simms, J.G., *War and politics in Ireland 1649–1730*, London 1986

——, 'The making of a penal law' in *Irish Historical Studies*, vol. 12, pp 105– 18

Smith, R.W. Innes (ed.), *English-speaking students of medicine at the university of Leyden*, Edinburgh & London 1932

Smith, W., *A pocket companion for free masons*, Dublin 1735

Smyth, Jim, 'Freemasonry and the United Irishmen' in Dickson, D., Keogh, D. and Whelan, K., (eds), *The United Irishmen: republicanism, radicalism and rebellion*, Dublin 1993

Spratt, Edward, *The new book of constitutions of the free and accepted masons*, Dublin 1751

Stewart, A.T.Q., *A deeper silence: the hidden roots of the United Irish movement*, London 1993

Stokes, George T., *Some worthies of the Irish church*, Dublin 1899

Tierney, Mark (ed.), 'The papers of James Butler II' in *Collectanea Hibernica*, no. 20, pp 89–146

Trench, Charles C., *Grace's card: Irish catholic landlords 1690–1800*, Cork 1997

Vicars, Arthur (ed.), *Index of prerogative wills*, Dublin 1897

Wakefield, Edward, *An account of Ireland, statistical and political*, London 1812

Wall, Maureen, *Catholic Ireland in the eighteenth century*, Dublin 1989

——, 'The catholic merchants, manufacturers and traders of Dublin 1778–1782' in *Reportorium Novum*, vol. 2, no. 2, pp 298–323

Warburton, John, Whitelaw, James & Walsh Robert, *History of the city of Dublin*, 2 vols, London 1818

Ward, Robert E. & Ward Catherine C. (eds), *The letters of Charles O'Conor of Belanagare*, Ann Arbor, Mich., 1980

Ward, R.E., Wrynn, J.F. & Ward, C.C. (eds), *The letters of Charles O'Conor of Belanagare*, Washington DC 1988

Watson's Dublin Almanac

Webb, John J., *The guilds of Dublin*, Dublin 1929; reprinted New York & London 1970

Weekly Miscellany

Weekly Newsletter

White, Terence de Vere, 'The free masons' in Williams T.D. (ed.), *Secret societies in Ireland*, Dublin 1973, Chapter 5

Whitelaw, James, *An essay on the population of Dublin*, Dublin 1805

Widdess, J.D.H., *An account of the schools of surgery*, Edinburgh 1949

——, *History of the Royal College of Physicians in Ireland*, Edinburgh & London 1963

Williams, Harold (ed.), *The correspondence of Jonathan Swift*, 5 vols, London 1965

Wilson's Dublin Directory

Index

The following abbreviations have been used: bp=bishop, abp=arch-bishop, Ld Lt=lord lieutenant and UIM=United Irishman. It has not been thought necessary to include in the index the names appearing in Appendix 12 (pp 184–6) nor the lists of freemasons in pages 134–7.